CISTERCIAN STUDIES SERIES: NUMBER TWO HUNDRED THIRTY

The Lives of Monastic Reformers, 2
Abbot Vitalis of Savigny,
Abbot Godfrey of Savigny,
Peter of Avranches,
and Blessed Hamo

CISTERCIAN STUDIES SERIES: NUMBER TWO HUNDRED THIRTY

The Lives of Monastic Reformers, 2
Abbot Vitalis of Savigny,
Abbot Godfrey of Savigny,
Peter of Avranches,
and Blessed Hamo

Introduced, translated, and edited by

Hugh Feiss, OSB
Maureen M. O'Brien
Ronald Pepin

α

Cistercian Publications
www.cistercianpublications.org

LITURGICAL PRESS
Collegeville, Minnesota
www.litpress.org

A Cistercian Publications title published by Liturgical Press

Cistercian Publications
Editorial Offices
161 Grosvenor Street
Athens, Ohio 54701
www.cistercianpublications.org

All four of these lives are translated from editions of E. P. Sauvage, the *Vitae* of Vitalis and Godfrey from "Vitae BB. Vitalis et Gaufridi, primi et secundi abbatum Saviniacensium in Normannia," *Analecta Bollandiana* 1 (1882): 355–410, and the *Vitae* of Peter of Avranches and Hamo from "Vitae B. Petri Abrincensis et B. Hamonis monachorum coenobii saviniacensis," *Analecta Bollandiana* 2 (1883): 475–560.

Biblical quotations are translated from the Latin.

1   2   3   4   5   6   7   8   9

Library of Congress Cataloging-in-Publication Data

Abbot Vitalis of Savigny, Abbot Godfrey of Savigny, Peter of Avranches, and Blessed Hamo / introduced, translated and edited by Hugh Feiss, OSB, Maureen M. O'Brien, Ronald Pepin.
    pages   cm — (The lives of monastic reformers ; 2) (Cistercian studies ; 230)
    "All four of these lives are translated from editions of E. P. Sauvage. the vitae of Vitalis and Godfrey from "Vitae BB. Vitalis et Gaufridi, primi et secundi abbatum Saviniacensium in Normannia," Analecta Bollandiana 1 (1882): 355–410, and the vitae of Peter of Avranches and Hamo "Vitae B. Petri Abrincensis et B. Hamonis monachorum coenobii saviniacensis," Analecta Bollandiana 2 (1883): 475–560."
    Summary: "This volume offers translations of the twelfth-century Latin vitae of four monks of the Monastery of Savigny: Abbot Vitalis, Abbot Godfrey, Peter of Avranches, and Blessed Hamo. Founded in 1113 by Vitalis of Mortain, an influential hermit-preacher, Savigny expanded to a congregation of thirty monasteries under his successor Godfrey (1122–1138). In 1147, the entire congregation joined the Cistercian Order. Around 1172, two monks of Savigny, Peter of Avranches and Hamo, friends but very different personalities, died. Their stories were told in two further vitae.The vitae of these four men exemplify the variety of people and movements found in the monastic ferment of the twelfth century."—Provided by publisher.
    ISBN 978-0-87907-230-8 (paperback) — ISBN 978-0-87907-693-1 (ebook)
    1. Cistercians—France—Savigny (Manche)—Biography. 2. Vitalis, of Savigny, Saint, –1122. 3. Godfrey, of Savigny, Abbot, active 1122–1138. 4. Peter, of Avranches. 5. Hamo, Blessed. 6. Benedictines—France—Savigny (Manche)—Biography. I. Feiss, Hugh. II. O'Brien, Maureen M. III. Pepin, Ronald. IV. Sauvage, E. P. Vitae BB. Vitalis et Gaufridi, primi et secundi abbatum Saviniacensium. V. Sauvage, E. P. Vitae B. Petri Abrincensis et B. Hamonis monachorum coenobii saviniacensis.

BX3455.A33   2014
271'.1202244—dc23
[B]   2014016177

To Anna Minore and Joanne Draper,
Amy Jaszkowiak, Ami Brogdon, and Dory Hammersley,
teachers whose *vitae* inspire their friends and students

Contents

Foreword

THE PERIOD OF 1050–1150 was a time of monastic experimentation and expansion. Monastics as different as Bruno the Carthusian and Stephen Harding, Gilbert of Sempringham and Hildegard of Bingen, Norbert of Xanten and Robert of La Chaise-Dieu left behind their old lives, began new lives, and sometimes created new forms of monastic living. One of the centers of experimentation was at the borders of Normandy, Brittany, and Maine. There Robert of Arbrissel, Bernard of Tiron, and Vitalis of Savigny embraced the life of hermit-preachers and attracted disciples, male and female, for whom they eventually had to provide a home and a rule. The three men devised different solutions for the rule to be followed by their disciples. At Savigny, Vitalis chose the Benedictine Rule. Under Godfrey, his successor, Savigny expanded to become a congregation of monasteries under the authority of the abbot of Savigny. In 1147 and 1148, when that authority was challenged during the English Civil War between King Stephen and Empress Matilda, Abbot Serlo committed Savigny and all its dependencies to the Cistercian Order. This incorporation of Savigny into the Cistercian Order is clear evidence of the vitality, the prestige, and the organizational strength of the Order of Cîteaux.

We know the first century of Savigny through four *vitae*, those of the first two abbots, Vitalis and Godfrey, and those of two monks of the generation following Godfrey, Hamo and Peter of Avranches. These *vitae* are here translated together into English for the first time. They were written to plant models of monastic sanctity in the memories of the Savigniacs. They were also written—or at least employed—in an unsuccessful effort to secure official, papal canonization of these four saints of Savigny. Because of their didactic and political nature, these *vitae* cannot be approached as straightforward, accurate historical accounts, even though they are major sources for the lives of the first two abbots and almost the exclusive sources of our knowledge of Hamo and Peter.

When one looks at a painting of monks, all dressed the same, occupying identical seats in a monastic choir—or when one attends services in a monastery today—it is tempting to imagine such a thing as a typical monk. These four *vitae* caution against such imagining. They present four very different people and four very different kinds of holiness. These different kinds of holiness presumably reflect both the uniqueness of the four saints and the different notions of sanctity that the different authors of the *vitae* espoused and wished to convey.

The portraits of the two abbots could not be more different: Vitalis, a man of humble background, became the chaplain to Robert of Mortain and a canon of a collegiate church that Robert founded at Evroult. Then, converted to the austere life of a forest-dwelling hermit, Vitalis became a powerful, peripatetic preacher who was tireless and fearless in calling people of all classes and conditions to reform their ways. Well connected with the powerful before his conversion, he was well connected afterward with other hermit-preachers. His wisdom, eloquence, and kindliness won over many; for them he established Savigny and an associated women's monastery. He was the abbot, but he does not seem to have ceased his preaching and travels. This preaching was hardly characteristic of the Cistercian observance that Savigny had embraced a quarter of a century before Bishop Stephen of Fougères wrote Vitalis's *Vita* in the 1170s. It seems likely that dedicated preaching was both a fact of Vitalis's life and a concern of Bishop Stephen's.

By contrast, Godfrey preached only within the monasteries of the Order, whose form of life he made more strict, as several contemporary observers noted. He is presented as a man who valued order, who had been a monk even before he came to Savigny and became Vitalis's assistant. Godfrey must have had charisma, because he presided over a phenomenal expansion of the Savigny congregation, which directly or indirectly founded over twenty monasteries during his eighteen years as abbot. Some of this expansion may have been facilitated by his aristocratic background, which made it easier for him to interact with potential benefactors.

Hamo, the subject of the next life, is portrayed as a very vigorous, gregarious man who traveled a great deal, was the confidant of royalty, and ministered to monasteries of women. Early in his monastic career he had ambitions to become a prelate, but some time spent serving lepers cured him of that, and later in life he turned down several appointments. He was a very successful fundraiser. The funds he raised sometimes went for good causes outside of the Savigniac congregation. He was also an enthusiastic collector and distributor of relics. He promoted the construction of a new church at Savigny. He seems to have tended toward worry about his own spiritual state and that of others. He had a knack for discerning others' spiritual condition and urged those he perceived to be in sin to repent and confess their sins. Perhaps to give balance to the account of Hamo's many activities and involvements, the author of this *vita* includes some chapters emphasizing Hamo's commitment to prayer and meditation, which led him to the summits of contemplation and ecstasy. Hamo thought a great deal about the afterlife and made his peace with death before it came to him.

The *Vita* of Peter of Avranches is also noteworthy for a vision of the afterlife in which a knight saw Peter at the side of Christ. Though Peter was a friend of Hamo, who sometimes served as his confessor, he was utterly different in personality. Peter was very serious, withdrawn from the world, and solitary. He had been interested in music as a young man, but once he became a monk his life took on a very penitential cast. After his entry into Savigny, he was never known to laugh. He did not allow himself to take an interest in nature or affairs outside the monastery. He was irked when Hamo brought him greetings from King Henry II. One of the aims of Peter's *Vita* is to show the contrasting forms of holiness found in Hamo and Peter. To this end, the author includes a ditty: "Peter of Avranches, who sheared sins like a sword; / Hamo, dovelike, pious and patient, and like a sheep." At Hamo's request, after Peter died he appeared to Hamo and told him that God had prepared many dwellings in heaven, and Hamo's would be greater than Peter's.

Thus these four *vitae* present at twelfth-century Savigny a diverse group of men who were able to live together in service of Christ.

Vitalis's fidelity to his unusual vocation to be a hermit, preacher, and monastic founder unpredictably led to the founding of a traditional but vital monastery and congregation, which before long was absorbed into the Cistercian Order. In the end, Savigny did not create something radically new, except insofar as each saint, canonized or not, is a new and unique way of following Christ. That may be the lesson of Savigny: whatever institutional innovations or failures do or do not occur, the most important thing is that there be saints.

These four *vitae* are translated here into English for the first time. As in *The Lives of Monastic Reformers, 1: Robert of La Chaise-Dieu and Stephen of Obazine* (2010), three of us have collaborated on the project. Hugh Feiss translated the *Vitae* of Vitalis and Godfrey and wrote the introduction, using materials researched by Maureen O'Brien. Ronald Pepin translated the lives of Hamo and Peter of Avranches. Ronald and Hugh then vetted each other's translations before turning the entire manuscript over to Maureen for a thorough editing before she submitted it to Fr. Mark Scott, OCSO, executive editor of Cistercian Publications, and more recently to his successor, Marsha Dutton. We are grateful to them for offering us the opportunity to contribute to the Cistercian Studies Series and for the help given us.

Abbreviations

AA SS	*Acta Sanctorum*, ed. Ioannes Bollandus, et al. Antwerp, Bruxelles, Paris, 1643–1894.
ABR	*The American Benedictine Review*, ed. Terrence Kardong, Richardton, ND.
ACW	Ancient Christian Writers Series. Westminster, MD, and New York: Newman/Paulist, 1946– .
CCSL	Corpus Christianorum, Series Latina. Turnhout: Brepols, 1954– .
CF	Cistercian Fathers Series. Kalamazoo, MI, and Collegeville, MN: Cistercian Publications.
CS	Cistercian Studies Series. Kalamazoo, MI, and Collegeville, MN: Cistercian Publications.
CSEL	Corpus Scriptorum Ecclesiasticorum Latinorum. Salzburg: Universität Salzburg, 1866–2011.
PL	J.-P. Migne, *Patrologiae cursus completus, series Latina*. 221 volumes. Paris, 1844–64.
RB	*Rule of Saint Benedict*.
SBOp	*Sancti Bernardi Opera*, 8 volumes, ed. Jean Leclercq, H. M. Rochais, and C. H. Talbot. Rome: Editiones Cistercienses, 1957–1977.
SCh	Sources chrétiennes series. Paris: Éditions du Cerf, 1942– .

Introduction

THE ABBEY OF SAVIGNY existed for almost seven hundred years, from 1112 until the French Revolution. The abbey began with the preaching of Vitalis, a court chaplain turned hermit, who settled his numerous followers in the newly founded monastery at Savigny, in northwestern France on the border of Normandy, Brittany, and Maine, southeast of Avranches and Mont Saint-Michel. Under Vitalis's immediate successors, Savigny grew to be a congregation of over thirty monasteries. In 1147, the abbey and all its dependencies were incorporated into the Order of Cîteaux.[1]

There is no comprehensive, modern history of the monastery and congregation of Savigny, even during the period 1112–1243, which is of concern here. Sometime after 1712, Claude Auvry, who served as prior at Savigny from about 1698 to 1712, wrote a lengthy history of Savigny from its beginnings to the mid-thirteenth century. Auvry's sources were the four lives translated here, the mortuary roll of Saint Vitalis, the *Chronicle* and cartulary of Savigny, the

---

1. For the period 1122–47, the text below refers to Savigny and its dependencies as a congregation but calls Cîteaux and the monasteries deriving from it the Order of Cîteaux. This approach is somewhat arbitrary on both accounts. As is indicated below, it is difficult to determine the relationship that existed between Savigny and its daughter and granddaughter houses, though the monastery of Savigny certainly exercised considerable sway over those other monasteries. Constance Berman, in *The Cistercian Evolution: The Invention of a Religious Order in Twelfth-Century Europe* (Philadelphia: University of Pennsylvania Press, 2000), has challenged, unsuccessfully it seems, the consensus that there was a Cistercian Order at the time when Savigny petitioned to join it in 1147.

Book of Miracles of Savigny, and passing references to Savigny in medieval and later historians.

Auvry's work, which runs to over a thousand pages in the edition published by Louis Laveille, has its limitations.[2] Much of Auvry's work concerns donations recorded in the abbey cartulary, and Auvry discusses them chronologically in connection with the time in office of each abbot. He describes all the abbots as devout men and in many cases learned as well. Many of the charters describe legal conflicts, which seem almost always to be settled in Savigny's favor. Useful as such information is for the history of families who were donors, it gives a somewhat mercenary cast to the story. Auvry, who was a devout Cistercian monk, seems at times to read Cistercian practices back into the period before Savigny joined the

---

2. Claude Auvry, *Histoire de la Congrégation de Savigny*, ed. Auguste Laveille, 3 vols. (Rouen: A. Lestringant; Paris: A. Picard, 1896–98). Laveille's edition of Auvry's three volumes is divided into six books, each of which is divided into chapters. In these notes, this work will be referenced by book (bk.) and chapter (chap.) rather than by volume and pages. At Vaux-de-Cernay in 1680, Auvry was sacristan, monk in charge of the granary, and acting superior when the prior and subprior were absent. He then spent over a decade as a confessor to communities of nuns before being appointed prior of Savigny. He retired to Vaux-de-Cernay, where he wrote all or part of his history.

Some influential sources for the early history of Savigny are found in a manuscript from Savigny, Paris MS Bibliothèque nationale fonds lat. 4862. One item in the manuscript is a version of the first revision of the *Chronicon* of Robert of Torigni, revised to include information about Savigny. Léopold Delisle recovered the interpolations about Savigny and published them as *Auctarium Savigneiense* in *Chronique de Robert de Torigni*, ed. Léopold Delisle, 2 vols. (Rouen: A. Le Brument, 1872–73), 2:156–63. Also in this manuscript is a miscellany of historical notes about Savigny. Étienne Baluze combined these notes with other historical entries he found in another Savigniac manuscript and with a history of the abbots of Savigny (*Indiculus abbatum*) up to 1243 and printed the three texts as *Chronicon Savigniacense: Miscellanearum liber secundus* (Paris, 1679), 314–23. In "'Et inter abbates de majoribus unus': The Abbot of Savigny in the Cistercian Constitution, 1147–1243," in *Truth as Gift: Studies in Honor of John R. Sommerfeldt*, ed. Marsha L. Dutton, Daniel M. La Corte, and Paul Lockey, CS 204 (Kalamazoo, MI: Cistercian Publications, 2004), 113–18, Francis R. Swietek and Terrence M. Deneen show that these texts are heavily dependent on other sources such as Robert of Torigni's *De immutatione ordinis monachorum*, the history of Fontaines-les-Blanches written by Peregrinus of Vendôme about 1200, and papal bulls. Another source for the early history of Savigny is the entry on Vitalis in Ordericus Vitalis, *Historia ecclesiastica*, bk. 8, chap. 27.

Cistercian Order, mentioning, for example, the practice of never starting a new monastery with less than an abbot and twelve monks.[3] At times, when more information is available, Auvry pauses to discuss a particular event in detail; for example, Vitalis's career, the building of the abbey's churches, the translation of the relics of Savigny's saints,[4] and the founding of new monasteries. The only other fairly comprehensive effort to study the early history of Savigny is that of Victor de Buck in the *Acta Sanctorum*. He devotes a great deal of effort to sorting out the number and filiation of the monasteries founded directly or indirectly from Savigny.[5] Other scholars, using much the same body of sources as was available to Auvry and de Buck, have studied particular episodes or questions concerning Savigny.

The goal of this general introduction is to provide a context in which to read the four lives translated in this volume. Because more information is available about the first two abbots, Vitalis and Godfrey,[6] they will receive more attention. The treatment of some of the abbots begins with an excerpt in which the brief *Chronicle of Savigny* or another contemporary document epitomizes their contribution. We have placed these quotations in italics.

Reformer Monks: The New Monasticism

As this book is being prepared for the press in 2014, there is great ferment and uneasiness in monastic and other intentional religious communities. On the one hand, many existing Roman Catholic religious orders cope with declining numbers and the need to amalgamate houses, provinces, and even entire orders. The decline of many Roman Catholic religious communities does not seem to be the result of criticism or disdain but rather of lack of interest

---

3. Capitulum 9, in Chrysogonus Waddell, ed., *Narrative and Legislative Texts from Early Cîteaux*, Studia et documenta 9 (*Cîteaux: Commentarii cistercienses*, 1999), 408.

4. Throughout we will refer to Vitalis, Godfrey, Hamo, Peter of Avranches, and William Niobé as the saints of Savigny, even though no pope ever canonized them.

5. Victor de Buck, "De BB. Gaufrido et Serlone, abbatibus, Guilelmo, novitio, et Adelina abbatissa, Saviniaci in Normannia," *Acta Sanctorum*, October 8 (Brussels: A. Greuse, 1853), 1019–41.

6. Vitalis's successor will always be referred to as Godfrey to distinguish him from others of the same name, to whom we will refer as Geoffrey.

among Catholics.[7] On the other hand, in the United States and elsewhere a movement that is sometimes called "the New Monasticism" is leading to the creation of new intentional communities. These communities are Protestant, Catholic, and ecumenical. They often draw inspiration and guidance not only from the Bible but also from the Rule of Saint Benedict, the example of Saint Francis, and Roman Catholic religious orders. There is great diversity in these experimental communities: some are returning to traditional practices that were generally abandoned forty or fifty years ago, some are open to innovation, some are austere, some live with the poor in the inner city, and many have a mixed membership of men and women, clergy and laity, celibate and married.[8]

---

7. Near the end of *God in Proof: The Story of a Search from the Ancients to the Internet* (Berkeley, CA: University of California Press, 2013), 224, Nathan Schneider gives a poignant example: "My first day there I noticed, out for perusal in the chapter room, a photocopy of the annual 'House Report': a one-page, rather dour document describing the state of things at the abbey. It said that there were 'twenty (20)' members, of whom only 'eight (8)' were able to live the full monastic life. No one was in formation. There were no new vocations. They had commissioned a major plan for environmental sustainability, but someone would have to be around to implement it. The report ended by declaring their total dependence on God, their determination to live out God's call, and the intimation that nothing short of a miracle could keep this place going for much longer."

8. For the history of Catholic religious orders and a sense of their present precarity, see Elizabeth Rapley, *The Lord Is Their Portion: The Story of the Religious Orders and How They Shaped Our World* (Grand Rapids, MI: Eerdmans, 2011). "The New Monasticism" and the "ecclesial movements" are discussed in many books and articles. Here is a sampling: *School(s) for Conversion: 12 Marks of a New Monasticism*, ed. Members of Rutba House, The New Monastic Library 1 (Eugene, OR: Wipf & Stock, 2005); Jon R. Stock, Tim Otto, and Jonathan Wilson-Hartgrove, *Inhabiting the Church: Biblical Wisdom for a New Monasticism*, The New Monastic Library 2 (Eugene, OR: Wipf & Stock, 2006); Jonathan A. Wilson, *Living Faithfully in a Fragmented World, Second Edition: From After Virtue to a New Monasticism*, The New Monastic Library 6 (Eugene, OR; Cascade Books, 2010); John Michael Talbot, *The Universal Monk: The Way of the New Monastics* (Collegeville, MN: Liturgical Press, 2011); Mary Forman, ed., *One Heart, One Soul: Many Communities* (Collegeville, MN: Liturgical Press, 2009); Brendan Leahy, *Ecclesial Movements and Communities: Origins, Significance, and Issues* (Hyde Park, NY: New City Press, 2011); Ivan J. Kauffman, *"Follow Me": A History of Christian Intentionality*, The New Monastic Library 4 (Eugene, OR: Cascade Books, 2009); Gerald W. Schlabach, *Unlearning Protestantism: Sustaining Christian Community in an Unstable Age* (Grand Rapids, MI: Baker/Brazos, 2010).

The phrase "the New Monasticism" figures in the title of Henrietta Leyser's classic study, *Hermits and the New Monasticism*.[9] Like our own times, that era within which Vitalis and the other saints of Savigny lived was a time of ferment and experimentation in monasticism. Although existing communities continued to thrive, new kinds of monasticism sprang up, first in Italy with Saint Romuald and Saint Peter Damian,[10] and then in what is today France. In the French Alps, Saint Bruno established the Grand Chartreuse in 1084. In Burgundy, in 1098, what would become the Cistercian Order began with the migration of a group of monks from one monastery, Molesme, to a new one, Cîteaux, though Molesme itself had eremitical connections. At Premontré, Norbert of Xanten (d. 1134), a canon turned hermit, established an enduring order of canons regular. In the Auvergne and Limousin, Robert of La Chaise-Dieu (d. 1067), Stephen of Obazine (d. 1159), and Stephen of Muret (d. 1124), and near the borders of Normandy, Brittany, and Maine, Vitalis of Savigny (d. 1122), Bernard of Tiron (d. 1116), and Robert of Arbrissel (d. 1116) withdrew into solitude, drew followers by their way of life (and in many cases their preaching),[11] and became founders of monastic communities.[12]

These founders and their associates struggled with complex issues: how to provide for and order the relationships among the men and women who became their disciples, how to make the

9. Henrietta Leyser, *Hermits and the New Monasticism: A Study of Religious Communities in Western Europe, 1000–1150* (New York: St. Martin's Press, 1984).

10. On these two pioneers, see Jacques Dalarun, *Robert of Arbrissel: Sex, Sin, and Salvation in the Middle Ages*, trans. Bruce L. Venarde (Washington, DC: The Catholic University of America Press, 2006), 24–26.

11. Leyser, *Hermits*, 69–77. Dalarun, *Robert of Arbrissel*, 33–34, points out the partial complementarity of this new eremitism and preaching: the personal asceticism of the hermit makes his call for repentance credible; as Jesus required of the seventy(-two), the hermit traveled without baggage and often with a companion.

12. On the adoption of an order and customs among the new movements of the first half of the twelfth century, see Leyser, *Hermits*, 87–96; *The Lives of Monastic Reformers, 1: Robert of La Chaise-Dieu and Stephen of Obazine*, trans. Hugh Feiss, Maureen M. O'Brien, and Ronald Pepin, CS 222 (Collegeville, MN: Cistercian Publications, 2010): "The Tripartite Life of Robert, Abbot of La Chaise-Dieu," 1.1 (*Lives, 1*, 73); "The Life of St. Stephen of Obazine," 1.24–26, 2.1–2, 2.11–13 (*Lives, 1*, 153–56, 163–64, 172–77); Carole A. Hutchison, *The Hermit Monks of Grandmont*, CS 118 (Kalamazoo, MI: Cistercian Publications, 1989), 17–22.

transition from a band of disciples gathered around a hermit or hermit-preacher to an organized community under a succession of leaders, how to relate to bishops and other clergy, and how to connect the communities that they founded into a federation.[13] As these hermitages developed into institutionalized communities, some took untraditional forms, such as Stephen of Muret's Grandmont and Robert of Arbrissel's Fontevraud; others assimilated to Benedictine models or were absorbed into the Cistercian Order. Others became canons regular.[14]

One can detect in the lives and foundations of some of these reformer monks an effort to return to pristine beginnings—to the Rule of Saint Benedict in its integrity, to the example of the Desert Fathers, to the *vita apostolica* of the church of Jerusalem as described in the early chapters of the Acts of the Apostles, and to the teachings of Jesus. In this sense they aimed to recover a golden age. For these new hermits, however, solitude meant something different than it had for the hermits who went into the Egyptian desert in the fourth century or even for Saint Benedict. The new hermits did not settle into places far removed from human habitation; for the most part they welcomed companions. What they wanted to leave behind was soft living and financial, legal, and social entanglements, so that they could live as "poor men of Christ and contribute to their own support and to meet the needs of the poor by the work of their hands."[15]

The titles of both this book, *The Lives of Monastic Reformers, 2*, and its predecessor, *The Lives of Monastic Reformers, 1*, are somewhat problematic.[16] Hermit-preachers like Vitalis did not aim to reform

---

13. According to Dalarun, *Robert of Arbrissel*, xii, Robert pioneered the centralized organization of later orders by making the abbess of Fontevraud superior over all the other monasteries in the congregation, whose superiors were prioresses answerable to her.

14. Leyser, *Hermits*, 87–96.

15. Leyser, *Hermits*, 18–28.

16. This discussion of "reform" is informed by Patrick Henriet, "Les trois voies de la réforme dans l'hagiographie érémitique du xiie siècle. Enquête sur la *Vita Bernardi Tironensis* (BHL 1251)," *Médiévales* 62 (2012): 105–22; Patrick Henriet, *La Parole et la prière au Moyen Âge* (Brussels: De Boeck Université, 2000), 256–63; Christopher M. Bellito and David Zachariah Flanagin, eds., *Reassessing Reform: A Historical Investigation into Church Renewal* (Washington, DC: The Catholic University of America Press, 2012); Martha Newman, "Reformed Monasticism

religious life or the church as a whole. Their aim was to convert hearts, to set people on a path of continuing conversion and growth that would lead them toward ever-greater perfection in the Christian life; theirs was a reform that was forward looking (*reformatio in melius*), even eschatological.

That some of those who responded to the preaching of these men wanted to become their followers and perhaps to enter religious life prompted Vitalis and some other preachers to found monastic or canonical communities for them, but Vitalis does not seem to have intended to reform existing monastic life. It is true that Marbod of Rennes wrote to Vitalis asking him to find a place in his congregation for a young woman who could not find a place in a traditional aristocratic community of nuns, so on this point Marbod did see Savigny as innovative.[17] Godfrey, his successor, opted for a stricter form of monastic life and was in that sense a reformer of the community Vitalis founded. There is no reason to think, however, that Savigny under Vitalis was "deformed," so that it needed moral or spiritual re-formation by Godfrey.

As it turned out, Robert of Arbrissel and Stephen of Muret's followers did form new institutional arrangements, but one might wonder to what extent they intended these new forms either to reform existing monasticism or to critique it. Bernard of Tiron certainly fought for the independence of Saint-Cyprien from Cluny, but it was to Cluny's politics, not its monastic observance, that he objected. The congregations of Obazine and Savigny joined the Cistercians in 1147–48, indicating that by then the two groups felt an affinity with the particular monastic form championed by Cîteaux, whose founders had undertaken an "enterprise of renewal and reform."[18] In their beginnings, however, Obazine, La Chaise-Dieu, and Savigny were informal communities that, when they needed a rule, chose the Rule of Saint Benedict.

There is another ambiguity about the idea of reform, which in medieval times usually meant embracing a life that was austere,

---

and the Narrative of Cistercian Beginnings," a paper delivered at the 48th International Congress on Medieval Studies (Kalamazoo, MI: Western Michigan University, May 11, 2013); and very helpful conversations with Robyn Parker of the University of Sheffield, who alerted me to Henriet's article.

17. PL 171:1474D–1475B; Henriet, *Parole*, 281.

18. Waddell, *Narrative and Legislative Texts*, 6.

withdrawn from the world, or devoted primarily to prayer, on an assumption (it can be called "the austerity assumption") that these ways of living are better than alternative forms that are moderate and missionary. This "austerity assumption" seems to have encouraged a drift toward traditional enclosure and disengagement in congregations like that of La Chaise-Dieu, which in its beginnings Marbod of Rennes had to defend against critics who argued that Casadeans had gone from better to worse when they went from being hermits to helping people in need. Was the imposition of a more enclosed way of life on the congregation of Savigny by Vitalis's successor, Godfrey, a de-forming of what Vitalis had envisioned, as well as a re-forming according to the "austerity assumption"? What about the thirteenth-century women's communities that cared for the sick, lepers, and women in difficulties—was their transformation into cloistered communities a reform?[19]

If reform is a complex and difficult idea, monasticism need not be. In Stephen of Muret's words, "Any Christians who have come together to live as one can claim the right to be called monks, even if the name is more particularly given to those who, like the apostles, kept a greater distance from the business of the world, giving their minds to the thought of God alone."[20]

Vitalis: Court Chaplain, Hermit, Traveling Preacher, Monastic Founder

> *This father was educated in the liberal disciplines from an early age. When he reached manhood he began to love poverty and put before his eyes the gospel saying, "Whoever does not renounce all that he possesses cannot be my disciple"* [Luke 14:33]*, just as it is said of Blessed Benedict that he*

---

19. Anne E. Lester, *Creating Cistercian Nuns: The Women's Religious Movement and Its Reform in Thirteenth-Century Champagne* (Ithaca, NY: Cornell University Press, 2011).

20. Carole Hutchison, introduction to Stephen of Muret, *Maxims*, trans. Deborah van Doel, CS 177 (Kalamazoo, MI: Cistercian Publications, 2002), xii. It is curious that Stephen of Muret thought that "the apostolic life" meant greater distance from the business of the world and single-minded concentration on God. On the definition of monasticism, see Hugh Feiss, "Monasticism, Definitions of: Christian Perspectives," in *Encyclopedia of Monasticism*, ed. William M. Johnston, 2 vols. (Chicago: Fitzroy Dearborn, 2000), 2:871–74, and criticisms in a review of the book by Bennett Hill in *Catholic Historical Quarterly* 87 (2001): 707–9.

despised the arid world with its flowers.[21] *So, having been snatched by the hand of divine mercy from the ruin of this falling world,*[22] *he led a strenuous eremitical life at a place called "The Lord's Rock" for almost seventeen years. While he did so, he had frequent visits from proven and upright people of his time, namely, Lord Robert of Arbrissel (who built the monastery that is called Fontevraud), Lord Bernard, and other renowned persons professing the same way of life. In the manner of the Holy Fathers they held very frequent colloquies at The Lord's Rock, discussing the state of holy church and what is useful for souls.*

How holy was the manner in which he conducted himself in his professed state of life, how much he disdained the world and loved poverty, how stingy he was with himself and how generous to those in need, how intent he was on fasts, vigils, prayers, and other holy activities the close and frequent gatherings of the people just mentioned indicates, for as the prophet says, "You will be holy with the holy one" [Ps 17:26].[23]

How faithfully and indefatigably he spread the divine word is attested by the unbearable labor and resulting exhaustion of those brothers of his who accompanied him, when while they sat and took turns in serving him, he never sat while he was preaching, and even when his hearers were worn out, they never saw him tired out. If someone wishes to capture in words how many plots of wicked men, how many indignities of thirst and hunger, how much heat and other bad weather he suffered, such a one will be exhausted with the futile effort. Wanting nothing earthly, he sought "not the things that are his" [1 Cor 13:5] *but the things of Jesus Christ, working only to restore peace among those in discord and to provide food and clothing for the needy, hospitality for the wanderers, pardon for the guilty, lawful marriages for prostitutes, and houses and other necessities for lepers. The Lord conferred such grace on him that although he undertook difficult and impossible things, with God's help he never failed to accomplish them.*

Therefore, when he had served zealously in these and other holy works of this kind for seventeen years, finally, forced by the entreaties of the large

21. Gregory the Great, *Dialogues*, 2. Prol. 1, ed. Adalbert de Vogüé, SCh 260 (Paris: Éditions du Cerf, 1979), 126; *The Life of St. Benedict by Gregory the Great; Translation and Commentary*, trans. Terrence Kardong (Collegeville, MN: Liturgical Press, 2009), 1.

22. Cyprian, *Ad Demetrianum*, ed. M. Simonetti and C. Moreschini, CCSL 3A.2 (Turnhout: Brepols, 1976); cited and trans. Allen Brent, *Cyprian and Roman Carthage* (New York: Cambridge University Press, 2010), 99: *inter ipsas saeculi labentis ruinas* ("in the midst of the very ruins of a decaying age").

23. This text is also cited by William Langland, *Piers Plowman*, B-Text, Passus V, ed. Walter K. Skeat, *The Vision of William Concerning Piers the Plowman*, 2 vols. (Oxford: Oxford University Press, 1979), 1:154, line 285.

multitude of brothers who had come to him because of his holiness, he became the father of more than 140 people of both sexes, judging it better, as Gregory wrote, to profit many than to live for himself alone.[24] *Once he was put in charge, however, he did not abandon his earlier poverty. He kept preaching just as much. He was a great founder of churches, a completely steadfast defender of the poor, a fierce denouncer of tyrants, and a just and humble pastor and most loving provider for the flock committed to him.*[25]

The founder of the monastery of Savigny was a remarkable man of rare talent, broad experience, boundless energy, and deep faith. He was born in Tierceville, about twelve kilometers from the episcopal see of Bayeux.[26] He may have been born or baptized on September 22, the feast of a saint named Vitalis. As an adult, this later Vitalis was chaplain to Robert of Mortain, who died in about 1095, so Vitalis must have been born by 1060. His parents, Rainfredus and Rohes, were dead by 1107, though in 1243 villagers in Tierce-

24. Mendicant orders have often cited the maxim *non sibi soli vivere, sed et aliis proficere.* The duty to serve incumbent on those who have the ability and call is a frequent theme in the writings of Gregory the Great. For example, in his *Pastoral Rule* 1.5 (PL 77:18CD), Gregory writes that when those blessed with gifts from God refuse positions of leadership in the church, "they lose the gifts, which they have received not just for themselves but also for others. Because they are thinking about their own profit and not that of others, they deprive themselves of the goods that they seek to have just for themselves" (*dona admittunt, quae non pro se tantummodo, sed etiam pro aliis acceperunt. Cumque sua et non aliorum lucra cogitant, ipsis se quae privata habere quaerunt, bonis privant*). See Cuthbert Butler, *Western Mysticism*, 3rd ed. (London: Constable, 1967), 176–88. For a similar statement about Robert of Arbrissel, see Baudri of Dol, "First Life of Robert of Arbrissel," par. 12, in *Robert of Arbrissel: A Medieval Religious Life*, trans. Bruce Venarde (Washington, DC: The Catholic University of America Press, 2003), 13.

25. Léopold Delisle, ed., *Rouleaux des morts du ixe au xve siècle* (Paris: Renouard, 1866), 282–84. The translation is by Hugh Feiss. Because the Latin text of this lengthy quotation is easily accessed on line (http://www.archive.org/details/rouleauxdesmorts00deliuoft [accessed November 28, 2013]), it is not included here. This brief biographical sketch was composed just after Vitalis's death and circulated to 208 monasteries, so it seems likely to be reliable. Stephen of Fougères quoted it in his *Vita* of Vitalis, and scholars since have relied on it.

26. What follows is a summary of the very careful reconstruction of the story of Vitalis's life in Jaap van Moolenbroek, *Vital l'ermite, prédicateur itinérant, fondateur de l'abbaye normande de Savigny*, trans. Anne-Marie Nambot (Assen/Maastricht: Van Gorcum, 1990), 148–211.

ville confidently pointed out their home, where Vitalis was born.[27] They had other children, including Osbert, who, the *Vita* 2.15 reports, fell off a roof at Savigny. Vitalis was sent to study when still a young boy. The most likely school would have been at the Benedictine monastery of Grestain,[28] the family monastery of the noble family of Conteville, lords of the area. After studying at Grestain, or perhaps directly from Tierceville, Vitalis probably went to study at the cathedral school of Bayeux, where he would have lived with the canons, whose number and dwellings the redoubtable Bishop Odo (bishop 1049–97) augmented.[29] From Bayeux, Vitalis may then have been sent elsewhere to gain the knowledge of rhetoric and law that Stephen of Fougères (d. 1178) attributes to him. Liège was a likely locale for such an education.

Having finished his education, Vitalis entered into the service of Robert of Mortain, who may have been the patron of his education. Count Robert, Bishop Odo's full brother, had many chaplains, traveled a great deal, and was often in the entourage of his half brother, Duke William of Normandy, known in England as the Conqueror. Traveling with Robert, Vitalis would have learned much about the world. Robert also paid his chaplains well. He wanted to make Mortain an important secular and religious center, and to that end in 1082 he had the collegiate Church of Saint-Evroult[30] and the monastic Church of Notre Dame consecrated in the presence of Duke William and five bishops. Once made a canon of Saint-Evroult, where Saint Firmat (William Firmatus) was buried, Vitalis was assured of an ample income.

Vitalis was now a wealthy and well-connected man. In 1095–96 he withdrew to become a hermit. He did so in a time of turmoil,

27. *Liber de miraculis*, referenced by Van Moolenboek, 352n3.

28. Grestain was a Benedictine Abbey founded by Herluin de Conteville (d. 1066) and his wife Ariette, mother of Duke William of Normandy. Herluin's son, Robert of Mortain, half brother of William and brother of Odo of Bayeux, was a principal benefactor.

29. John Marshall Carter, "'Fire and Brimstone' in Anglo-Norman Society: The Preaching Career of Vital of Mortain and Its Impact on the Abbey of Savigny," ABR 34 (1983): 169–72.

30. There are photographs of this beautiful church in Lindy Grant, *Architecture and Society in Normandy, 1120–1270* (New Haven, CT: Yale University Press, 2005), 153, 158–59. The church was rebuilt early in the thirteenth century. The church at Savigny probably had much in common architecturally with Saint-Evroult.

when Robert Curthose, the duke of Normandy, had little control over his nobility, a council at Rouen declared a Truce of God, and there was a serious famine. While all this was happening, the hermit life was thriving in the forests of western France, and the ideal of voluntary poverty was exerting a strong attraction.

The letter attached to Vitalis's mortuary roll reports that Vitalis embraced the life of solitude and poverty at a place called *Domini Petra* (*Dompierre*, "Rock of the Lord"),[31] somewhere in or near the triangle delineated by Fougères, Savigny, and Passais-la-Conception, near the border of Maine and Normandy and not far from the border with Brittany. Living austerely, like one of the Desert Fathers, he held conversations with like-minded men, over some of whom he exercised authority. It was an apostolic life, thought to replicate the life of Jesus and his disciples, but apostolic also in that it imitated the life of the church in the Acts of the Apostles, where possessions were shared and the apostles gave themselves to preaching.

Vitalis was an indefatigable preacher before and after he founded Savigny. His manifest voluntary poverty enhanced his credibility. According to Ordericus Vitalis, his preaching and his example were an urgent call to interior conversion addressed to men and women of all classes, urging them to abandon sin and lead disciplined, simple lives. Preaching this message brought him both physical discomfort and opposition from knights and churchmen. One of the purposes of his preaching was to bring peace and reconciliation and put an end to the armed conflicts that brought misery to the poor. In his preaching missions, he showed concern for the needy and particularly for prostitutes, whom he called to conversion and for whom he provided means to enter into lawful marriages.[32]

Around 1105, Count William of Mortain underwrote the establishment of a religious community just outside Mortain. He and other secular and religious figures endowed it with lands and rights. The community, of which Vitalis was the prime mover, may have

---

31. Hippolyte Sauvage, *Saint Vital et l'Abbaye de Savigny*, 3rd ed. (Mortain: Armand Leroy, 1895), 42–43, described what he believed were the site and ruins of Dompierre.

32. On Vitalis's preaching see Carter, "Fire and Brimstone," 176–85; Hugh Feiss, "*Seminiverbius*: Preaching in the *Vita* of Vitalis of Savigny," ABR 63 (2012): 257–66; Henriet, *Parole*, 268–82, 407–11.

been for women, for canons regular, or for brothers dedicated to care of the poor. But this new foundation was placed in jeopardy when in 1105 King Henry I of England (1068–35) invaded Normandy, poised to battle with his older brother, Duke Robert Curthose (1054–34), and his supporter, Count William of Mortain (ca. 1084–p. 1140). Vitalis sought to help negotiate a peace, but the effort failed, and Duke Robert and Count William lost the battle.[33] The donations to the new monastery were thus annulled; it seems to have ceased to exist, and its goods were transferred to the Abbey of Saint-Étienne in Caen.

Vitalis and his followers then withdrew to a hermitage in a wooded area twenty kilometers southwest of Mortain. Bernard of Abbeville (1046–1116) was nearby, but by 1109 he and his followers had departed to their monastery at Tiron and had erected wooden buildings there. Vitalis himself may have been reluctant to start another monastery, but the growing number of his disciples and their need for a more stable life and religious discipline evidently persuaded him of the need. By 1113, with donations from Raoul de Fougères (ca. 1070–ca. 1120) and other magnates and the approval of Henry I, the monastery of Savigny was a reality.[34]

So from about 1113 to his death in 1122, Vitalis was abbot of the men's monastery at Savigny, to which was joined before long a women's priory, although in later centuries it was known as

---

33. H. Sauvage, *Saint Vital*, 36–37.

34. For the relevant charters, see Van Moolenbroek, *Vital*, 257–63. Jacqueline Buhot, "L'abbaye normande de Savigny, chef d'ordre et fille de Cîteaux," *Le moyen âge* 46 (1936): 7–8, evokes the setting of the new monastery. The lords of Fougères and their families remained devoted supporters of Savigny throughout the period here under consideration (1112–1244). Auvry, *Histoire*, makes frequent references to their generosity toward the abbey; e.g., bk. 3, chap. 4; bk. 4, chap. 4; bk. 4, chap. 25; bk. 5, chaps. 4, 12, 15; bk. 6, chaps. 10, 18, 27, 28, 33. Bennett Hill, "The Beginnings of the First French Foundations of the Norman Abbey of Savigny," *ABR* 31 (1980): 132, reached a similar conclusion about the counts of Mortain: "In the course of the twelfth century every generation of the family supported the abbey and the Congregation of Savigny." He explores the contributions of both the Counts of Mortain and the Fougères lineage in "The Counts of Mortain and the Origins of the Norman Congregation of Savigny," in *Order and Innovation in the Middle Ages*, ed. William C. Jordan, Bruce McNab, and Teofilo Ruiz (Princeton, NJ: Princeton University Press, 1976), 237–53.

"l'Abbaye Blanche."[35] Vitalis did not cease preaching, but during these years he devoted a great deal of attention to putting Savigny on a sound political, economic, and religious footing. It seems that the community grew beyond its financial means, a fact that prompted Vitalis to recover from the Abbey of Saint-Étienne at Caen the original donations made around 1105 by William of Fougères.[36] In 1119 he obtained support and a privilege from Pope Calixtus II.[37] At the time of his death the monks were working to support themselves by the work of their own hands as much as they could, but they also relied on other sources of income of the kind that monasteries had traditionally depended on. After Vitalis's death, Godfrey and later abbots at Savigny alleviated the economic stress of the community by sending out colonies of monks to make new foundations, but those foundations in their turn also often experienced great financial need.[38]

The new monastery at Savigny followed the Rule of Saint Benedict. The brothers owed obedience to their abbot, their vows were permanent, and they were required to celebrate the divine office.[39] They wore habits of undyed wool. Lay benefactors received from the monks of Savigny and from the monks of other monasteries

35. Van Moolenbroek, *Vital*, 198–99, writes that it is incorrect to say that the superior of this women's monastery was Adeline, sister of Vitalis. He says there was an Abbess Amerline, mentioned in Vitalis's mortuary roll, who was a member of his family and was deceased by 1122. This relative of Vitalis is not to be confused with another woman named Adeline, who had a reputation for sanctity, died before 1181–86, and was buried at Savigny. She and the hermit-become-novice William Niobé were counted among the six saints of Savigny. When the relics of the other five were moved into the new church in 1243, hers remained in the chapel of Saint Katherine. Her relics may have been moved into the church after a fire in 1705. See H. Sauvage, *Saint Vital*, 48–52. On other early women's foundations from Savigny, see Auvry, *Histoire*, bk. 4, chap. 5; bk. 6, chap. 29.

36. See E. P. Sauvage, ed., *Vita Vitalis* 1.15, in "Vitae BB. Vitalis et Gaufridi, primi et secundi abbatum Saviniacensium in Normannia," *Analecta Bollandiana* 1 (1882): 355–410 (hereafter *Vita Vitalis*), and the documents in Van Moolenbroek, *Vital*, 140–44, 266–67, and also Mary Suydam, "Origins of the Savigniac Order: Savigny's Role within Twelfth-Century Monastic Reform," *Revue Bénédictine* 86 (1976): 101–6.

37. See Sauvage, *Vita Vitalis* 2.12; Van Moolenbroek, *Vital*, 189–90, 267–68.

38. Cf. de Buck, *De BB. Gaufrido*, 1014.

39. Van Moolenbroek, *Vital*, 267.

with which Savigny had prayer confraternities prayers for themselves and their families as well as the possibility of burial at the monastery. The monks of Savigny also prayed for the whole world while at the same time offering practical charity to their neighbors. Vitalis dedicated the monastery of Savigny, like the earlier failed foundation near Mortain, to the Trinity at a time when new monastic groups were dedicating their churches to Mary. We know, however, that Vitalis died during Matins of the Blessed Virgin, so devotion to Mary was not lacking at Savigny.[40]

According to the mortuary roll, at the time of death Vitalis was abbot of 140 religious, both men and women. Some members were certainly from aristocratic backgrounds. We know no details of the makeup of the community of women during his lifetime. In these early days Savigny was an original creation. Although founded in a remote forest, it seems during Vitalis's life to have been more involved in preaching and charitable work than were most monasteries. The emergent community existed because of its founder's positive and persistent character. He was fearless in calling people to conversion, and he was equally accessible to the poor and the powerful. His combination of rigorous zeal and deep compassion for all made him a sympathetic figure then as it does now.

Godfrey (1122–38):
Founder of Abbeys and of a Congregation

> *He built many monasteries and imposed customs that were stricter than heretofore.*[41]

No one has done for Godfrey, the second abbot of Savigny, what Van Moolenbroek has done for Vitalis—collected and analyzed

---

40. Janet Burton, ed. and trans., *The Foundation History of the Abbeys of Byland and Jervaulx*, Borthwick Texts & Studies 35 (York: Borthwick Institute for Archives, University of York, 2006), xxxiv–xxxvi.

41. Baluze, "Chronicon Savigniacense," 310: *Hic multa monasteria aedificavit et consuetudines prioribus altiores imposuit. Altiores* usually means "higher" or "more noble." Since other contemporaries report that Godfrey's customs were stricter or harsher, here *altiores* has been interpreted accordingly.

every shred of evidence about the man.[42] The *Chronicle* of Savigny sets the parameters of his abbacy:

> 1122: Our father Dom Vitalis, abbot and founder of this holy monastery, died on the sixteenth of the Calends of October. [September 16]
>
> 1138: Dom Godfrey, the second abbot of this monastery, died the eighth of the Ides of July.[43] [July 7]

Godfrey's *Vita* does not provide many details about his life before or during his abbacy, and what it says may not be completely accurate. According to his *Vita*, Godfrey was from a noble family who lived in Bayeux. He was well educated and studied at Paris before joining the Abbey of Cerisy-la-Forêt, where he remained for some time. He then transferred to Savigny, to which he was drawn by the zeal of Vitalis, whose assistant he became. He was highly esteemed by King Henry I of England. He founded many monasteries, acted as their *visitator* (though not, perhaps, in a formally determined way), and according to chapter 114 of his *Vita* began a General Chapter for all abbots of the Savigniac congregation, held for three days annually at Savigny on the feast of the Holy Trinity. It is generally thought that this General Chapter was established in 1132.[44]

Several sources report that when Godfrey became abbot, he imposed stricter observances on the monks of Savigny. Robert of Torigni wrote,

---

42. See Van Moolenbroek, *Vital l'ermite*. The most protracted study of Godfrey's life is that found in bks. 3 and 4 of Claude Auvry, *Histoire*. For a summary of Godfrey's life and contribution to Savigny's history, see Buhot, "L'abbaye normande," 11–17. Not without reason, she calls him "Geoffrey le fondateur de l'Ordre Savignacien" (17).

43. Baluze, *Chronicon Savigniacense*, 314.

44. Auvry, *Histoire*, bk. 4, chap. 16, thinks the General Chapter was established at least by 1132. He reports that in that year a group of hermits from Fontaine in the archdiocese of Tours asked to join the congregation of Savigny. Godfrey sent Odo to be their first abbot. Their leader Geoffrey and some of the other hermits continued to live as hermits. Their second abbot, Gilbert, was also a religious from Savigny. The seventh or eighth abbot, Peregrin, wrote a history of the community, whence Auvry derived this information.

Vitalis, the hermit, an outstanding sower of the word, built a monastery on the border of Normandy and Brittany, in the settlement of Savigny; he imposed modern observances on his monks, somewhat like those of the Cistercians. Godfrey of Bayeux, a monk of Cerisy, a well-educated and devout religious, succeeded him. He built many monasteries and imposed customs on the Savigniacs that were stricter than what they had had before.[45]

Ordericus Vitalis also reports Godfrey's imposition of stricter discipline: "When he [Vitalis] died, Godfrey of Bayeux succeeded him. He was zealous for immoderate innovations and imposed a heavy yoke on the neck of his disciples."[46] Ordericus and Robert do not report what these new and stricter observances were. One may conjecture that Vitalis, who continued his itinerant preaching after Savigny was founded, may have permitted some of his followers to accompany him on his journeys or to

---

45. *Chronique de Robert de Torigini, abbé du Mont-Saint-Michel: Suivie de divers opuscules historiques*, ed. Léopold Delisle (Rouen: Librairie de la Société de l'Histoire de Normandie, 1873), 2:189: *Vitalis heremita, optimus seminiverbius, in confinio Normanniae et minoris Britaniae, in vico Savinneio, monasterium aedificans, modernas institutiones, in aliquibus Cisterciensibus similes, monachis suis imposuit. Huic successit Baiocensis Gaufridus, Cerasiensis monachus, vir admodum litteratus et in religione fervens. Hic multa monasteria aedificavit, et consuetudines prioribus arciores Savinniensibus imposuit.* Bruce Venarde, in a note to his translation of Dalarun's *Robert of Arbrissel*, 37, and in another note to his translation of documents pertaining to Robert, *Robert of Arbrissel, A Medieval Life* (Washington, DC: The Catholic University of America Press, 2003), 120–21, comments that *seminiverbius* is a rare word applied to Paul in the Vulgate version of Acts 17:18 (Greek: *spermologus*), where, he says, it means "chatterbox." Venarde says that in Christian documents the word has a positive meaning and was usually applied to teaching to pagans. The word is applied to Robert of Arbrissel in three places, twice in Baudri of Dol's *Vita* of Robert and once in the *Vita* by Andrew, a religious of Fontevraud.

46. *Historia ecclesiastica* 8.26 (PL 188:644B); *The Ecclesiastical History of England and Normandy*, trans. Thomas Forester, 4 vols. (London: Bohn, 1854), 51–53: *Quo defuncto, Bajocensis Goisfredus, ac Cersiacensis monachus, successit; qui et ipse immoderatis adinventionibus studuit, durumque jugum super cervices discipulorum aggregavit.* This text is cited by the editor of the *Vitae* of Vitalis and Geoffrey (Sauvage, *Vita Vitalis*, 404n2); Auvry, *Histoire*, bk. 3, chap. 2, discusses Godfrey's intensification of austerities and Ordericus Vitalis's reaction to them.

make preaching expeditions of their own.[47] It is also possible that during his lifetime the new monastery offered some of the scope for individual choice and idiosyncrasy that eremitical life permits. As Vitalis's assistant, Godfrey may have been partly responsible for maintaining discipline when Vitalis was away. In any case, he had time to think about how he would like observance to be at Savigny if and when he was in charge. His vision for Savigny may have been influenced by the observances in the Order of Cîteaux and other monastic reform movements.

Godfrey did indeed found many monasteries. When he succeeded Vitalis as abbot in 1122, Savigny was a single abbey, to which two priories were subject.[48] When he died in 1138, Savigny was head of a congregation of twenty-four abbeys, twenty-three of which had been founded during his abbacy, eighteen of them directly from Savigny.[49] These abbeys included

Furness, founded in 1124 at Tulketh; moved in 1127 to Furness, which founded Rushen (1134), Swineshead (1134–35), Calder (1135 and 1142–43), Holy Cross (1169), and Fermoy (1170)[50]

Beaubec, 1127, which founded Lannoy (Briostel) in 1135–37, and Bival (1128–54), a woman's community that founded a number of daughter houses

47. On the presence of active ministry and contemplative withdrawal at Savigny in the twelfth century, see Kathryn L. Reyerson, "The Way of Mary or That of Martha: Conceptions of Monastic Life at Savigny, 1112–1180," in *The Medieval Monastery*, ed. Andrew MacLeish, Medieval Studies at Minnesota, 2 (St. Cloud: North Star Press, 1988), 34–42.

48. De Buck, *De BB. Gaufrido*, 1024, adds a third: Villers-Canivet, a women's community that he argues was established by 1127.

49. This list is based on de Buck, *De BB. Gaufrido*, 1014–30. Included here are monasteries founded before 1138 and their foundations before 1200. Auvry, *Histoire*, bks. 3–4, also details the founding of monasteries during Godfrey's abbacy. The total of eighteen foundations from Savigny does not include women's monasteries. Founding a monastery was often a protracted process, involving donations, sending a founding community under an abbot, sometimes moving to a new site when the original site proved unsuitable, and building and blessing a church.

50. According to Janet Burton, "English Monasteries and the Continent in the Reign of King Stephen," in *King Stephen's Reign, 1135–1154*, ed. Paul Dalton and Graeme J. White (Woodbridge, UK: Boydell and Brewer, 2008), 98–114, by 1147

Vaux-de-Cernay (1127),[51] which founded Breuil-Benoît (1137)

Inch-Courcy (1127–30, 1180)[52]

Chaloché (1128)

Fourcamont (1129), which founded Lieu-Dieu (1191)

Saint-André en Goffern (1130), which founded Tironnel (1149–51)

Neath (1130)

La Boissière (1131)

Aulnay (1131), which founded Croxden (1170–79)

Quarr (1131–32), which founded Stanley (1151–54)

Fontaine-les-Blanches (1132)[53]

Basingwerk (1131–33)

Combermere (1133), which founded Dieulacres (1146–1214), Whalley
(1172–1206), Jervaulx (1145–50)

---

there were thirteen Savigniac abbeys in England and Wales and one on the Isle of
Man. Savigny founded Neath (1130), Basingwerk (1131), Quarr (1132), Comber-
mere (1133), Stratford Langthorne (1135), Buildwas (1135), Buckfast (1136), and
Coggeshall (1140). From Furness were founded Rushen on the Isle of Man (1134),
Swineshead (1134–35), and Calder/Byland (1135). The story of Calder/Byland is
recounted below.

51. According to Auvry, *Histoire*, bk. 4, chap. 7, and Hill, "Beginnings," 142–43,
Arraud, the first abbot, had been a member of a Benedictine monastery before
joining Savigny under Vitalis. Arraud died in 1145 and was buried in the chapter
room. During his abbacy, Vaux-de-Cernay founded Breuil-Benoît.

52. According to Colmán Ó Clabaigh, "The Benedictines in Medieval and Early
Modern Ireland," in *The Irish Benedictines: A History*, ed. Martin Browne and
Colmán Ó Clabaigh (Dublin: Columba Press, 2005), 90–91, this, the first Savigniac
house in Ireland, was founded at Erenagh (Carrig) in County Down, perhaps at
the urging of Saint Malachy. The first monks seem to have come from Tulketh
(Furness). Reportedly the first abbot (Evodius) had a premonition that the monastery would be destroyed and replaced by a foundation at Inch. The monastery
was destroyed by John de Courcy when he conquered Ulster. In 1180–87, he
founded a Cistercian house at Inch in reparation. The other Irish Savigniac Monastery, Saint Mary's, Dublin, was founded from Savigny in 1139. After the Savigniac
congregation was merged with the Cistercians, it was affiliated with Combermere
Abbey and then, in 1156–57, with Buildwas.

53. Auvry, *Histoire*, bk. 4, chap. 19.

Calder I (from Furness) (1134–40); made daughter of Savigny after moving to Hood (1138), then Old Byland (1142), then Byland (1177); Calder II (resettled from Furness, 1142–43)

Rushen (Isle of Man) (1134), which founded Mirescog (1176)

Swineshead/Hoyland (1134–35)

Longvilliers (1135)

Stratford (1135)

Buildwas (1135), which founded Strata Marcella (1179–1230)

Lannoy (Briostel) (1135–37)

Buckfast (1134–36)

Breuil-Benoît (1137), which founded La Trappe (1140).

This is an impressive list of foundations. Savigny's growth was not as rapid as that of the Cistercian Order, but if compared, for example, to Engelberg, which did not make a foundation from the time it was established in 1120 until the nineteenth century, it is noteworthy. If, however, when Vitalis founded Savigny he had with him 140 disciples, both men and women, and the number of religious at Savigny was 140 or more when Godfrey became abbot, the founding of so many monasteries is not so astounding.

In 1124, two years into Godfrey's abbacy, the church begun by Vitalis was dedicated. Five bishops presided at the dedication: Turgisus of Avranches, Richard of Coutances, Richard of Bayeux, John of Séez, and Hildebert of Le Mans.[54]

The constitutional standing of Savigny under Vitalis and Godfrey in relation to its daughter houses and their daughter houses is not spelled out in the sources, nor is the relationship of Savigny and its progeny to their diocesan bishops. Auvry says that Godfrey visited the daughter houses of Savigny every year,[55] although he may be mistaken about the visitations being annual.[56] Scholars have different views of the question of Savigny's oversight of its daughter

---

54. Delisle, *Auctarium Savigneiense*, 2:160; Auvry, *Histoire*, bk. 3, chap. 4.

55. Auvry, *Histoire*, bk. 4, chap. 15.

56. Bennett Hill, *English Cistercian Monasteries and Their Patrons in the Twelfth Century* (Urbana, IL: University of Illinois Press, 1968), 96–97.

houses, but it may be that Savigny's relationship to its daughter and granddaughter houses was more immediate and comprehensive than that between Cistercian houses.[57] On the other hand, the evidence suggests that Savigny and its daughter houses, like the Cistercians, were not fully exempt from diocesan control until after the congregation was amalgamated into the Cistercian Order and Cistercians themselves received papal exemption from diocesan control.[58] Savigny accepted revenues from churches, tithes, and mills, while the early Cistercians did not. When they joined the Cistercian Order the Savigniacs were allowed to keep these revenues. This fact may not have weakened the Cistercian Order, but it did require allowing differences of observance.[59]

John of Coutances, a churchman, wrote a book titled *De computo ecclesiastico* that studied in detail the ways in which to compute the date of Easter and make other calculations. He sent it with a covering letter addressed "To Abbot Godfrey, Prior Richard and the Monks of Savigny." He indicates that the monks had requested that he write such a compendium. He tells them,

> If you, my blessed lords and true philosophers, whose true philosophy spreads far and wide in things human and divine, see anything useless in this little work, correct it or notify me to correct it. I know your holy and venerable community has many upright and erudite men, who if it had pleased you could have completed this undertaking more adequately and who can correct it where needed.[60]

---

57. Suydam, "Origins," 94–108. Against Buhot and others, Hill, *English Cistercian Monasteries*, 85–97, argues strongly that there was very limited Cistercian influence on the customs of Savigny during the abbacies of Vitalis and Godfrey. Perhaps with reference to the question of exemption from episcopal control, Hill writes in "Beginnings," 131n2, that Suydam "unsuccessfully attempts to assess the Congregation's administrative and spiritual role in the twelfth-century reform movement."

58. Francis R. Swietek and Terrence M. Deneen, "The Episcopal Exemption of Savigny, 1112–1184," *Church History* 52 (1983): 285–98.

59. Anselme Didier, "Savigny et son affiliation à l'ordre de Cîteaux," *Collectanea Ordinis Cisterciensium Reformatorum* 9 (1947): 358.

60. Joannes Constantiensis, "Epistula ad Gaufridum," PL 163:1479–82. J.-P. Migne reprinted the book from Martène's *Anecdota*, 1:362, and assigned it to the year 1137. Auvry describes the contents of the book in *Histoire*, bk. 4, chaps. 23–24.

Such flattering prose need not be taken too literally, but the book is complex enough to indicate that there were learned monks at Savigny.

At the time of Godfrey's death in 1138, there was tension between Savigny and Furness. Furness had established a foundation at Calder in 1135 under an abbot named Gerald, but the foundation was destroyed by Scottish armies sent into northern England by King David of Scotland after the death of Henry I in 1135. In 1138 when the monks returned from Calder to Furness, the monks there would not receive them back. Various reasons, all of them speculative, have been adduced to account for this inhospitable refusal: Gerald may have been unwilling to resign his abbacy, and the presence of two abbots in one place might not have been workable; the monks of Furness may have thought that the vow of stability required that Gerald and his companions stay at Calder and rebuild there; Furness may not have felt able to support additional monks; and the original reason for the foundation at Calder may have been some sort of tension or schism at Savigny.

In any case, with the help of Archbishop Thurstan of York, the monks from Calder settled later in 1138 first at a hermitage at Hood, near Thirsk, then in 1142 at Old Byland, which turned out to be too close to Rievaulx Abbey, and finally, in 1177, at Stocking, where they built Byland Abbey, whose ruins remain to this day. In the General Chapter of 1141, they successfully petitioned to be removed from the filiation of Furness and put under that of Savigny. When Abbot Gerald died in 1142, Abbot Roger replaced him, remaining in office until 1196. Meanwhile, in 1142–43 Furness colonized Calder a second time. In 1149–50, Hardred, abbot of Calder II, strove to have Calder II recognized as the motherhouse of Byland, but when Abbot Serlo came to England in 1150, Hardred renounced this claim. After Serlo resigned, Furness appealed unsuccessfully to his second successor as abbot of Savigny, Richard (1153/54–58), to have Byland placed in its filiation.[61]

---

61. Burton, *Foundation History,* xviii–xxiv; Burton, "English Monasteries," 98–114; Auvry, *Histoire,* bk. 4, chap. 21; Hill, *English Cistercian Monasteries,* 98–101, sees in this troubled history a symptom of the lack of constitutional clarity in the Savigniac congregation. For the dating of the various events, we have followed those given in Burton's introduction to *The Foundation History.*

Summing up Godfrey's life and contribution to Savigny, Claude Auvry wrote,

> Saint Godfrey did not follow in everything the pattern that Saint Vitalis, his predecessor, had set. As this saintly founder had had a special vocation to preach the word of God and received from the pope a plenary power of doing so everywhere, he devoted himself particularly to the conversion of souls in various provinces of Christendom, and God confirmed his words with a great many miracles. For his part, Godfrey stayed within the enclosure of his monasteries, where he governed in the spirit of the Rule of Benedict, so we see no hint in his story that he or any of his religious had preached publicly.[62]

It is difficult to evaluate Godfrey's contribution to the polity of the Savigniac congregation. Under him the Order expanded rapidly, and he is credited with having established structures for governance: annual General Chapters and visitations. Neither of these institutions seems to have worked very well, however, perhaps because it fell to the abbot of Savigny to visit all the houses of the congregation each year—an impossible task. Furthermore, all the abbots in the British Isles were expected to come to Savigny each year, a task which though not impossible was impractical because such a journey was often dangerous, time consuming, and expensive, especially during the civil war that broke out in England at around the time of Godfrey's death. Savigniac houses both in England and on the continent were to be found in the territories of both contenders for the English throne—King Stephen and Empress Matilda, whose husband Geoffrey of Anjou was conquering Stephen's territories

---

62. Auvry, *Histoire*, bk. 4, chap. 28: "S. Geofroy ne suivit pas tout à fait la conduite que St. Vital, son prédécesseur, avoit tenue de son temps. Comme ce saint fondateur avoit eu une vocation particulière pour prêcher la parole de Dieu, et reçu des papes un plein pouvoir de la répandue partout, il s'appliqua particulièrement à la conversion des âmes en diverses provinces de la chrétienté, et Dieu confirma ses paroles par un grand nombre de miracles; au lieu que S. Geofroy se renferma, pour ainsi dire, dans l'enceinte de ses monastères, qu'il gouverna selon l'esprit de la règle de S. Benoît aussi ne voyons-nous en aucun endroit de son histoire que ni lui, ni ses religieux aient prêché publiquement" (2:298–99).

on the continent—a situation that undermined the cohesion of the Savigniac congregation.

Royal and Baronial Patrons

After the 1106 Battle of Tinchebray, William, count of Mortain, forfeited his position for having supported the unsuccessful revolt of Duke Robert Curthose. King Henry I then made his nephew, Stephen of Blois (1096–1154), count of Mortain. Hence as a young man Stephen may have had occasion to meet Vitalis. In 1125, Stephen was married to Matilda of Boulogne (d. 1152), heiress to the county of Boulogne. The couple became important benefactors of Savigny, which was located in Stephen's county of Mortain. Stephen then negotiated the founding of a monastery by monks from Savigny in his English territory of Lancaster; in 1127 the community settled at Furness.[63] Stephen went on to found the Savigniac abbeys of Buckfast (Devon) and Longvilliers (Boulogne), and his queen founded Coggeshall on land she inherited in Essex.[64] Stephen seems to have been more than conventionally pious. His conduct, writes David Crouch, shows him "to have been one of the most prominent early propagators of the Christian and ethical knighthood preached in the next reign by Stephen de Fougères, bishop of Rennes,"[65] author of the *Vita* of Vitalis. An important Anglo-Norman baron, Earl Ranulf I of Chester, was a notable patron of Savigniac monasteries in his vast territory. According to Bennett Hill, he contributed to the founding of Basingwerk, Combemere, and Dieulacres.[66]

Empress Matilda, daughter of Henry I, and Stephen's rival for the throne, was benefactor of two Savigniac nunneries, Saint-Saëns

---

63. David Crouch, *The Reign of King Stephen, 1135–1154* (Harlow, UK: Longman, 2000), 11–22; R. H. C. Davis, *King Stephen* (London: Longmans, 1967), 8.

64. Crouch, *Reign*, 317.

65. Crouch, *Reign*, 319.

66. Hill, *English Cistercian Monasteries*, 30 (and the chart between 30 and 31). He also writes that Ranulf founded Calder, but we find no confirmation of this statement. On the founding of monasteries during Stephen's reign in England, the foundations of Stephen, Empress Matilda, and Ranulf of Chester, see Christopher Holdsworth, "The Church," in *The Anarchy of King Stephen's Reign*, ed. Edmund King (Oxford: Clarendon, 1994), 212–29.

and Bondeville.[67] Otherwise, she was not an important patron of Savigniac monasteries, though she was a generous patron of many religious houses. She withdrew in 1148–49 to Rouen in Normandy, where she often stayed at a priory of Bec, Notre-Dame-du-Pré, which her father, Henry I of England, had founded. After her death in 1167 she was buried at Bec.[68]

Abbot Evan (1138–40)

Abbot Godfrey died in 1138 or possibly 1139.[69] His successor was Evan, who was elected to Savigny after being abbot of Furness from 1126 on. Henry I died in 1135, so by the time Evan became abbot at Savigny, the war for the throne of England between Stephen and Empress Matilda had been underway for several years. The war spilled over into the area where Savigny was located.[70] According to Auvry, Evan was a native of Normandy and had returned to Savigny in 1136.[71] Perhaps his experience in England and his first-hand knowledge of Furness and the conflict over Calder recommended him to the electors. By the time of his election the British Isles were particularly important to the Savigniac congregation, as ten of its twenty-four abbeys were there.

---

67. Grant, *Architecture and Society*, 23, 38. Other Savigniac monasteries of women included, besides l'Abbaye Blanche (founded by Vitalis), Villers-Canivet, Bival, and Gomerfontaine.

68. Grant, *Architecture and Society*, 631; Marjorie Chibnall, *The Empress Matilda: Queen Consort, Queen Mother and Lady of the English* (Oxford: Blackwell, 1995), 128–37, 177–90.

69. De Buck, *De BB. Gaufrido*, 1011, gives evidence for the two dates and opts for 1138; Auvry, *Histoire*, bk. 4, chap. 28.

70. Lindy Grant, "Savigny and its Saints," in *Perspectives for an Architecture of Solitude: Essays on Cistercians, Art, and Architecture in Honour of Peter Fergusson*, ed. Terryl Kinder (Brepols: Turnhout, 2005), 109, suggests that Savigny "suffered an eclipse in the mid-twelfth century when the Angevins took control of Normandy, for the order had become closely associated with King Stephen. But Henry II soon once more extended ducal patronage and protection to it and fell under the spell of Haimon, master of the *conversi* at Savigny, who was widely regarded as a holy man."

71. Auvry, *Histoire*, bk. 4, chap. 30; F. R. Swietek and T. M. Deneen, "The Date of the Merger of Savigny and Cîteaux Reconsidered," *Revue d'histoire ecclésiastique* 101 (2006): 567.

Abbot Serlo (1139–53; d. 1158)

At Clairvaux . . . Serlo, who had been abbot of Savigny; a man outstanding in life, speech, and knowledge of the Scriptures.[72]

Robert of Torigni gives this version of Serlo's life:

> After Evan of England, who ruled the monastery for only a short time, Godfrey was succeeded by venerable Serlo . . . who had been a disciple of Godfrey in the world and had entered the monastic life with him first at the monastery of Cerisy and then, having left that monastery, sought a greater form of religious life at Savigny. Because the monasteries subject to him did not submit to him as he wished, by the authority of Eugene, the Roman Pontiff, he submitted himself and all his monasteries to the Cistercian Order, and then, after a few years, for the sake of being more free to spend time with God, he left behind care of the monasteries and secluded himself at Clairvaux, spending time with himself and with God. He was succeeded as head of Savigny by Richard de Courcy, who was prior of that monastery.[73]

Serlo is said to have been born near Bayeux and to have been a disciple of Godfrey. Serlo entered Cerisy-la-Forêt with Godfrey, then transferred with him to Savigny in 1113, one year after that monastery was founded by Vitalis. By the time he became abbot of Savigny, he had had over twenty-five years of experience in living in a monastery. In 1144 he obtained papal protection for Savigny.[74]

---

72. Baluze, "Chronicon Savigniacense," 314: *Anno Domini MCLVIII obiit apud Claramvallem V Idus Septembris Domnus Serlo, qui fuerat Abbas Savigneij, vir vita et sermone atque Scripturarum scientia conspicuus.*

73. Robert of Torigni, *De immutatione*, 189–90: *Cui, post Evanum Anglicum, qui parvo tempore eidem monasterio praefuit, successit venerabilis Serlo de Valle Badonis juxta Baiocas, qui fuerat praedicti Gaufridi in seculo discipulus et monachatum susceperat prius cum eo in monasterio Cerasiensi, sed relicto illo monasterio, pro majori religione expetierat Savinneium. Hic, quia pro velle suo non ei obtemperabant monasteria sibi subdita, auctoritate Eugenii Romani pontificis, subdidit se et omnia monasteria sua Cisterciensi ordini, et exinde post paucos annos, ut Deo liberius posset vacare, relicta cura monasteriorum, in monasterio Clare Vallis, Deo et sibi vacans, delituit. Cui successit in regimine Savinneii Ricardus de Curceio, prior ejusdem loci.* See Delisle, *Auctarium Savigneiense*, 2.161–62. On Evan see Auvry, *Histoire*, bk. 4, chap. 4.

74. The confirmation is in the bull *Desiderium quod*, issued by Pope Lucius II on December 5, 1144. A second bull, *Quia igitur (Habitantes in domo)*, which was as-

Serlo seems to have found it difficult to hold the Savigniac congregation together. Contemporary witnesses report that some English abbots had become lax about making the arduous and time-consuming trek to the annual General Chapter; others were restive under the authority of the abbot of Savigny. Only three English abbots attended the 1147 chapter at Savigny. Burdened with worry about this lack of cohesion, Serlo and Osmund of Beaubec[75] went to the Cistercian General Chapter of 1147 and asked in the presence of Saint Bernard and the Cistercian pope Eugene III (1145–53) that the Savigniac monasteries be incorporated into the Cistercian Order. At the same General Chapter, the congregation of Obazine (successfully) and the Gilbertines (unsuccessfully) also petitioned to join the Cistercian Order. The confirmation occurred in *Pax ecclesiae*, a privilege addressed by Pope Eugene to Serlo on September 19, 1147.[76] After the March 1148 council that met at Reims, Eugene III issued a more solemn document on April 10, 1148, *Apostolicae sedis*, specifying that all the Savigniac monasteries were now permanently Cistercian and were to obey Serlo and his successors.

---

signed the same date, includes provisions for living under the Rule of Saint Benedict, disciplining abbots, monks, and *conversi*, and forbidding schisms. It seems to have been a forgery written between 1148 and 1153. Such are the conclusions of two studies by Francis R. Swietek and Terrence M. Deneen, "Pope Lucius II and Savigny," *Analecta Cisterciensia* 9 (1983): 3–26; "A Savigniac Forgery Recovered: Lucius II's Bull *Habitantes in Domo* of December 5, 1144," in Studiosorum Speculum: *Studies in Honor of Louis J. Lekai, O. Cist.*, ed. Francis R. Swietek and John R. Sommerfeldt, CS 141 (Kalamazoo, MI: Cistercian Publications, 1993), 363–87. De Buck, *De BB. Gaufrido*, 1012–13, and Auvry, *Histoire*, bk. 5, chaps. 1–19, regarded *Quia igitur* as authentic.

75. Swietek and Deneen, "Date," 553–55. This article considers the sequence of events in 1147–48 that led to the incorporation of the congregation of Savigny into the Cistercian Order. The authors examine the dates of the incorporation in light of the radical redating of the emergence of the Cistercian Order proposed by Berman, *The Cistercian Evolution* (see n. 1 above), with which they do not agree. Burton, *Foundation History*, xxv–xxvii, also provides evidence undermining Berman's theory. According to Auvry, *Histoire*, bk. 4, chap. 6, and Hill, "Beginnings," Osmund was the first abbot of Beaubec (founded 1127–28) and remained in that office until 1156.

76. Swietek and Deneen, "Date," 558–60. In the momentous year of 1147, William Niobé, a saintly hermit who seems to have asked to become a novice at Savigny, died (Delisle, *Auctarium Savigneiense*, 2.162).

Although Serlo placed Savigny and its congregation in Saint
Bernard's hands, scholars dispute what role Bernard played in the
union of Savigny and the Cistercians. R. H. C. Davis believed that
Bernard was hostile to King Stephen because Stephen did not support Bernard's candidate for the archbishopric of York.[77] Davis also
believed that Stephen had encouraged Furness to free itself from
the control of Savigny. Jacqueline Buhot believed that it was because
Serlo was so taken with Bernard that he asked for the merger.
Francis R. Swietek, for his part, thinks that Bernard's role in the
merger was only "peripheral."[78] Christopher Holdsworth, on the
other hand, marshals evidence to show that from at least 1144
Bernard and Serlo were planning on a merger. He provides as evidence a possible visit of Bernard with Serlo at Savigny in 1144, the
close and inconvenient proximity between some new Cistercian
foundations and existing Savigniac houses, and shifting political
alliances between the two monastic groups and their patrons on
both sides of the English civil war. He agrees with Chrysogonus
Waddell that expanded versions of the *Carta caritatis* and of the
story of the beginnings of Cîteaux were prepared to facilitate the
assimilation of the Savigniacs.[79] In any case, Savigny was assigned

---

77. The appointment of the archbishop of York was highly contested throughout the 1140s. Stephen's brother, Bishop Henry of Winchester, supported the
candidacy of a relative, William Fitzherbert, to whom Saint Bernard was vehe-
mently opposed. Bernard supported the candidacy of the eventual winner in the
struggle, the Cistercian Henry Murdac. For a summary of this conflict see Crouch,
Reign, 301–10.

78. Francis R. Swietek, "The Role of Bernard of Clairvaux in the Union of
Savigny with Cîteaux: A Reconsideration," in Bernardus Magister: *Papers Presented
at the Nonacentenary Celebration of the Birth of Saint Bernard of Clairvaux, Kalamazoo,
Michigan*, ed. John R. Sommerfeldt, CS 135 (Kalamazoo, MI: Cistercian Publications, 1992), 289–302; Chrysogonus Waddell, "Toward a New Provisional Edition
of the Statutes of the Cistercian General Chapters, ca. 1119–1189," in Swietek and
Sommerfeldt, Studiosorum, 400–1.

79. Christopher Holdsworth, "The Affiliation of Savigny," in *Truth as Gift*, ed.
Dutton et al., 43–88. It is difficult to unravel the political dimensions of the ten-
sions that arose in the Savigniac congregation in the 1140s. R. H. C. Davis inter-
prets the situation as follows. The founder of Byland, which applied in 1147 to be
removed from the filiation of Furness and placed under Savigny, was a supporter
of the Angevins (that is, of Empress Matilda and her husband, Geoffrey of Anjou).
Western Normandy, including Savigny, had fallen to Geoffrey in 1142. Neath and
Quarr, which with Byland were the only Savigniac monasteries represented at the

to the filiation of Clairvaux, and Bernard sent Thibaud from Clairvaux to be prior of Savigny to instruct the monks of Savigny in Cistercian observances.[80] Whatever the cause for opposition, Peter of York, abbot of Furness, appealed to Eugene III, asking that Furness be allowed to remain in the same observance in which it was founded, even though Savigny itself had joined the Cistercians. Archbishop Hugh of Rouen and Bishop Arnulf of Lisieux settled this challenge, with Pope Eugene issuing a mandate, *Cum omnibus*, on October 10, 1149, that squelched the English Savigniac houses' attempt at independence. When Abbot Peter was forced to resign, Richard of Bayeux, who had been a monk of Savigny, succeeded him as abbot of Furness.[81]

After the union of 1147, some Cistercians wanted to prohibit adding new communities to the Order. A decree of the General Chapter of 1152 issued a prohibition against the founding or incorporation of new communities. Between 1147 and Serlo's resignation in 1152–53, eight new monasteries were added to the Savigniac filiation.[82] Some of the language of the forged bull *Quia igitur* (*Habitantes in domo*) may have been meant to protect Savigny's new foundations and its capacity to continue to grow. It seems deliberately to omit references to Cistercian norms and to encourage expansion when it declares, "First it is set down that you observe

---

1147 chapter at Savigny, had as patrons Earl Robert of Gloucester and Baldwin de Redvers, earl of Devon, respectively, both of whom were prominent supporters of the Angevin cause. Davis conjectures that Stephen encouraged Furness and the other Savigniac monasteries in England to resist the hegemony of Savigny and incorporation into the Cistercian Order. Saint Bernard and Pope Eugene III were supporting the Angevins by the time of the merger, and this fact may have made the Empress Matilda and her supporters receptive to the Cistercian takeover of Savigny (Davis, *King Stephen*, 101–3; De Buck, *De BB. Gaufrido*, 1015–18).

80. De Buck, *De BB. Gaufrido*, 1015–18.

81. Swietek and Deneen, "Date," 562; de Buck, *De BB. Gaufrido*, 1018; Hill, *English Cistercian Monasteries*, 101–15, traces the repercussions of the union of the Savigniac congregation with the Order of Cîteaux down to the end of the twelfth century and concludes that the union with the Savigniac monasteries brought no benefits to the Cistercians but instead introduced alien customs (e.g., accepting tithes) that led to corruption and dissension. His conclusion seems to go a considerable way beyond the available evidence.

82. De Buck, *De BB. Gaufrido*, 1030–40.

inviolately the monastic order according to the *Rule* of blessed Benedict and the relevant enactments of the rule, that in the future you not depart from the state of religion which is known to be thriving in your congregation through the grace of God, but by striving to become better you advance in the increase of your order and religious way of life."[83]

Another sticky issue in the amalgamation of the congregation of Savigny with the Order of Cîteaux was the possession of *spiritualia*, that is, the ownership of churches and church revenues. The monasteries of Savigny had them; the Order of Cîteaux forbade them. It seems that the Savigniacs quietly kept possession of their *spiritualia*, and when asking for papal confirmation they discreetly left them out of their list of properties. At the same time, they renewed efforts to obtain confirmation and protection from secular lords. When, however, litigation at the papal court increased during the pontificate of Alexander III (1159–81), the Savigniac houses applied for papal confirmation of their *spiritualia*. Alexander III may have inadvertently approved such possessions early in his reign. Then he became adamantly opposed to such possessions, but finally in 1174–80 he allowed Savigniac houses an exception from the rule, provided that the *spiritualia* had been in their possession before the amalgamation with the Order of Cîteaux. Over the next two decades, this distinction between spiritual properties acquired before and after the merger dissolved, and Savigniac houses began to seek confirmation of recent acquisitions.[84]

Another issue was the status of the abbot of Savigny in the hierarchy of the Cistercian Order. Historians have long thought that at the amalgamation in 1147 Serlo obtained for the abbot of Savigny a place just after the abbots of the first four daughters of Cîteaux and a permanent position among the definitors—advisors to the

83. Swietek and Deneen, "A Savigniac Forgery," 366–67 with commentary on 370–72: *In primis siquidem statuentes ut ordinem monasticum secundum beati Benedicti regulam et instituta regulae competentia inviolabiliter observetis, nec a statu religionis qui per Dei gratiam in vestra congregatione vigere cognoscitur in posterum declinetis, sed in melius proficiendo in ordinis ac religionis augmento proficere studeatis.*

84. Francis R. Swietek and Terrence M. Deneen, "'Ab antiquo alterius ordinis fuerit': Alexander III on the Reception of Savigny into the Cistercian Order," *Revue d'histoire ecclésiastique* 99 (1994): 1–28.

Abbot General who assumed an important place in the General
Chapters. Swietek and Deneen have argued convincingly against
both of these claims.[85] After the 1147 General Chapter, Serlo stayed at Clairvaux in hope
of being allowed to resign his abbacy. Bernard was inclined to allow
this resignation if the monks of Savigny would agree. They preferred to keep Serlo, but fearing that they could not, they designated
two possible successors, both of whom declined. Bernard then sent
Serlo back to Savigny. In 1153, Serlo returned to Clairvaux and was
succeeded at Savigny by William, who was abbot for less than a
year. Serlo led an edifying and quiet life at Clairvaux until his death
in 1158.[86] André Wilmart identified thirty-four of Serlo's sermons
surviving in manuscripts and edited one of them. Lawrence
Braceland edited and translated three more and pointed out the
existence of a few more fragments of Serlo's writings.[87]

Abbot Richard de Courcy (1153–58) to
Abbot Joscelin (1163–78)

> *He [Richard de Courcy] defended the rights of the church of Savigny
> steadfastly during the entire time of his abbacy. . . . He resigned,
> advancing no cause except his own insufficiency.*[88]

Richard had been prior under Serlo before the union with the
Cistercians. Contemporary documents say he grew up in the abbey
from his youth and was a wise and discerning person.[89] He resigned

85. "Et inter abbates," 89–118.

86. Delisle, *Auctarium Savigneiense*, 2.161–63; de Buck, *De BB. Gaufrido*, 1013–14.

87. André Wilmart, "Recueil des discours de Serlo, abbé de Savigni," *Revue
Mabillon* 11 (1922): 26–38; Serlo of Savigny and Serlo of Wilton, *Seven Unpublished
Works*, ed. and trans. Lawrence C. Braceland, CF 48 (Kalamazoo, MI: Cistercian
Publications, 1988); Lorna E. M. Walker, "Hamo of Savigny," 49n14, gives refer-
ences to a series of studies of Serlo's sermons by M. Pigeon.

88. Baluze, *Chronicon*, 311: *jura ecclesiae Savigniacensis toto suo tempore constanter
defendit. . . . cessit, nullam praetendens causam nisi suam insufficientiam.* See Auvry,
Histoire, bk. 3, chap. 6, which says that Richard was prior for ten years under
Godfrey, then again in 1150–51 under Serlo.

89. Swietek and Deneen, "Date," 569–70. On whether there was an abbot named
William who held office briefly between Serlo and Richard, see the note to chap. 22

the abbacy after five years, pleading his own inadequacy. He was succeeded by Alexander of Cologne, who had been a monk of Clairvaux and had served as abbot of Grandselve.

In 1172, Henry II traveled from Ireland to England and then to Normandy, where he met with papal legates first at Savigny, then at Avranches, and finally at Caen regarding the assassination of Thomas Becket. The legates are reported to have written, "it pleased us to gather for the meeting at the monastery of Savigny, where we could be helped by the prayers of religious men."[90] Henry II may have chosen Savigny for this consultation because of his family's benefaction to Savigny and its foundations and because of his personal ties with Hamo, a monk of the community.[91]

> In the year of the Lord 1173 Blessed Hamo passed to the Lord and a new church was begun at Savigny.[92]

In 1173 the old church begun by Vitalis and finished by Godfrey partially collapsed, and a new one was begun. As they so often did, the lords of Fougères contributed generously to the project.[93] This church was an avid wish of Hamo, one of Savigny's saints. He had prayed to God, received a sign, and heard a heavenly voice assuring him that his wish would be granted (chap. 52).[94] In 1243, his relics would be moved to the new church for which he had prayed. Hamo and his friend Peter of Avranches, another of the saints, died in 1172–73.

---

of the *Life of Hamo*, and Burton, *Foundation History*, xiii, xvii, xx, and especially 28 n. b and 56 n. c. The same note to chap. 22 of Hamo's *Vita* also discusses whether Abbot William of Toulouse was abbot a first time (1161–64) between Abbots Alexander and Joscelin as well as in 1178–79.

90. The letter containing the papal delegates' words is preserved by Roger of Hoveden and cited in *Chronique de Robert de Torigini*, 32n4.

91. Francis R. Swietek, "King Henry II and Savigny," *Cîteaux* 38 (1987): 14–23.

92. Baluze, *Chronicon*, 311: *huius tempore, videlicet anno Domini MCLXXIII, beatus Haino [sic] migravit ad Dominum et nova ecclesia Savigniacensis incepta est.*

93. Auvry, *Histoire*, bk. 6, chap. 18.

94. References in parentheses are to chapters to the lives of Hamo and Peter translated in this volume.

Hamo

According to the author of his *Vita*, Hamo, a native of Brittany, was an attractive, kindly, and "simple" man (chaps. 36; 43; 46), who was a model of monastic virtue, particularly humility (chaps. 1; 18–19). He was in charge of the *conversi* at Savigny and often did ministerial service in convents. He was a skilled confessor and discerner of hearts (chaps. 2; 38–42; 46–48) and in that capacity was an advisor to royalty (chaps. 20–21; 41), particularly to King Henry II of England (chaps. 20–21; 27; 31–32). Hamo was an ardent collector of miracle-working relics (chaps. 11–15; 22–26; 42–45), the beneficiary of eucharistic miracles (chaps. 3–10),[95] a fundraiser, a builder of churches (chap. 52), and a champion of the poor (chaps. 16–17). Perhaps to keep the reader from drawing the conclusion that Hamo was too much on the road and too involved in the world, his hagiographer writes that he was "an indefatigable adherent to the contemplative life" (chap. 37), and several times he applies to Hamo the phrase "he returned to himself," typically used with reference to contemplative experience (chaps. 3; 10).

Peter of Avranches

Hamo was Peter of Avranches's lifelong friend and one of his confessors (chaps. 4; 15). Peter, though, was a much more silent (chap. 5), solemn (chap. 6), and solitary (chap. 11) person, who had no use for Hamo's familiarity with the powerful of this world (chap. 8). Peter had the gift of tears (chap. 14), avoided conversations, and sought to remain in the peace and routine of the cloister (chap. 9). Once a knight who had had a vivid vision of the afterlife came to Savigny to talk with the monk whom in his vision he had seen standing next to the throne of God. The knight had been assured

---

95. Both relics and eucharistic miracles appear prominently in accounts of the spiritual experience of other saintly people in the decades after Hamo's death. See, for example, Marie d'Oignies (ca. 1177–1213): Vera von der Osten-Sacken, *Jakob von Vitrys "Vita Mariae Oigniacensis": Zu Herkunft und Eigenart der ersten Beginen* (Göttingen: Vandenhoeck and Ruprecht, 2010), 54–61; Brenda Bolton, "Mary of Oignies: A Friend to the Saints," in *Mary of Oignies, Mother of Salvation*, ed. Anneke B. Mulder-Bakker (Turnhout: Brepols, 2006), 199–220.

that the Lord heeded that monk's prayers. Peter, by then quite feeble, was living in the infirmary. The knight told him of his vision (chaps. 10–11).[96]

After his death, probably in 1172, Peter appeared to Hamo to assure him that a place was prepared for him in heaven, one that excelled in splendor the place that Peter occupied (chap. 15).[97] He was buried not in the common cemetery of the monks but in a more fitting place (chap. 15), from which his bones were moved to the new church at Savigny in 1243.

Building a Shrine to Savigny's Saints

> In 1220, under Abbot Raoul (1208–21) occurred the dedication of the Church of the Holy Trinity and of Saint Mary of Savigny. It was done by five bishops and innumerable devout and holy people.[98]

In 1181, midway in the abbacy of Simeon d'Evreux, "Richard, bishop of Avranches, dedicated the basilica of Saint Katherine."[99] The next year, the bodies of the saints of Savigny were moved from the old church to the new chapel of Saint Katherine, which stood to the south of the dormitory near the cemetery and had its own cloister. Peter, abbot of Clairvaux, and Ralph II of Fougères joined Abbot Simeon and a large crowd for the transferal. The remains of the saints were placed together in one carved stone sarcophagus.[100]

---

96. Ronald Pepin, "Visions of Heaven and Hell in the Life of Peter of Avranches, Monk of Savigny," ABR 63 (2012): 378–83.

97. Visions of the afterlife were also a feature of accounts of saintly lives around the time that Peter's *Vita* was written. See von der Osten-Sacken, *Jakob von Vitrys*, 180–82; Thomas of Cantimpré, "Supplement to the Life of Mary of Oignies," in *Mary of Oignies*, 143, 149–50.

98. Baluze, "Chronicon Savigniacense," 318: *In hoc anno [1220] fuit dedicatio Ecclesiae sanctae Trinitatis sanctaeque Mariae de Savigneio. Facta fuit a quinque Episcopis et a populo innumerabili in devotione sancto, sexto Idus Maij.* The five bishops were the archbishop of Rouen and the bishops of Avranches, Bayeux, Coutances, and Sées.

99. Baluze, *Chronicon,* 315: *Anno Domini MCLXXXI, V Kal. Junii dedicata est basilica sanctae Katherinae a Domno Ricardo Abrincansi.*

100. Lindy Grant, "Savigny and its Saints," 110–12.

Simon's successor, William III de Douvres (1187–1205/8) was remembered as "a religious man and very energetic in temporal affairs." [101] "In 1200 the community of Savigny entered for the first time into the new church on the day of the Assumption of Blessed Mary." [102] The abbey church, many years in the building, was far enough advanced for the monks to begin using the choir. Hamo of Landécot had urged the building of a church where the monks would have more room and the abbey's relics would be kept and displayed. His death in 1173 meant that his relics could be displayed with those of the other saints of the Savigny congregation: Vitalis, Godfrey, Peter of Avranches, and William Niobé. Vitalis's *Vita* was written slightly before the church was begun. Hamo's was written just afterward.

Although all that remains of the church now are the lower courses of the radiating chapels on the east end, the south wall of the nave, and the west wall of the transepts, the church was in use in Auvry's time and up until the French Revolution, so several descriptions of it are extant. The church was patterned after the new church at Clairvaux, which, breaking with earlier Cistercian practice, had at the east end a rounded ambulatory with radiating chapels that made it possible for pilgrims to visit the remains of Saint Bernard and for priests to celebrate private masses. The church at Savigny was 247 feet long and 80 feet wide. Ten large cylindrical columns supported the nave. Like Clairvaux, Savigny had nine radiating chapels. They were trapezoidal, set into the polygonal wall of the east end. The east end did not align with the nave, so a space filled with a trapezoidal bay stood on the eastern end of the nave. Each transept held two chapels facing east. Over the crossing there was a tower (not usual in Cistercian churches, but perhaps present in the earlier church at Savigny), but there were no towers on the west end. A large rose window was in each transept. The central cloister lay on the south side of the church, with the dormitory on the east and the refectory on the west. By the mid-nineteenth century the only large masonry remnant still standing was the

101. Baluze, *Chronicon*, 311: *vir religiosus et in temporalibus strenuissimus.*

102. Baluze, *Chronicon*, 316: *Conventus Savigneij in Ecclesiam novam in die Assumptionis beatae Mariae primo intravit.*

doorway to the refectory, which had been built a decade or so before the church was begun.[103]

Stephen of Lexington (1229–43)

He did many good things both in this house and in its whole filiation, aroused religious fervor there very much, increased the monastery of Savigny to over forty monks and more, and adorned the abbey with many buildings. This good man, everywhere circumspect, led by the Holy Spirit, carried the bodies of the saints of the monastery from the chapel of Saint Katherine, where they had rested for a long time, to the greater church with much honor. On that occasion, the Lord deigned to make known many noteworthy miracles.[104]

Stephen of Lexington was the brother of Henry, bishop of Lincoln. He studied at Paris and Oxford and was a student of Edmund of Abingdon. He entered Quarr Abbey in 1221 and was abbot of Stanley from 1223, in which capacity he was sent to reform the Cistercian houses in Ireland. When that mission was finished he assumed the abbacy of Savigny in 1229. After he later became abbot of Clairvaux, he was instrumental in founding the Collège de Saint-Bernard in Paris, a *studium* for Cistercians there. He was deposed by the abbot of Cîteaux for his role in that endeavor. He was appointed bishop of the Isle of Man but died before he received the news. He died at Ourscamp in 1257.[105]

---

103. Grant, *Architecture and Society*, 154–55; H. Sauvage, *Saint Vital*, 70–72. On page 76, H. Sauvage gives a drawing of the doorway into the refectory. There are photographs of it in Grant, *Architecture and Society*, 152–53, with the probable date of the refectory given as the 1150s or 1160s.

104. Baluze, *Chronicon*, 312–13: *hic multa bona tam in hac domo quam in tota generatione fecit, fervorem religionis ibidem amplius excitavit, conventum Savigniacensem usque ad quadraginta monachos et amplius augmentavit, ipsam abbatiam multis aedificiis decoravit. Hic bonus vir, undique circumspectus, corpora sanctorum, praesentis monasterii, Spiritu Sancto edocente, de capella beatae Katherinae, ubi multo tempore quieverant, ad majorem Ecclesiam cum multo honore reportavit.*

105. Auvry, *Histoire*, bk. 6, chap. 34; Maur Standaert, "Étienne de Lexington," *Dictionnaire de spiritualité* 4 (1961): 1502–4; Stephen of Lexington, *Letters from Ireland, 1228–1229*, trans. Barry W. O'Dwyer, CF 28 (Kalamazoo, MI: Cistercian Publications, 1982), 3–14.

In 1242 Stephen obtained permission from the Cistercian General Chapter to move the bodies of Savigny's saints to the new church. He also secured permission to have lamps always burning before them. When the tomb in the chapel of Saint Katherine was opened, the bodies of the saints were found interred in individual coffins with a name of a saint on each. They were displayed for veneration there in the chapel until their new resting place was ready. Even more than their translation fifty years before, this one was a very public celebration. While two abbots had presided over the earlier translation, this time an archbishop and five bishops presided.

The relics were placed in the new church in elevated gilded and enameled tomb chests. Vitalis and Hamo were placed on either side of the altar of the Blessed Virgin in the center of the ambulatory, and Peter of Avranches's relics were placed to the south, between the last pillar of the ambulatory and the first pillar of the nave. The relics of Godfrey and William of Niobé were placed opposite Peter on the north side of the ambulatory. It was customary thereafter to carry the relics in procession on the Tuesday after Easter and on May 1. A monk was commissioned to write an account of the translation and the miracles of healing and celestial fire that accompanied it.[106]

From accounts of the building and dedication of the church at Savigny, Lindy Grant draws several conclusions. Savigny remained an important and well-connected abbey after it joined the Cistercian Order. It was alert to developments within the Order. In embracing the public veneration of its saints in its church, Savigny was returning to its roots. Vitalis had gone among the people as a preacher, and crowds had come to listen. Now they came to venerate his relics.[107]

---

106. Grant, "Savigny," 112–13; Auvry, *Histoire*, bk. 6, chaps. 29, 31; H. Sauvage, *Saint Vital*, 47–50. H. Sauvage provides a diagram of the ambulatory and the tombs of the saints. Calvinists pillaged Savigny in 1562 and destroyed the tombs. After the destruction of the monastery following the French Revolution, the relics of the saints were divided between the nearby parish churches of Savigny-le-Vieux and Landivy.

107. Grant, "Savigny," 113.

Lorna E. M. Walker has discovered that there are two versions of Hamo's *Vita* and reconstructs their relationship as follows.[108] The earlier version, which is found only in British Library MS Cotton Nero A XVI, contains material not found in the other manuscripts of the *Vita* used by E. P. Sauvage in preparing his 1882 edition. The first version was written very soon after Hamo's death in 1173, the second some seventy years later. The first version emphasizes Hamo's *simplicitas*, his intelligent but self-doubting integrity of heart. It calls him a skilled "confessor and searcher of hearts," skills he exercised not just for England's Henry II but also for the *conversi* at Savigny, the nuns of the L'Abbaye Blanche, and the empress Matilda. The first version of the *Vita* might have been prepared soon after Hamo's death for Henry II, with the hopes of encouraging him to contribute to building the new church at Savigny, a project dear to Hamo's heart. The manuscript, however, does not have the décor of a presentation copy, and Henry II would probably have been unhappy with the intimate details it contains about himself and his mother.

It is easier to conjecture the reason for the preparation of the mid-thirteenth-century second edition of the life. The material left out of that version concerns Hamo's relations with Henry II. As the second version of Hamo's *Vita* was prepared under Stephen of Lexington with a view to Hamo's canonization, it was apparently thought desirable to eliminate references to Hamo's close connections with Henry II, since that relationship might not have endeared Hamo to Pope Innocent IV. Also eliminated was Hamo's criticism of some of his fellow monks' lack of devotion to the Eucharist.[109]

---

108. This and the next paragraph summarize the research and conclusions of Lorna E. M. Walker, "Hamo of Savigny and his Companions: Failed Saints?" *Journal of Medieval History* 30 (2004): 45–60. On a similar failed initial effort under the first abbess of Fontevraud to secure the canonization of Robert of Arbrissel, which led to a reworking of Robert's *Vita*, and on subsequent failed efforts, see Dalarun, *Robert of Arbrissel*, xv, xx. Dalarun thinks that Robert anticipated being revered as a saint (8, 141). The *Vita* of Bernard of Tiron may also have been written to secure Bernard's canonization: see Geoffrey Grossus, *The Life of Blessed Bernard of Tiron*, trans. Ruth Harwood Cline (Washington, DC: The Catholic University of America Press, 2009), xii–xiv.

109. The chapters that E. P. Sauvage indicates are found only in the Cotton manuscript are the last half of 10, 14, 16, 18–21, 23–25, 27–28, and 31–45.

In 1244, after Stephen of Lexington had departed to become abbot of Clairvaux, Raoul III of Fougères sent a request to Pope Innocent to ask for the canonization of the five saints of Savigny: Vitalis, Godfrey, William of Niobé, Hamo, and Peter of Avranches. Some or all of the lives of the first four of these men may have been written with a view to their canonization.[110] Raoul's postulation emphasizes the miracles worked through the saints, some of which he had witnessed himself. There is no evidence that the pope responded. Savigny had waited too long. They no longer had the patronage of the English crown. When Stephen of Lexington moved to Clairvaux, he seems to have given priority to the canonization of his former teacher, Edmund of Abingdon, who was canonized in 1247. The pope may have thought that the saints of Savigny were of merely local interest, and then the Cistercian Chapter of 1268 put a moratorium on seeking canonizations for its members.

Be that as it may, there is evidence of approved veneration of the saints at Savigny in the eighteenth century, though in the nineteenth century Hippolyte Sauvage was unable to find any churches dedicated to Savigny's saints or any mention of them in the lists of saints of the neighboring dioceses. He found, however, that *Vitalis* was a frequently given first name in the region.[111]

---

110. That the *Vitae* were written with a view toward canonization is a reasonable inference but not an incontrovertible fact. Henriet, *Parole*, 269–70, 8, 141, so cautions regarding the *Vita* of Vitalis, and similar caution is required regarding the *Vita* of Waltheof (Waldevus, d. 1159), written by Jocelin of Furness about the second abbot of the Cistercian community of Melrose. This life of a Cistercian by a member of the Savigniac filiation offers some interesting points of comparison with the lives of Savigny's four saints. For an account of the *Vita Waldevi* see Helen Birkett, *The Saints' Lives of Jocelin of Furness: Hagiography, Patronage, and Ecclesiastical Politics* (York: York Medieval Press, 2010), 12–21, 115–38, 201–25. Another possible reason for writing a saint's life was to supply readings for the divine office in honor of the saint.

111. H. Sauvage, *Saint Vital*, 50–59.

The Life of Blessed Vitalis of Savigny

Introduction to
The Life of Blessed Vitalis of Savigny

The Author, Sources, Purpose, and Date

Stephen of Fougères (d. 1178) was an official at the court of Henry II of England[1] from 1156 and bishop of Rennes in Brittany from 1168. Robert of Torigni writes in his chronicle for 1178, "The death of Stephen, bishop of Rennes, an upright and well-educated man. . . . He wrote many poems and songs for fun and for human acclaim; and because the One who has mercy on men knew he was going to die soon, he warned him to refrain from such things and do penance. He wrote the *Vita* of Saint Firmat, the bishop, and the *Vita* of Saint Vitalis, the first abbot of Savigny."[2] Stephen had also been a canon of the Church of Saint-Evroult in Mortain[3] from

1. T. A. M. Bishop, "A Chancery Scribe: Stephen of Fougères," *Cambridge Historical Journal*, 10, no. 1 (1950): 106–7.

2. *Obiit Stephanus, vir honestus et litteratus, episcopus Redonensis. . . . Ipse enim multa ritmico carmine et prosa jocunde et ad plausus hominum scripserat; et quia miserator hominum eum in proximo moriturum sciebat, monuit eum a talibus abstineret et poenitentiam ageret. Scripsit etiam vitam S. Firmati et vitam S. Vitalis primi abbatis Savigneii.* (*Chronique de Robert de Torigni, abbé du Mont-Saint-Michel suivie de divers opuscules historiques,* ed. Léopold Delisle, 73–74 [Rouen: Librarie de la Sociète de l'Histoire de Normandie, 1873]; cited by E. P. Sauvage in "Vitae BB. Vitalis et Gaufridi, primi et secundi abbatum saviniacensium in Normannia, nunc primum editae studio et opere E. P. Sauvage," *Analecta Bollandiana* 1 [1882]: 355–410, here 355) (hereafter cited as *Vita Vitalis*).

3. Count Robert of Mortain founded the collegiate Church of Saint-Evroult at Mortain in 1082. Ordericus Vitalis, *Ecclesiastical History,* ed. and trans. Marjorie Chibnall, 6 vols. (Oxford: Oxford University Press, 1969–80), 4:330–31; cited by Lorna E. M. Walker, "Hamo and His Companions: Failed Saints?" *Journal of Medieval History* 30 (2004): 45n1.

1165/66 to 1168, where Firmat, an eleventh-century hermit, was buried and honored as a saint and where Vitalis himself had been a canon. When Stephen became bishop of Rennes, he had a chapel constructed in his episcopal palace and dedicated to Mary and Saint Firmat.[4]

In his prologue to the *Vita* of Vitalis, and again in book 1, chapter 7, Stephen says that his sources include vernacular writings and the recollections of trustworthy men.[5] He also says he drew on Vitalis's mortuary roll, particularly the cover letter.[6] He knew the *Historia ecclesiastica* of Ordericus Vitalis and may have drawn on the written lives of Robert of Arbrissel and Bernard of Tiron (who, he mentions, met with Vitalis when they were all living as hermits) as well as on other contemporary documents and hagiographical accounts.[7] Jaap van Moolenbroek, however, thinks that Stephen's task in writing the *Vita* was limited to taking material that had been collected and then supplied to him by the monks of Savigny, giving it a proper literary form, and attaching edifying commentary.[8]

In the prologue to the first book on Blessed Vitalis, Stephen indicates that his motives for writing are to make known the life of a great man and to make sure that future generations will have a written record of that life. At the beginning of book 2 he says that he has been forced to write more than he had intended by some

---

4. Van Moolenbroek, *Vital*, 54–56. The *Vita* of Saint Firmat is found in the AA SS, April 2 (Antwerp, 1675): 334–41.

5. Sauvage, *Vita Vitalis*, 2.1, 2.6, 2.13.

6. Sauvage, *Vita Vitalis*, 2.13.1; *Rouleau des morts du ixe au xve siècle*, ed. Léopold Delisle, Société de l'Histoire de France (Paris, 1866); *Rouleau mortuaire du B. Vital, abbé de Savigni*, éd. phototypique, ed. Léopold Delisle (Paris, 1909); Van Moolenbroek, *Vital*, 61.

7. Sauvage, ed., *Vita Vitalis* 2.13.2. See *Robert of Arbrissel, A Medieval Religious Life, Documents*, trans. and annotated Bruce L. Venarde, Medieval Texts in Translation (Washington, DC: The Catholic University of America Press, 2003); Jacques Dalarun, *Robert of Arbrissel: Sex, Sin*; Geoffrey Grossus, *The Life of Blessed Bernard of Tiron*, trans. Ruth Harwood Cline (Washington, DC: The Catholic University of America Press, 2009). Compare, for example, the story about Vitalis's school companions calling him "the little abbot" with the incident in Geoffrey Grossus's *Vita* of Bernard of Tiron, chap. 7 (trans. Cline, 14), where other boys "jeered and called him a monk." The same *Vita*, chaps. 49–50 (trans. Cline, 56) contains a description of Bernard's preaching. See Patrick Henriet, *La Parole et la prière au Moyen Âge* (Brussels: De Boeck Université, 2000), 270–71.

8. Van Moolenbroek, *Vital*, 66.

people who have inquired among Vitalis's surviving disciples and want Stephen to extend his text. That those persons are said to have inquired among Vitalis's disciples seems to indicate that they were not among those disciples, but that fact would not mean they were not monks of Savigny who came to the monastery after Vitalis's death. In fact, Van Moolenbroek believes that it is obvious that the monks of Savigny commissioned the life, because (1) right at the beginning Vitalis is introduced and praised as the first abbot of Savigny (Prol.1), a "devout religious house" (bk. 1.1.5), and (2) the life itself says little about the seventeen years he spent as a hermit, and that little is taken from the letter attached to Vitalis's mortuary roll (bk. 2.12–14).[9]

The monks may have wanted a *Vita* to provide readings for the divine office. They may also have commissioned Stephen to write a *Vita* of Vitalis to prove Vitalis's sanctity and provide evidence supporting Stephen's canonization.[10] In any case, the author's aims are hagiographic, as he makes clear in the prologue. His aim is to

9. Van Moolenbroek, *Vital*, 52.

10. According to Van Moolenbroek, *Vital*, 72–75, in favor of this hypothesis is the role played by hagiographic texts in the canonization of Saint Bernard in 1174. As Bernard was buried at Clairvaux, so Vitalis was buried at Savigny, which after the merger of the two orders was placed in the filiation of Clairvaux. It is even possible that readers are to think that the monk who had the vision of Vitalis being taken up into heaven (bk. 2.18) was Saint Bernard himself. Van Moolenbroek, however, thinks that the arguments against this hypothesis are stronger. For one thing, it was still possible for a canonization to occur locally with the concurrence of several bishops, as occurred for Saint Firmat at Mortain in 1156, though there do not seem to have been any further local canonizations in the archdiocese of Rouen. Second, Hamo, who died in 1173, had undertaken the construction of a grand monastery church, which would have left few funds for the expensive process of a papal canonization. Third, Savigny did not have the support at Rome for Vitalis's canonization that Clairvaux had for Bernard's; the priority of the Cistercians at that time was the canonization of Malachy of Armagh.

Walker, "Hamo of Savigny," 45–60, explores a possibility that Van Moolenbroek left open: that whatever the reasons for the writing of Stephen's *Vita* of Vitalis in the 1170s, in 1243 the monks of Savigny used it in a concerted effort to obtain papal canonization of four of their number: Vitalis, Geoffrey, Hamo, and Peter of Avranches. Their attempt failed. Walker suggests that one reason for the failure may have been that the priority of Stephen of Lexington, formerly abbot of Savigny and now abbot of Clairvaux, was the canonization of Edmund of Abingdon (canonized 1247), whose process may have been held up because of the questionable miracles attributed to him.

describe the virtues and charisms of a saint, the miracles he worked, the prophecies he uttered, and the veneration he received after his death. However improbable some of the things he recounts, he wants the reader to know that they really happened (bks. 1.11; 2.6, 2.7) while somewhat distancing himself by saying "this is what reliable people told me."

Converging evidence indicates that Stephen wrote the *Vita* of Vitalis near the end of his own life. Why the monks of Savigny chose him to write it is not evident. Presumably the monk who wrote the *Vita* of Hamo could have written it, but perhaps the monks of Savigny thought that having a well-connected bishop write their founder's life would give the *Vita* and them more prestige.

Outline and Style of the *Vita*

Stephen's *Vita* of Vitalis has a discernible structure. It contains two books; the first seven chapters of book 1 tell of Stephen's early life. Then, skipping over his seventeen years as a hermit, chapter eight concerns the founding of Savigny. The last seven chapters in this book tell of some of his religious ministries, in no obvious chronological order, though the last event is known to have taken place in 1118. Book 2 is longer, perhaps because other people who knew Vitalis provided new materials (bk. 2.1.1). An event that can be dated to 1119 appears in chapter 12 of book 2. Then come two chapters excerpted from his mortuary roll (bk. 2.13–14), with a final miracle in the chapter after that (bk. 2.15). The remaining chapters tell of his death, translation, burial, and miracles associated with those events.[11] The overall structure is as follows:

1.1   Prologue: Family and Birth

1.2–4   Childhood and Education

1.5–7   Chaplain to the Count of Mortain

1.8   Petition to Raoul de Fougères to Build Savigny

1.9   Converting Prostitutes

---

11. Van Moolenbroeck, *Vital*, 58.

In Vitalis's *Vita*, Stephen of Fougères does not flaunt his learning. He employs many biblical quotations and allusions but does not make much use of classical allusions. His style and vocabulary seem designed to make his work accessible to a wide spectrum of those who could read Latin. He does not use many complex rhetorical devices, though he does play on Vitalis's name in book 1.1.3, saying that Vitalis valued this life (*vitam*) little but animated many others

---

12. On this story of the way people in England who did not know Vitalis's language understood his preaching, see Henriet, *Parole*, 276–77.

toward better lives. He also in one place invokes the monastic *topos* of the desert wasteland (bk. 1.1.4). In an aside to the reader, he draws a rather forced comparison between Vitalis's run-in with the octopus and the efforts of Pharaoh to kill the Hebrew children and of Herod to kill the newborn Christ (bk. 1.3.3).

Stephen's favorite rhetorical device is apostrophe. Many times after a paragraph of narration he breaks out in enthusiastic exclamations (bks. 1.1.2, 1.3.2, 1.7.2, 1.10.2, 1.13.2, 1.14.2), some explicitly addressed to Christ (bks. 1.2, 1.15.2; 2.10.2), Vitalis himself (bk. 1.1.5), the monks of Savigny (bk. 1.1.3), or the reader (bk. 2.2.2). These passages are a way of drawing readers into the story and pointing out the moral that they should be drawing.

What the *Vita* Reveals about Vitalis

Stephen's *Vita* is clearly a work of hagiography. It is not a biography. He wrote it fifty years after Vitalis died, under the auspices of the monastery Vitalis had founded. It aims to show Vitalis's sanctity: his voluntary poverty, his fearless dedication to preaching,[13] his concern to help the poor and sinners, and his readiness for martyrdom. Nevertheless, it does provide some important historical information. Twelve of the first twenty-seven chapters mention Vitalis's preaching. To depict Vitalis as a peripatetic preacher did not serve any immediate institutional goal of the enclosed monks at Savigny, but they wanted it included because it was true. Additionally, as the *Vita* includes four mentions of Vitalis's activity in England (three of which involve preaching), it seems clear that Vitalis had a special connection with England.

In the details of Stephen's account, a number of facts seem historically sound. Vitalis's parents' names were Reigfredus (Rainfredus) and Rohardis (Rohes), and Vitalis himself was born in Tierceville. His family was not of the nobility. It seems plausible that he was educated away from his home territory and then became chaplain at Mortain. Stephen does not mention that Vitalis, like him, was a canon at Mortain, though the fact is known from other sources.

---

13. Feiss, *"Seminiverbius"*; Carter, *"Fire and Brimstone"*; Henriet, *Parole*, 272–82, 407–11.

The story that Henry, the youngest son of Raoul de Fougères, resisted his father's wish to give Vitalis some of his inheritance to
found a monastery may have come from Henry himself, who in
1150 retired to become a monk of Savigny. Vitalis's mortuary roll
agrees that he helped prostitutes enter into lawful marriages. He
is known to have been a peacemaker,[14] and independent evidence
exists of the court case described in *Vita* 1.15.

The plots that Stephen describes against Vitalis's life seem less
credible, but the letter attached to the mortuary roll corroborates
(*reis veniam*) Vitalis's compassion for prisoners and the presence of
his blood brother at Savigny. The story of the nun who used threads
from his clothes to cure illnesses is evidence that a women's community already existed at Savigny during Vitalis's lifetime. Ordericus
Vitalis's account of Vitalis's death, however, differs somewhat from
Stephen's, and the presence of a monastic community at "the Rock
of the Lord" by the time of Vitalis's death is doubtful.

Translation

What follows is a translation of E. P. Sauvage's edition of the *Vita*.
As his edition is accurate and well annotated, we have emended
very seldom. The numbering and titles of the chapters come from
his edition, but some longer chapters have been divided into num-
bered paragraphs. The aim throughout has been to create as literal
a translation into smooth-flowing English as possible. In order to
do so, it has sometimes been necessary to divide long, complicated
sentences. Nevertheless, Anthony Esolen, a skilled translator, notes
the danger of imposing such divisions: "when you break up those
sentences into three or four separate sentences, the effect is dis-
joined; the essential relations between words and images and scriptural allusions are lost."[15] Every effort has been made to avoid these
dangers.

14. Henriet, *Parole*, 277–80. The chaotic political situation in which Vitalis lived
resembles the surroundings in which Stephen of Obazine and Robert of La Chaise-
Dieu lived and ministered; see *The Lives of Monastic Reformers, 1*, trans. Feiss,
O'Brien, and Pepin, 13–15, 121–22.

15. Interview with Kathleen Naab, www.Zenit.org, Sept. 29, 2011 (accessed
September 30, 2011).

The author sometimes uses an odd sequence of tenses. So, for example, in book 1, chapter 10, Stephen writes, *Cum igitur vir Dei sermonem faceret, praefatus vir ad ejus pedes advolvitur* ("When the man of God finished his sermon [imperfect subjunctive], the man throws [present indicative] himself at his feet"). At other times when he is narrating a story, the author switches from past to present tense to give the story more immediacy. In instances of the first sort, we have smoothed out the sequence of tenses, and in cases of the second, we have sometimes put the story into the past tense. In other cases, however, as in book 1, chapter 14, we have left the tenses as Stephen wrote them.

In the text the author often uses the pronouns *he* and *him* or does not specify the subject of the verb. In some of these cases, the name of the subject has been inserted.

The Life of Blessed Vitalis of Savigny

Prologue

1. As the authority of the angel testifies, "it is good to hide the secret of the king, but it is honorable to reveal and praise the works of God."* Therefore, we have decided to make heard in a more evident written form what we have found written in the vernacular concerning the venerable man who was the first abbot of Savigny, as well as what we know from the recollections of trustworthy men. The life and works of many men who built holy church with their words, deeds, and examples are read. Hence, it is very shameful that the life of so great a man be passed over in sterile silence and that transmission of knowledge about him to future generations should have no written support.

*Tob 12:7

2. Desiring to write about the life of this man, we humbly implore the Lord's clemency, so that he "who made the tongues of infants eloquent, and loosened the tongues of the mute for words,"* and granted to the ass, the beast of burden of the foolish prophet, to form human words to convince him of his folly,* will grant us an abundance of words, so that what the mind conceives the tongue will be able to bring to birth arranged by a truthful pen.[1] For God, whose

*Wis 10:21

*Num 20:28, 30

---

1. *stylo*: the word translated as "written form" in paragraph 1.

nature is unwaveringly good and who always seeks opportunities to bestow a benefit, never ceases to carry into effect on behalf of human beings the overflowing abundance of his goodness, so that invited by his benefits they may be ashamed to be subject to the devil's tyranny and to fail to give thanks to so great a benefactor.

3. Hence it is that to this man about whom we have decided to write he conferred the gift of his grace. Through his saving doctrine Vitalis granted salutary medicine to souls poisoned by the infectious venom of the ancient* serpent, and when they had been healed of their wounds he showed them the way of salvation. Hence by his words and life Vitalis spent the talent entrusted to him by the father of the family* for the advantage of many, and disdaining the warnings of men he did not hide his lighted lamp under a basket of fear.* Leaving these matters aside, however, let us get on with the work that we have set before ourselves. Let us bring forth knowledge to the glory of the Lord and the advantage of our readers, seeking to please the Lord alone, asking a reward for our work from him from whom the secrets of the heart are not hidden, to whom mute things speak,* and to whom all silent things answer.

veternosi

*Matt 25:14-28

*Matt 5:15;
Mark 4:21;
Luke 11:33

*2 Pet 2:16;
cf. Num 22:28,
30

End of the Prologue

Book One

Chapter 1. The Beginning of the Life of Saint Vitalis, the First Abbot of Savigny

1. In the province of Bayeux there is a certain designated district that its inhabitants call Tierceville.[1] In this village lived a man named Reigfredus, who married a wife named Rohardis. They strove to serve the true Lord diligently. Perceiving the Lord's commands with attentive ear, they devoutly fulfilled them. They were alert to opportunity to support the poor and needy and lavished alms, according to what is written, "Give alms, and all things will be clean for you."* At night they gave them hospitality, which is known not to be at the bottom of the list of works of mercy.* About this the apostle said, "When they had extended hospitality to angels, they pleased God."* Rendering to the church the revenues sanctioned by canon law without any pride or procrastination*[2] and providing for their own life by just labors, with great earnestness

*Luke 11:41

*Matt 25:35-36; RB 53

*Heb 13:2

*sine aliquo typho vel procrastione

---

1. According to Hippolyte Sauvage, Tierceville is about nine kilometers from Bayeux. See *Saint Vital et l'Abbaye de Savigny*, 3rd ed. (Mortain: Armand Leroy, 1895), 358n2.

2. This phrase echoes RB 31.16: *sine aliquo typho vel mora*. In his edition, *Vita Vitalis*, in *Vitae BB. Vitalis et Gaufridi primi et secundi abbatum Savigniacensium in Normannia, Analecta Bollandiana* 1 (1882): 358, E. P. Sauvage corrected *typho* to *typo*, which usually means "figure" or "recurrent fever." This translation has restored

they offered to God the worship due him. While they were applying themselves to these and similar holy deeds, they bore a son. They derived great joy from his birth and, as was fitting, devoted the greatest care to his nurture.

2. This infant, washed in the font of sacred baptism, was named Vitalis. O name significant of a great grace! O the ineffable kindness of God! O unutterable providence of the Creator! O who is able to marvel worthily at the height of divine counsel? O who can penetrate to its depths? Through human beings divine power does what seems good to it; though they are unaware of it, it often does things that benefit salvation. I believe that it was not without reason* that incomprehensible divine wisdom wished this infant to be called with such a name. I think that by this name it already indicated in advance that he would be made a sharer in the heavenly life.*

*in vacuum

*see, e.g., 1 Cor 9:23; Heb 3:1

3. I say that deservedly he merited being distinguished by such a name, for he valued the passing life little, with the loving eagerness of his soul yearned for heavenly life, and by his word and example sought to enliven many toward that better life. Rightly he shone with such an appellation, for with wise argument he laid bare the deceits of the devil and by his wholesome advice drew many back from the latter's noxious mouth[3] and took care to return them to the heavenly life after restoring them to their earlier health. Rejoice, church of Savigny, and be glad that you merited having such a great and wise founder. I say, rejoice, all you who dwell at Savigny, and exult, and recognize as fulfilled in you what is said through the prophet Isaiah: "The strangers will eat in desert places

---

the original reading. Hereafter this edition will be cited as E. P. Sauvage, *Vita Vitalis.*

3. Hellmouth was a common iconographic theme in medieval art; see, for example, the Winchester Psalter, fol. 39r.

turned into abundance."* Where formerly wild beasts   *Isa 5:7
had their dens* and the birds of the air made their   *see Zeph 2:15
nests,* there many voices now sound praises to God.   *Luke 13:19
Where perhaps robbers plotted against the blood of
the innocent, now there is pursuit of divine contemplation. The land that vipers, thistles,* and sterile trees   *Gen 3:18
occupied* is now watered with the tears and weeping   *see Job 24:20
of holy men.

4. Why add more? The place that once remained
uncultivated and uninhabitable responds to the hands
of the cultivator and now supplies food to the disciples
of Christ. The power of God is magnified because in
the desert it produced water from the rock for the
Children of Israel;* his all-powerful mercy is glorified   *Num 20:8-11;
because he changed the empty solitude⁴ into provi-   1 Cor 10:4
sions for his servants. As I say these things, I conceive
a fire in the very depths of my heart. I truly confess
that I am filled with an extreme transport of joy. Who
unless weak in mind may not rejoice at seeing such a
great community of servants of God devoutly render
praise to God and assiduously engage in the work of
God?⁵

---

4. *vastam solitudinem*: Num 14:3, Deut 32:10 (*in loco horroris et
vastae solitudinis*), a favorite phrase of Cistercian authors. See
Burton, *Foundation History*, xxxiii–xxxiv. It emphasized the Cistercian desire to be apart from ordinary society, their connection with
the biblical accounts of going into the desert and with the desert
monastics of late antiquity, and their embrace of poverty; Janet
Burton and Julie Kerr, *The Cistercians in the Middle Ages* (Rochester,
NY: Boydell Press, 2011), 5, 15–16, 57–59; Christopher Kelly, "The
Myth of the Desert in Western Monasticism: Eucherius of Lyon's
In Praise of the Desert," *Cistercian Studies Quarterly* 46, no. 2 (2011):
129–41. For a subtle analysis of such imagery and a history of its
interpretation, see Nicolas Schroeder, "*In locis vaste solitudinis.*
Représenter l'environnement au haut Moyen Âge: l'exemple de
la Haute Ardenne (Belgique) au VIIᵉ siècle," *Moyen Âge* 116 (2010):
9–35.

5. *divino opere*: the divine office or Work of God (*opus Dei*); see
RB 19.2.

5. O Vitalis, venerable man, with God's help you were the beginning for all these, and by the wisdom handed on to you by God, by God's will you prepared this place for all of them. You transmitted to those who came after you the example of good remembrance. Rightly your memory is revealed in the mouth of peoples, for it is known that through you God built such a devout religious house to the praise of his name. Now let this digression suffice and let my pen return to what it proposed.

Chapter 2. Given to the Study of Letters, He Had a Gift for Learning Them

When therefore this infant reached the age at which he could be suitably imbued with letters, his parents handed him over to the study of letters. Divine goodness had granted him intelligence and innate mental ability. Already then, by a certain boyish prescience, those with whom he attended school called him "the little abbot" and showed him a corresponding reverence, insofar as that age allows. In fact, all loved him, and all regarded him as pleasant. In all these things I recognize your works, O Christ! You so extol your saints that even from their cradles you pour into some of them the copious dew of your spirit, and I know that it is in your gift to elevate whomever you wish. In regard to this child, it is told that when he was still small, by the divine mercy he worked a miracle, which it would be very unsuitable to pass over in silence.

Chapter 3. When He Went to the Bathing Place, a Fish Wanted to Drown Him

1. It happened that one day in summertime, when the students, his comrades, set out for the water to bathe, they led this young boy with them for the same

purpose. When they had entered the water and begun to bathe themselves, behold, a certain fish hooked itself to his back and, holding him tight, wanted to drown him. When his companions saw this, seized with fear, they jumped out as fast as they could and left him alone struggling in the water with the fish. When they had gone away, sad and stunned, they filled the air with their shouts and loud wailing and called on God and holy Mary with repeated cries. Seeing the boy in the water with the fish and not daring to come anywhere near him, they lamented bitterly. After being stunned by this shocking event, they suddenly saw the boy coming out of the water with the fish still clinging to his back, quite unwilling to let him go.[6] When they saw this, their grief suddenly turned into joy. Those who had previously wept in grief felt unalloyed joy, because they saw the one whom they were afraid they were losing rescued from danger.

2. O how great the malice of the ancient enemy! O how his wickedness was always eager to harm Vitalis! I think the enemy already had a presentiment that sometime it would happen that through Vitalis's teaching he would suffer the loss of many of his followers. For this reason, if he could, he endeavored to snuff Vitalis out and remove his life from their midst. However, because it is written, "There is no wisdom, there is no knowledge, there is no counsel against the Lord," * and because "the Lord guards all those who love him," * the devil could not accomplish what he began, because the Lord mightily rescued his servant from his snares.

*Prov 21:30
*Ps 144:20

6. E. P. Sauvage, *Vita Vitalis*, 361n1, plausibly suggests that the fish was some sort of octopus, implying that Vitalis was bathing on the ocean shore. For some musings on octopus attacks on people see Francis Buckland, *Log-Book of a Fisherman and Zoologist* (London: Chapman and Hall, 1876), 170–79 (available from Google Books).

3. I also think about this aspect of his deed: as fisher-
men pull fish from a stream, so this man Vitalis was
going to snatch people from the world. Pay attention,
reader, and carefully consider that this event also fulfilled the words of Truth, "The servant is not greater
than his lord."* Just as the devil wished through his
minions to kill the newborn Christ immediately* and
wanted through Pharaoh to kill the male children of
the Hebrews in the water,* so, I believe, he strove to
drown this boy so he could not benefit anyone with
his teaching.

*John 13:16;
15:20
*Matt 2:16

*Exod 1:22

Chapter 4. Because of Love of Wisdom He Left His Native Place

Now nearly grown up, in order to devote himself
more freely to the task of acquiring wisdom, for love
of it Vitalis strove to leave his native soil and go to
fresh territories.[7] He did not waste his time there but
concentrated with all his might on listening to wisdom. He did not receive it lazily or with a deaf ear but
installed it in the depths of his heart with a tenacious
memory. And so, imbued with a considerable amount
of knowledge, he returned home. His return brought
no little joy to his relatives and friends. Frequently
meditating on the divine law, he diligently distributed
its riches to those who did not have them. He was also
not ignorant of human laws. He was knowledgeable
in rhetorical devices and the elegance of Ciceronian
eloquence. Because it is written, "Hidden wisdom and
unseen treasure—what use is either?" * he did not
want to hide the good things he had but made them

*Sir 20:32

---

7. E. P. Sauvage, *Vita Vitalis*, 362n1, observes that according to
Ordericus Vitalis, *Historia ecclesiastica* 8.2 (PL 188:559), Odo, the
bishop of Bayeux (1049–97), whose mother was the mother of
William the Conqueror, sent teachable clerics to study in other
cities where the study of philosophy was flourishing.

public for the benefit of many. He did not wish to be silent regarding the truth out of fear of anyone or because of threats but freely spoke up in rebuke of the straying deeds of the wicked; he sought always to have the companionship of good people and from a tender age loved a holy life.

Chapter 5. A Count Made Him His Chaplain

Since he was endowed with so much wisdom and charming eloquence and had outstanding morals, the Count of Mortain,[8] who was rightly informed of these things about him, wished to have him with him and made him his chaplain. His wisdom affected Normans and Bretons and reached the French and the Angevins, and also crossed to the English, who inhabited the places across the sea. And while he spent a long time at the court of that prince, he tried to please his will without displeasing the Creator. For he had read what was written, "Render to Caesar the things that are Caesar's, and to God the things that are God's."* To the count he rendered suitable service and to God the worship due him. The Lord gave him so much grace that the count and countess conferred on him every honor and the entire family household held his sermons in veneration. None presumed to contradict what he said. All hung on his words and reverently obeyed what he said, like disciples obeying their master.

*Matt 22:21; Mark 12:17; Luke 20:25

8. Mortain was an important county. Robert (d. 1095) was half brother of William the Conqueror and Odo of Bayeux. His wife was Mathilda of Montgomery. Robert's son William, count of Mortain, forfeited his possessions when he rebelled against Henry I. Henry I later bestowed the county on his nephew, Stephen of Blois, who succeeded him as king of England (1135–54). Upon Stephen's death, his surviving son, William, became count of Mortain while Henry of Anjou, grandson of Henry I, became king of England. When William in turn died childless in 1159, Henry II took back the title of count of Mortain.

Chapter 6. He Consoled the Sorrowing Countess

Because of the authority of the one who reported it, we must not by our silence pass over what one of his disciples reported. One time he found the countess weeping, afflicted with great sorrow and sobs. He carefully inquired about the cause of her sorrow, and by her disclosure he learned that the count had demeaned her and dared to strike her with blows. The venerable man, moved to pity by her sorrow, said he took it ill that the count had presumed to inflict such things on her and that the bond of obligation between him and the count was dissolved if the latter did not take care to refrain from inflicting such injury on the lady.

Chapter 7. The Count Submitted to Being Whipped at His Hands

1. Once it happened that Vitalis left Mortain and did not inform the count of his departure. When this departure was reported to the count, he went after Vitalis without delay. When the count had given a pledge to make satisfaction, he had Vitalis return. The cause of this separation remains hidden; it has been revealed to no one but these two. When they had returned and privately entered the chapel, however, the count began to beseech the venerable man, imploring him for mercy so that he would not hesitate to strike him with blows as he saw fit. Then the prince took off his clothes and stood before Vitalis naked. The venerable man, standing over the count, punished him with sharp blows.[9] The prince humbly implored him to

9. *acribus verberibus*: The phrase occurs in RB 30:3. Regarding the occurrence of such whippings in the twelfth century, see E. P. Sauvage, *Vita Vitalis*, 364n1, referring to Robert Pullen, *Sententiarum librum* 7.3 (PL 186:914).

have mercy on him, but the venerable man chastened him as he wished with cutting blows. 2. O man endowed with supreme liberty! O man distinguished by great authority! The statement of the apostle is true that says, "Where the Spirit of God is, there is liberty."* Truly he was free. Even the countess did not fear to open her sorrow to him. The count was not ashamed to submit humbly to a whipping at his hands. In faithfully translating into the Latin tongue these things that we found written in the vernacular, we have handed them on in a clearer text. What we have submitted we know from trustworthy men who recount them. Note, though, that thus far we have been describing a man who walked upon the earth. Now we will try to describe someone who was suspended above the earth like an eagle and was intent on lofty things.

*2 Cor 3:17

Chapter 8. The Petition for Building Savigny

When he decided to build the monastery of Savigny on the border of Normandy and Brittany, he knew a place suitable for gaining souls. Petitioning for its construction, he laid his request before Lord Raoul de Fougères,[10] in whose grant the place lay. With the help of Raoul's wife, he obtained the place and the woods adjacent to it by the grant of Raoul and his two older

---

10. According to E. P. Sauvage, *Vita Vitalis*, 364n4, Raoul de Fougères was one of the companions of William the Conqueror. His wife was Avicia, daughter of Richard, the count of Brion, by whom he had five sons and many daughters. The eldest son, William, died before the year of this foundation (1112: see the charter in Van Moolenbroek, *Vital*, 272–74), but Raoul, Mainonius, Henry, and Robert were still alive. Henry is here rightly called "younger," not "youngest." Later, when his brothers had died, Henry succeeded his father, Raoul (ca. 1120–24). He in turn had four sons. He withdrew from secular affairs, became a monk at Savigny during the abbacy of Serlo (d. 1158), and died shortly thereafter.

sons. But a younger son named Henry was unwilling
to grant, either for prayer or for payment, what they
had granted. But all things [lie within the scope] of
God's power, for it is truly written, "The Lord will
reign for you, and you will be silent."* What a man
did not wish to do, God accomplished by his mercy.
The holy man looked at Henry with the indignation
of spiritual zeal and proclaimed that one who would
not assent to his petition would fulfill it in no good
spirit. When he went back, the boy was seized with
an illness, and as it advanced, he was wracked with
severe pains. For this reason, he sent for the man of
God,[11] and because of the great need Vitalis returned
to him quickly. Then the boy, corrected by his illness,
did not delay to do what earlier, when he was well, he
had not wanted to do. And so his pains lessened and
he returned to good health. Afterward, he left the
world, entered monastic life in the same house, and
there, in holy religion until his last day, he died.

*Exod 14:14

*Chapter 9. He Converted Prostitutes from Their
Notorious Trade*

Divine generosity gave Vitalis a great gift of grace
for converting women prostituted by the unspeakable
mire of lechery.[12] When he found women given to this
shameful occupation, drawing them with the sweet
title of daughters and gentle encouragement, he converted them from their filthy shame. Once they were
converted and had gone on to pledge marital chastity,

---

11. *vir dei*: a phrase used in the Bible of prophets (e.g., 1 Sam
2:27; 9:6-10; 1 Kgs 12:22; 13:1-13; 17:18, 24 [Elijah]; 2 Kgs 4:9, 25
[Elisha]), and by Gregory the Great of Saint Benedict, *Dialogues*,
2.1.4, ed. Adalbert de Vogüé, 132.39–40; 2.1.5, ed. de Vogüé,
132.50; 2.1.6, ed. de Vogüé, 134.67, etc. The phrase is used of
Vitalis in this *Vita* in chaps. 1.8, 1.10, 1.11, 1.13; 2.3, 2.4, 2.8, and
2.12.

12. On this, see Dalarun, *Robert of Arbrissel*, 82–93.

he gave them into marriage. Thus those whom he had found selling their souls in shameful commerce with men and had snatched from notorious depravity he left legitimately joined in marriage, wealthy in the community of the faithful who supported them because of his preaching. By the witness of the gospel we know for certain that "the Lord received publicans and sinners,"[13] cured demoniacs, and freed those in difficulty from what troubled them.

And now we know that by the care of the servant of God sinful women were rescued from the abominable abyss of an evil trade and restored to conjugal chastity by his urging and advice. He who then cured people himself now does these things through his servant. As the scribes and Pharisees were scandalized by his reception of sinners, however, so perhaps there will be someone who on hearing these things will criticize with an ill-meaning heart or think that Vitalis could not have done such things. Whoever is not afraid to chomp at Vitalis's deeds with venomous teeth will learn that it is not now possible to harm Vitalis with a venomous tongue, but one saying such things is covered in a mound of sin. Anyone can understand easily from what follows what abundant grace Vitalis had in restoring and reforming peace among those who were at odds.

Chapter 10. Some Knights Who Did Not Want to Pardon an Enemy

1. One day when Vitalis was occupied in public preaching, a certain knight[14] was present who had handed over another to be killed. For that reason, the

---

13. For example, Luke 15:2.

14. *miles*: this translation uses *knight* throughout, though some of the armed thugs with whom Vitalis deals do not resemble the noble knights of later medieval romance.

brothers of the dead man were trying to kill the knight in order to avenge the blood of their brother. When the man of God had finished his sermon, the knight threw himself at his feet. When the saint inquired what troubled him, he learned the cause from the knight. Without delay Vitalis summoned them and, broaching the topic of making peace, spoke with one of them to ascertain if he hated the knight so much. He said that he hated the knight so much that the extent of his hatred could not easily be put into words, and it was hard to bear the sight of him alive. While the saintly man was still reflecting how, if this were so, he could uproot the flame of hatred from his heart, the man responded with something like this: "If I had one foot in paradise and the other in hell, I would gladly take my foot from paradise so that in hell I could gain vengeance at will."

2. O hard heart! O heart blinded by wickedness! O diabolical anger! O perverse wrath! O anger satisfied only by the death of another! It is written, "The wrath of a man . . . does not effect the justice of God."* How can someone effect the justice of God when he has a heart infected with such evil that he seeks to revel in the death of another? When the man of God heard this statement, he declared that the man was full of an evil spirit and immediately ordered him to get out of his sight. When the man had left but not gone very far, however, Vitalis ordered him to be called again. When he had been called, he had the knight prostrated at the man's feet in the shape of a cross and had a sharp cutting sword handed over into the man's hands, saying, "Look, now avenge the blood of your brother, if you can; if God allows it, complete what you want so much."

A marvelous thing! When he raised his hand with the sword to gain vengeance, suddenly the sword fell and his hand and his whole body trembled. Rendered feeble, he collapsed at Vitalis's feet. The one who earlier had proudly refused to obey the words of the man

*Jas 1:20

of God now lay before him with the neck of his pride[15] broken. Stunned by this event, what the man had earlier disdained to do when admonished by prayer, now that he knew God's power, he willingly completed by forbearing to punish. And so the man of God, having restored peace among those whom he had found at odds, left them peacefully bound together in friendship.

Chapter 11. A Man Unwilling to Be Reconciled with His Adversary through His Warnings

At another time discord arose among some people at London when a certain wealthy man gravely wounded in a hostile meeting had lost the fight. Vitalis approached this man for the sake of concluding a peace with those who were in discord. But the wealthy man disdained to lend an ear to his words; in fact, having entered his own house, he strove to defend himself with arms. Fortified with spiritual weapons, the man of God urged this man to make peace with his adversary regarding what the other had committed against him. When the wealthy man refused to do that, he was gripped with pain; drooling from his mouth, he shook uncontrollably. Thus through the mediation of the man of God, peace and concord were established between the wealthy man and his adversaries.

We are describing things that are true, although we did not see them. We do not restrict divine power from being able to do these things. Since it is known that God has done much greater things, indeed has made everything, why should one not believe that he could also do these things through his servant? Saying

---

15. *superbiae fracta cervice*: the idea of a stiff neck (*dura cervix*) often occurs in the Old Testament to designate pride and stubbornness: e.g., Exod 32:9; 33:3, 4, 9; Prov 29:1.

these things, we strive to protect ourselves with a wall of caution, lest we deviate from the truth. We entrust the whole matter to God, for whom nothing is impossible. In fact, if we pay careful attention to what is primary, we know devoutly that Vitalis had power over unclean spirits. For as the words of the fathers testify, when lust is trampled down, when anger is removed, when holy chastity is put on, and when the soul is made lovely with the beauty of peace, the spirits of fornication are excluded, and the miracle is greater just as the soul is more precious than the flesh.

Chapter 12. He Predicted the Frightful Death of a Man Unwilling to Listen to Him

A certain armed man arrived, and another man who was attending Vitalis's preaching saw him. The armed man was the other man's enemy and was constantly seeking his death. Seized with fear, the listening man hastened to the feet of the holy man. Recognizing the cause of his fear, the holy man ordered the armed man who had arrived to take his place outside the church and so, if he wished, to attend to the word of God with the rest. When the armed man repeatedly pushed toward Vitalis and disdained to listen to him, that most excellent man, muttering and alight with fiery zeal, with his hand extended toward the altar, with the glorious Virgin Mary as his witness, proclaimed that there was no way that the armed man would leave this world by a good death. After he had said that, the outcome proved it true; as it is written, his words did not fall on the ground.*

*1 Sam 3:19

Not long afterward, when the armed man was in the middle of a shameful act in the forest with the wife of another man, he was caught by her husband and slain in an awful death. His body, eaten by dogs, had no proper burial. From this story one may take care not to hold the words of holy men in contempt, because when they are provoked by awareness of the disdain of the wicked, the Holy Spirit who dwells in them is grieved,* and contempt is an affront to his grace, opposition to which certainly cannot turn out well.[16] For notice that the unhappy man who disdained the words of the holy man perished, destroyed by a most evil death. If he had chosen to listen to his words humbly and decently, he would have lived in good health interiorly and by avoiding his shameful act would not have incurred so terrible a death.

*Eph 4:30

Chapter 13. He Exposed the Tricks of the Devil

1. Another time also, when Vitalis was similarly occupied in preaching and the people were listening to his words with great attention, in his address he introduced these words: "Be careful and pay close attention: and whatever you hear do not abandon what you have begun. The enemy of all good is very upset because you receive the word of God so devoutly. As a result he never ceases to plot maliciously how to distract you from what you are hearing." After his admonition, the noise of shouting is heard outside. A cry is raised that the village is burning. Astonished by this shout and not remembering well the words of the man of God, the people immediately go out, but they see nothing of what they heard. When they return in confusion, the servant of God addresses them as follows: "Did I not tell you that you should not leave here because of the things you were about to hear? See, the devil would gladly have done even more if he could have. But from this he gained no profit, because he was not able to harm you."

2. Alas, how great is the weakness of the human race! Alas, how slight or nonexistent their stability!

---

16. E. P. Sauvage, *Vita Vitalis*, 368n2, observes that the meaning of this sentence is not clear.

Alas, how fast they fail, how quickly they fall! Alas, when a reason appears, how slight the push that forces them away from what they had proposed. O how great the devil's wickedness! O how full of deceit his malice! O how boldly his temerity is always causing harm! Truly, he is tortured, inflamed, and shaken by prods of envy when he knows that something is withdrawn from him and submitted to the gentle yoke of Christ. One learns this fact from the words of the evil spirits when they were speaking in the gospel to the Lord: "What have we to do with you, O Christ, Son of the Living God? You have come before the time to torture us."* But, O diligent man! O man full of wisdom! I will speak. I will say what I feel. I do not think this man lacked the spirit of prophecy, for he could predict the horrible death of a man and expose the tricks of the devil.

*Matt 8:29

Chapter 14. He Placed Little Value on Care of the Body

1. How little Vitalis valued the care of the body and how much concern he had for expending the talent of the word of God entrusted to him stand out clearly in one deed of his that I include here. One time he needed to go from the place where he was staying to other places. Having undertaken the journey, he entered a wood, but he lost track of the right way. Wandering, he roamed with his companions through its trackless places, enduring a fast for three days. Having emerged at last on the fourth day, he enters a certain village, and, neglecting hunger, he occupies himself with preaching. He prolongs his sermon almost to midday until, because a monk who was with him was complaining, the people realize how long he was fasting.[17] For it is written, "Behold, the eyes of the

17. The odd mix of present and imperfect tenses reproduces the Latin.

Lord are upon those who fear him and on those who
hope in his mercy, so that he feeds them in their hun-
ger."* I think he is nourished with interior sweetness   *Ps 32:18, 19
of spirit and cares little or nothing for the nurture of
the body.

2. What of this? What will the sluggishness of
negligent pastors reply? What will sinking idleness
answer—those who are ready to stuff their stomachs
with delicate foods, those who are slow and sluggish,
I may say to speak, but also to meditate?[18] What Scripture says applies to them: "Woe to pastors who feed   *Ezek 34:2
themselves,"* and "silent dogs cannot bark."* They   *Isa 56:10
happily pride themselves over a place of honor,* and   *Matt 23:6;
they rarely or never apply themselves to the word of   Mark12:39;
preaching in order to gain souls, because while they   Luke 14:7-8;
care only about passing things, they rarely or never   20:46
ponder the nature of their office. Truly this man
showed that he thought very differently, because he
strove to scatter the seeds of God's word with such
watchful zeal.

*Chapter 15. Spurning the Counsel of Men, He Committed
His Cause to the Will of God*

1. How strong an advocate and lover of truth he
was the little page that follows shows. A controversy
arose between him and the abbot of Caen regarding
part of the district of Mortain, which, after he had
accepted in gift from the count, Vitalis had in turn
given to that monastery.[19] A day for pleading the case

---

18. The punctuation of this sentence has been altered slightly
to improve the sense.

19. Van Moolenbroeck, *Vital*, 140–45, explains the background
of this litigation. Around 1105, William of Mortain and others
offered donations for founding a monastery for men near Mortain.
Since no monastery existed yet, Vitalis transmitted these possessions to the monastery of St.-Étienne in Caen. By 1118 Vitalis had

was set. When that day arrived, they entered into the matter of the case. When Vitalis had been admonished by the words of his adversaries, he entered the church alone and there gave himself to prayer for a long time. When he had finished, he returned. Having declared what stood as true, he committed his case to God's will. The abbot just mentioned, pondering within himself that perhaps it was the will of God that Vitalis should receive what he asked, agreed to his petition and, putting an end to his complaint, ended the case. It is certainly clear from this that the Lord prosecuted the case of his servant, who spurned the reed staff,* that is, the help of men, because he did not wish to place his hope in a human being but fled to the Lord when need arose.

*Isa 36:6; Ezek 29:6

2. O how good you are, Lord, to those who hope in you! For you said, "Whatever you ask for in faith, believe you will receive" it,* and you fulfilled that for your servant. What are those afflicted by monstrous desire going to say here? Those who, stirred by the fires of avarice, even attack others' possessions with lawsuits and violence? Surely if their hearts were touched within them, perhaps by pulling out the monstrous vice they would try to be freed from its dominion. So that my discourse will not induce boredom in the reader by its length, however, let this first book be ended, so that the reader may then gain the strength to read the rest more devoutly.

*Matt 21:22; Mark 11:24

---

founded his own monastery five years earlier and was hard pressed to provide for its material needs. So he asked that the donations be returned to him. An ecclesiastical council decided in Vitalis's favor. Henry II's charter confirmed this decision.

Book Two

Chapter 1. [Introduction]

I had decided to end this work with a few things,
but because you force me and have diligently inquired
about his life from those of his disciples who still remain, I have set aside the other things I was doing and
will take care to make note of still other things that
can be known from their report. As above I described
some of his virtues, now it remains for me to show
how much patience and love he extended to his enemies. Because surely Scripture cannot be wrong,
which says, "All who wish to live devoutly suffer persecution," * and there can be no Abel who is not tried
by the malice of Cain,* this man had many adversaries, but his patience overcame them.

*2 Tim 3:12
*Gen 4:1-16

*Chapter 2. Envious Men Who Were Upset by His
Proximity Wished to Kill Him*

1. When Vitalis had begun to inhabit the place already mentioned, some men annoyed by his proximity
were enflamed with the fire of malice. Thinking that
they would not have the woods near the place for their
use as they had previously, they tried to root him out.
One day when he was traveling, other men, as advised
by the malicious ones, were lying hidden in an ambush
and attacked him with arrows. As the arrows rained

down thickly around him, God's power kept him safe and sound. Having launched their arrows in vain, the men were thunderstruck by what had happened. They left their hiding places, came to him, and confessed their crime. They gained a quick pardon from him.

2. Here what will our pride say? What will our arrogance answer? Provoked by some slight word or even a sign, if we cannot do anything else, we surely bear a detestable grudge in our heart and we cannot look our rivals in the face. If ever we find an opportunity to avenge ourselves as we desire, however, we vomit up the pernicious poison that we had hidden, *Matt 5:44   even though the Lord says, "Love your enemies." *

Chapter 3. Some Men, Following the Orders of a Certain Knight, Wanted to Kill Him

A knight was once grieving that because of Vitalis's admonitions the offerings of the faithful were being taken to a place he did not want them to go. He was trying to deliver Vitalis to death. Having heard that he was passing by, the knight sent after him sons of pestilence,[20] that is, wicked men who were to carry out his orders in this regard. They came to a certain stream that the man of God had already crossed. They could not cross it, and, detained there by the power of God, they stayed there, foiled in all their efforts. One of them, however, more evil than the others and more ready to inflict harm, mounted on a stubborn horse, intervened. He began to rebuke them for being lazy, for they had not finished what they had begun. Blinded by wickedness, he climbed a bridge with his

---

20. *filii pestilentiae*: Saint Augustine uses this phrase in *De civitate Dei* 16.11, ed. Bernard Dombart and Alfonsus Kalb, CCSL 48 (Turnhout: Brepols, 1955), 513, line 2. According to James Craigie Robertson, *History of the Christian Church*, rev. ed., 8 vols. (Cooper Union, NY: Pott, Young and Co., 1874), 5:82 n., the antipope Anacletus described his enemies as *filii pestilentiae*.

horse, but intercepted by the just judgment of God, he fell into the water. By the divine judgment, he barely escaped the danger, and his horse drowned.

One of the other men, astonished by this miracle and moved to compunction of heart, started praying and humbly asked the Lord and the man of God to allow him to cross over. Granted what he requested, this man came to Vitalis and confessed his guilt. He immediately received pardon. He then led Vitalis to the rest, who had remained, unable to cross. Vitalis readily pardoned them in the same way, saying that he did not flee death but wished that he might be killed so that he could go to his Lord. With these words he showed that he was willing to undergo martyrdom for the love of God if there was anyone who would presume to inflict it. He was prepared to die for Christ so he could be crowned with the palm of martyrdom. We can gather, then, that although he did not yet undergo suffering in his body, in his mind he was prepared to receive it. This is recognized as a form of martyrdom: a mind that always keeps the rule of faith unimpaired and is always devoutly ready to undergo martyrdom.

Chapter 4. Some Who Envied Him Formed a Faction against Him

1. Once in the land of England a council was held in which many personages of the church came together. Among them were some said to have formed a conspiracy for the death of Vitalis.[21] When the man of God was informed of this fact, he was prepared to die for the sake of truth. He did not fear to go there; trusting in God, he refused to avoid their wicked plots

---

21. The Council of London was called at Michaelmas, 1102, by Anselm of Canterbury. E. P. Sauvage, *Vita Vitalis*, 373n1, refers to Matthew Paris (1200–59), *Historia Anglorum*, ed. F. Madden, 3 vols., Rolls Series (London: Longman, 1866–69), 1:191.

by hiding himself. Therefore, he came to the place of the council, climbed to an elevated spot, and began to sow the seeds of God's word. One of the evil party, however, lodged an accusation against him. When Vitalis had uttered two statements, this man reproached as lies his words, which had been heard by the whole council. When Vitalis made a third statement, the man's evil tongue was restrained from further criticism. In admiration of the virtue of Vitalis's word, which the man had first condemned, he now uttered praises in the hearing of the assembly. Having confessed his guilt, with the rest of the conspirators he asked pardon, saying that Vitalis could not have spoken such things except by the presence of the Holy Spirit.

The Lord gloriously magnified his servant by causing those present at the council to praise him as much as they had been attacking him. There is no stronger testimony than when someone who has tried to bring an accusation of a crime speaks praises. Vitalis kindly pardoned those over whom he was completely victorious because God turned their wicked counsel into good for the glory of his name. This, then, is the perfect victory of the saints over their enemies, when the latter abandon their wickedness, convert to good, and become advocates of the truth that they had assailed.

Notice that we have in part shown the virtue of Vitalis's patience, but we have not been silent about the depths of love that he extended toward his enemies. That he patiently bore persecution belonged to patience; that he with great kindness pardoned his persecutors belonged to love.

2. It is pleasant to remember that memorable deed of Moses and to ponder in this event something similar to it. Certainly when Moses wished at God's command to lead the children of Israel out of Egypt, Pharaoh did not want to release the people. Moses was then compelled by the impudence of the king to afflict that land with plagues. When Moses had cudgeled Pharaoh by turning the waters into blood and by pro-

ducing frogs, however, the magicians did similar things. But when they had proceeded to a third test and a plague of stinging insects came, the magicians failed. When the power of all their art failed, they said, "This is the finger of God."* Something similar occurred here. Once and again hostile words are uttered in condemnation of the holy man, but the third time his assailant is restrained from the wickedness of his effrontery and attributes his words to the Holy Spirit.

*Exod 8:19

Chapter 5. He Freed Those Sentenced to Death

Once, when the holy man was traveling through parts of England in order to preach and was pouring out words of salvation to the inhabitants, it happened that two condemned men were being led to hang. While they were being led along, he met them. He immediately took pity on them and, following the pattern of Blessed Nicholas,[22] absolved them and sent them away from this justice. The agents of justice did not presume to oppose his will.

Chapter 6. He Restored a Man to Life

It is pleasant to insert here a memorable event that happened to reach us by the report of our predecessors. One time certain knights went away, unwilling to acquiesce to Vitalis's words and refusing to be reconciled with their adversaries. But on their journey they met a serious obstacle. One of them, falling from his horse, tumbled to the ground and lay there as though dead. When Vitalis was informed of this fact, he traveled

22. Saint Nicholas of Myra (and later of Bari) was a much beloved saint. He was particularly celebrated as a helper for those who were in dire straits. Jacobus de Voragine preserves the story of how Nicholas saved three soldiers and three princes from execution. See *The Golden Legend*, trans. William Granger Ryan, 2 vols. (New Haven, CT: Yale University Press, 1993), 1:23–24.

there. A huge crowd of people accompanied him on the way to see such a sight. When he came to the place, he urged them to turn to prayer that God would deign to show his power to the glory of his name and the benefit of the onlookers. It happened. When the prayer was finished, Vitalis spoke to the man.

At Vitalis's voice, the man stirred, as though waking up from a heavy sleep. He was ordered to tell where he was and what he knew about what had happened to him. He answered that for his merits he had been assigned to the infernal places, but the merits and prayers of the holy man had restored him to life. He promised to renounce warfare completely and thereafter to live out his life in holy religion. The holy man arranged to send the man to a certain abbey so that dwelling there he could end his life in a holy way of living. He was zealous to submit to its demands, and there for a long time he faithfully lived a holy way of life. Do not let the novelty of the things we have inserted here cause anyone to think that these are our invention, for we have described not things of our own but things approved by the witness of trustworthy people and handed on to us.

Chapter 7. He Consumed a Spider in the Most Holy Mystery[23]

1. One day when he stood at the sacred altar during the sacred mysteries, withdrawn from human gaze, a spider slipped down into the sacred chalice. Perhaps this happened to show Vitalis's virtue. He was not able to drive it away; a human hand could not help. Therefore, armed with faith, he received it with the most holy sacrament and suffered nothing grim from it. And what wonder? Because he believed that he was

---

23. A similar story occurs in the slightly earlier *Tripartite Life of Robert, Abbot of La Chaise-Dieu*, 3.13. See *The Lives of Monastic Reformers, 1*, 98.

truly receiving the body and blood of the Lord, he trusted, not without reason, that such a great mystery could also overcome every poison. As Truth testifies, "All things are possible to one who believes."* For this reason he said to his disciples, "If you have faith like a mustard seed, you will say to this mountain, 'Move yourself into the sea,' and it will happen."* Hence it is that Paul proclaimed the same thing when, through a great proclamation, by naming each one separately, he showed that they pleased God.[24]

    *Mark 9:22

    *Matt 17:19

2. I am about to say marvelous things, and perhaps because of their greatness they will seem doubtful to some people. But I swear to God, whom I desire to serve with all my mind's intent, that what we insert here is not our own but what we have learned through the report of trustworthy men living in holy religion. One day, when the holy father was occupied in spreading the word of God to the people, that same spider is said to have gone out of his foot. And rightly so! It was fitting that what he had wondrously received should go out wondrously. He who could go forth from his mother without breaking the seal of her womb,[25] who wished, contrary to the usual course of

24. This seems to be a reference to Heb 11:4–12:2.

25. The idea that Mary remained physically a virgin during childbirth (in partu), as well as before and after, was widespread among Christian writers in the Middle Ages; see, for example, Ludwig Ott, Fundamentals of Catholic Dogma, trans. Patrick Lynch, ed. James Bastible (Cork: Mercier Press, 1962), 205–6. According to J. N. D. Kelly, Jerome, His Life, Writings, and Controversies (New York: Harper & Row, 1975), 106, 307, at the time of his attack Against Helvidius (ca. 383), Jerome, a committed champion of Mary's virginity, did not endorse the idea of Mary's virginitas in partu. By the end of his life, he had come to accept the idea, probably because of the influence of Ambrose and Augustine. See also Luigi Gambero, Mary and the Fathers of the Church, trans. Thomas Buffer (San Francisco: Ignatius Press, 2005), 208–9 (on Jerome, who Gambero doubts fully endorsed the idea of Mary's virginity in partu), and 368–69 (on Gregory the Great); Luigi Gambero,

Exod 17:1-7 things, to draw water for his people from a rock, could show such a great miracle in his servant. Let the believer hear this in order to be made more ardent and devout. Let one who is doubtful hear this in order to be more strongly fortified in faith. Let all hear it so that all may recognize the power and faith of the man and that the Lord's grandeur may be glorified for them.

Chapter 8. A Woman Admonished in a Dream about Preparing Food for Him

There was a certain knight whose wife, it was said, was not faithful to their marriage bond. The holy man, whose custom it was to call back to chastity people who strayed in this way, was at Coutances. He arranged to have hospitality at her house, although it was far from that town. When he had undertaken the journey but before he reached there, the sun was setting and the day was over. As the time approached, those among whom he had decided to be a guest were napping on a couch. The woman, already asleep, was awakened in a vision by an excited voice, which ordered her to prepare food for the holy man. But chided by her husband's voice that[26] she had been awakened by a phantom, she lay down again. Again the same voice admonished her and commanded that she prepare the things it had specified because the man would remain there the whole day.

When this had happened three times, the messenger of the holy man arrived and announced that the man of God was at hand. Thus the outcome of the

---

Mary in the Middle Ages, trans. Thomas Buffer (San Francisco: Ignatius Press, 2005), 30 (on Ildephonse), 64 (on Alcuin), and 75–77 (on Paschasius Radbertus); Miri Rubin, *Mother of God: A History of the Virgin Mary* (New Haven, CT: Yale University Press, 2009), 22–33; for Thomas Aquinas on the topic, see *Summa theologiae* 3.28.2.

26. The Latin text has *quasi*, which I have corrected to *quia*.

event proved that woman had not been disturbed by a phantom but had seen true things in a vision. And rightly was she admonished about preparing the things he needed, since the reason he came was to bestow on her wholesome counsels for life, so that she who was being ruined by a shameful reputation[27] might be called back by his words to safe boundaries.

Chapter 9. He Made Shepherds Safe from Robbers; Thieves Are Captured

One time a war was raging in areas where some shepherds were pasturing the flocks of the holy man. These shepherds, terrified of incursions of robbers, asked him to be transferred elsewhere so that what they were guarding would not be carried off from them by the intruders' violence. The holy man reassured them and promised to make restitution to them for any damage they suffered from robbers. After the shepherds accepted his assurance, they remained there and suffered no harm from robbers. Thieves came in the night, however, entered the building where the flocks were kept, and led out many cattle, but they could not force out of the courtyard the cattle they had led out. They spent the whole night driven around by an aimless spirit and consumed by fruitless labor. They accomplished nothing at all. Recognizing in such a miracle the power of God, and carrying rods,[28] they confessed their sins and submitted themselves to the holy man, from whom they merited to receive pardon.

27. E. P. Sauvage, *Vita Vitalis*, 377, prints the phrase as *infami nota exurebatur*. This translation has emended *infami* to *infamia*. Ronald Pepin points out a similar passage in the *Life of Hamo*, chap. 42: *infandas criminum notas* ("unspeakable signs of her sins"). Both instances refer to sexual sin.

28. E. P. Sauvage, *Vita Vitalis*, 378n1, suggests that the rods indicate the thieves' readiness to submit to punishment.

Chapter 10. Hairs from his Clothes Restored Sick People to Health

1. We must not negligently pass over what a certain nun, whom Vitalis had established in a holy way of life, has a habit of reporting. She says that one time one of her sisters took hairs from the clothes of the holy father. These she mixed with water and distributed to the infirm and feverish to drink. They testify that when they drank this potion, they were restored to their former health. We read that the woman with a hemorrhage was restored to her former health by touching the hem of the Lord's garment.* We also read that the sick were placed in the streets so that when Peter went by they could be restored to health by his shadow.* He who through himself or through the supreme head of the apostles did these things could then also do wondrous things through his Vitalis by endowing him with power.

2. O Lord, how wonderful you are always in your saints.* So that the virtue of the saint would become more gloriously known, you not only wished to perform miracles through his presence, but also, in order to show his virtue, you willed to aid those in want through the tiniest things connected with him.

*Matt 9:20; Luke 8:43

*Acts 5:15

*Ps 67:36

Chapter 11. When He Was Preaching in England, People Who Did Not Know French Understood His Words

Let us add another miracle also. There is no doubt that following the example of earlier believers, by the merits of his servant through a sudden inpouring at the working of the Spirit, he put into the hearts of his hearers knowledge of an unknown tongue.* For one time when he was staying in England, it happened that when he was situated in a church among an innumerable multitude of people, as was his wont, he gave a sermon. Although many there did not know French, God deigned to pour such an abundance of his gra-

*Acts 2:4-6

cious bounty into the minds of his hearers that as long as that sermon lasted they all understood the French that he was speaking. When the sermon was finished, however, that grace did not remain in them. By this one should know that although for that hour his hearers were rightly enabled to understand the words of the Holy Spirit that proceeded from his mouth, they were then deprived of that understanding for a wholesome reason, namely, so that afterward they would not spend that grace in vain chatter.

Chapter 12. By the Command of the Lord Pope, He Gave a Sermon at the Council of Rheims

1. It seems that one should not omit from its place that Vitalis elicited fear and reverence from kings, princes, and the powerful of this world not only because of his outstanding holiness but also, according to the statement of holy Job, by smashing their jaws he snatched from their teeth the spoils* and booty of the poor with a mighty hand and an outstretched arm* of independent authority. Leaving aside a great many examples of the pope's discernment regarding the man of God, one example will suffice to show this. When the lord pope had invited Vitalis to a general council that was to be celebrated in the city of Rheims, he enjoined him to give a sermon in the council assembly.[29]

> *Job 29:17
> *see Ps 135:42; Jer 21:5, 32:21; Ezek 20:33-34

2. As he was departing after the council, as a covenant and mark of singular friendship,* the blessed man was granted many gifts by which, thenceforth comforted for all time, he was renewed by the affection of such a great father. The lord pope also bore testimony to him before many people that in the entire cisalpine

> *loco foederis et singularis amicitiae

29. Calixtus II, who in September 1119 issued a decree promising papal protection of Savigny and commending Vitalis and the monastery to the protection of several bishops and lay magnates. See Van Moolenbroeck, *Vital*, 267–69 (PL 163:1120D–1121B).

region he had found not one other person who speaking directly had made clear to him with such severity of sharp criticism, without alloy of flattery or fawning, all the things that he judged blameworthy in the apostolic office.[30]

3. It should not be passed over in silence that in the council just mentioned Vitalis acquired from the lord pope for the church of Savigny the dignity of this privilege: if the whole diocese of Avranches even together with its bishop will for whatever reason be deprived of the Mass and the rest of the divine services, the church of Savigny nevertheless will fully complete all that pertains to the divine service, unless it has committed a specific capital fault so that it deserves to be interdicted and prohibited from the divine services.[31]

Chapter 13. A Brief Epilogue

1. Therefore, having treated at some length the life of the saint, making a kind of summary, let us still briefly take note of certain of his virtues according to what is written in his mortuary roll.[32] Last, let us come to his death. As we said above, this father, educated from childhood in the liberal arts, came to the age of manhood. Placed amid an abundance of things, he began to love poverty. At the same time he set before his eyes the gospel statement, "Whoever does not renounce everything he possesses cannot be my disciple," *just as it is said of Saint Benedict, "he despised as arid the world with its adornment."[33]

*Luke 14:26

---

30. *ipso apostolico*; it could also mean the episcopate more generally.

31. E. P. Sauvage, *Vita Vitalis*, 380n1, observes that Paschal II had already granted such a privilege to Savigny. The peculiar verb tenses are in the Latin.

32. Léopold Delisle, ed., *Rouleaux des morts*, 281–344.

33. Gregory the Great, *Dialogues* 2, 126.

2. Therefore, snatched by the hand of divine mercy from the ruin of this falling world,[34] he vigorously lived the eremitical life in a place called "The Rock of the Lord" for almost seventeen years.[35] He was not without frequent visits from proven and upright persons of his time, namely, Dom Robert of Arbrissel, who built the monastery that is called Fontevraude, and Dom Bernard of Tiron, along with other renowned persons of the same profession. In that place, "the Rock of the Lord," as was the custom of the holy fathers, they held very frequent colloquies,[36] in which they discussed the state of holy church and matters of use to souls. With what holiness Vitalis conducted himself in that profession, how greatly he despised

---

34. Horace, *Carm.* 3.3.7–8, http://www.thelatinlibrary.com /horace/carm3.shtml (accessed July 16, 2014), echoed by Cyprian, *Ad Demetrianum*, 20.380–81 (PL 4:559B); *Ad Donatum* 14 (*Opera*, ed. W. Hartel, CSEL 3 [Vienna, 1868], 14); see also Bruno, *Letter to the His Carthusian Brothers* (ed. Maurice Laporte, *Lettres des premiers chartreux*, 1, SCh 88 [Paris: Éditions du Cerf, 1962], 82); Hugh of Saint Victor, *Quid vere diligendum est*, in Hugues de Saint-Victor, *Six opuscules spirituels*, ed. Roger Baron, SCh 155 (Paris: Éditions du Cerf, 1969), 96–99; trans. Hugh Feiss, in *On Love*, Victorine Texts in Translation 2 (Turnhout: Brepols, 2011), 180; *De Vanitate* 2 (PL 176:731BC); Charles Sidney Smith, *Metaphor and Comparison in the Epistulae ad Lucilium of L. Anneas Seneca* (Baltimore: J. H. Furst, 1910), 124–26.

35. E. P. Sauvage, *Vita Vitalis*, 353n1 and 383n1, cites Auvry, *Histoire*, to the effect that Vitalis left the court of the count of Mortain about 1093 and a year later went with some companions to the forest of Fougères. Around 1095 Vitalis received permission to leave the diocese of Avranches from Bishop Turgisius, to whom the territory of Savigny was subject. The forest of Savigny was donated to Vitalis in 1112, as a charter of Raoul de Fougères indicates (see the text in Van Moolenbroeck, *Vital*, 272–74). Then Vitalis began to build a monastery and church. In charters Vitalis is called *frater* or *eremita*. So the seventeen years extend from the end of 1094 to the beginning of 1112.

36. *collationes*: the title of a book of Cassian, which contains reports of discussions with various Desert Fathers. The point is that these modern hermits held colloquies like those Cassian had with the hermits of the Egyptian desert.

the world and loved poverty, how stingy he was to himself and how generous to the needy, how intent he was in fasts, vigils, prayers, and other holy works, the familiar and frequent gatherings around him of the persons just mentioned show. As the prophet says, *Ps 17:26   "You will be holy with the holy one."*

Chapter 14. He Tirelessly Scattered the Seeds of God

1. His brothers who accompanied him with unbearable labor and the exhaustion it induced give proof of how faithful and tireless a dispenser of the divine word he was.[37] While they sat and succeeded one another in service to him, they never saw him sit when he preached, and even though his hearers were often worn out, they never saw him tired out. If anyone wants to capture in words how many plots of evil men, how many annoyances of thirst and hunger, how much heat and other bad weather he bore in carrying out that office, the inquirer will be worn out from his useless effort. Wanting nothing earthly, he sought "not *Phil 2:21   what is his own, but what is Christ's."* He worked very hard to restore peace among those who were at enmity and to provide food and clothing for the needy, hospitality for the wandering, pardon for the guilty, lawful marriages for prostitutes, homes and other necessities for lepers. The Lord bestowed so much grace on him that, although he undertook difficult and impossible things, by God's help he never lacked results.

2. When Vitalis had devoted himself to these and similar holy works for seventeen years, finally, compelled by the prayers of the brethren, a considerable number of whom had flocked to him because of his holiness, he became the father of more than 140 per-

---

37. The sentence could also be translated, "His brothers who accompanied him give proof of how faithful and tireless a dispenser of the divine word he was, with unbearable labor and the exhaustion it produced."

sons of both sexes. He decided that, as Gregory said, it was more excellent to profit many than to live for himself alone.[38] When he was placed in charge, however, he did not abandon his earlier poverty; he still engaged in preaching, he was a great founder of churches, a most constant defender of the poor, a sharp critic of tyrants, a just and humble pastor, and a most kindly provider of the flock committed to him. I will add here still another miracle so that it will not be passed over in silence because of our negligence.

Chapter 15. His Brother Fell from a High Place but Was Not Hurt

One time when carpenters were busy building the dwellings at the monastery of Savigny, a board fell from high up. The saint's brother in the flesh fell to the ground with it, but the holy man raised his eyes and hands, and his brother suffered no injury from the fall. Those present when this thing happened were struck with wonder and moved to the praise of God.

Finally, having run through these few things, let us turn our pen from his virtues to his death.

Chapter 16. His Death

1. At the time determined for Vitalis to receive the fruit of his labors from God who gives the reward, some cause required him to set out for "the Rock of the Lord."[39] Suddenly he began to be troubled by bodily pain. The servant of God, however, tried not to yield to the pain of his illness or skip the customary prayers even a little. In fact, on the very night he died, the sixteenth of the kalends of October AD 1122,[40] he

38. Cf. *Regula pastoralis* 1.5 (PL 77:18C–19C).

39. This is the place where the author said Vitalis spent seventeen years living as a hermit (bk. 2.13).

40. September 16, 1122.

arose first for Matins, struck the signal to wake the brothers, sang the regular Matins, and began but did not finish the Matins of Saint Mary. When the monk who was going to read the lesson asked for a blessing from him, he spoke this blessing for him: "May the intercession of Saint Mary the Virgin join us to the company of the angels." When he finished, he gave up his spirit.

2. On Sunday he had offered the holy sacrifice to the Lord. After that, on the second night, as we believe, his spirit ascended to the Lord, victorious forever. It is reported that as his spirit journeyed, a bright cloud appeared there and a sweet odor filled the house in which these things took place. And it was right indeed that at his passing a sweet odor appeared, for his preaching poured into the world the scent of eternal life, so that one could say, "We are the good odor of Christ in every place."* Therefore, when the holy man had left the world, people from different places gathered at his passing.

*2 Cor 2:15

Chapter 17. People from Le Teilleul Wanted to Take His Body but Could Not

When Vitalis's body was carried through their midst, the people of Le Teilleul[41] wanted to keep it.[42] Although many took it one after another, all their effort was in vain. Although they tried three times to move the bier from the place where it had been set down, they could not budge it. When they were completely exhausted, two monks came forward and easily

41. Le Teilleul was located south of the modern-day town of Mortain and east of Savigny. From the text it seems that it must have been located between "The Rock of the Lord," where Vitalis died, and Savigny.

42. Compare a similar story about Stephen of Obazine in *Lives*, 1, 231–32; similar quarrels over possession of the body of a saint are told of Saints Martin of Tours, Romuald, Firmat, and Robert of Arbrissel; see Dalarun, *Robert of Arbrissel*, 135–36.

lifted it; rejoicing, they carried it on their own shoulders to their abbey. Out of reverence for the holy father, for three days with psalms and prayers they kept his body unburied. I believe that by this obvious miracle God made it known that he did not wish to deprive the church of Savigny of its own shepherd. How justly and modestly he treated his subjects can be estimated from the filial love of their eyes, which were focused on him now dead and could scarcely be pulled away from him.

Chapter 18. *The Assumption of His Soul*

On the same day that the blessed man departed to the Lord, with the approval of divine mercy the glory of his assumption was graciously revealed to the bodily eyes of a certain monk who was separated from the monastery of Savigny by a large tract of territory and was not professed for the same house. This man was in everything a person of honorable religion and renowned sanctity. While he was seated with other brothers in a certain place, he suddenly jumped up from his seat and with his eyes and hands raised began to run around among them. The brothers who were present with him looked on with great puzzlement. They did not, however, in any way dare suddenly to correct or rebuke him whom they knew to be a man of such holiness and respect. They decided instead to wait for the outcome. When the venerable man quieted down after the short space of an hour, calling himself back within the boundaries of his accustomed gravity and humility, he began to think carefully about the vision he had had. The brothers began urgently to insist that he immediately divulge to them what had happened to him. He responded to them, "At the hour you saw me rejoicing and jumping, the blessed abbot Vitalis, released from the prison of the flesh, was assumed into heaven with inexpressible glory, while the choirs of angels sang. Therefore, I had to join in the rejoicing over his glory with all the striving of my body and the feeling of my mind."

Chapter 19. A Certain Sick Man Received His Health under His Bier

During the interval the monks kept Vitalis's body, God, who had adorned his servant with virtues during his lifetime, also glorified him with miracles after he was dead. A certain man, badly held back by illness of his ears and hands, with very many prayers obtained permission to lie under the bier and received his health there and went away happy.

Chapter 20. A Person Who Offered the Sacrifice of the Mass for Him Smelled a Pleasant Scent

1. The Lord continues to multiply his wonders around the dead body of his servant, so that the faith of those who see or hear rejoices and their affection is consoled. A person who served at his funeral rites offered the Holy Sacrifice to the Lord for him. While he stood at the holy altar, he sensed a fragrance of great sweetness. Coming from the place where his as-yet-unburied body lay, that fragrance spread out sweetly. And so while his soul, released from the prison of the body, returned to its homeland, as we believe, the Lord filled the place where these things were happening with an odor of sweetness. Thus when they were thinking of handing his body over to burial so that his merits might be shown, a wonderful smell refreshed the servant of God.[43] Rightly indeed did his body give off this smell, for armed with the

---

43. This is an odd statement: *servum Dei mirifica redolentia exhilaravit*. One is tempted to correct *servum* to *servus* so that the meaning would be "the servant of God refreshed with a wonderful scent."

beauty of purity he had trod underfoot the stench of vices, and leaning upon virtues he had turned aside from the squalors of sins. Better, a hundred times better, is he buried with the beauty of virtues rather than being defended from worms by being smeared with myrrh and aloes. Virtues protect and exclude the poisons of the venomous serpent, but myrrh and aloes, although they protect a corpse from corruption, do not free the soul from punishments.

2. What harm does it do to him now, when his soul rests in the heavens, that sometimes, with his feet hardened with calluses from rough work, his bare foot traveled through various regions spreading the word of God and he tamed his body with rough sackcloth? Rather, he rejoices now all the more gloriously as then he bore heavier things for the love of God, for whenever the effort increases so does the reward of the work. O, what a good exchange to purchase by labor in time a blessed kingdom without end!

Chapter 21. The Tomb in Which His Body Was Placed

It seems quite absurd to pass over without amazement what is related about the tomb[44] in which Vitalis's body was placed. His tomb had been placed in the church of the community * of Blessed Mary of Savigny. As the inhabitants of the place testify, when many of their predecessors had tried to move it, nothing had resulted from their efforts. When some people reported this to the blessed man, doubtless full of the spirit of prophecy, he responded, "Leave it be. Leave it be, because the Lord is keeping this for me." Finally, on the occasion of his burial, it was taken with such ease from the church to the place of his burial that it

*parochiae

---

44. In the chapter title the word is *mausoleum*; here it is *sepulchrum*. Both words seem better translated as *tomb* rather than as *coffin*.

seemed as if it weighed nothing. He is handed over[45] for burial in the oratory of the same church that he had founded, in the northern part of it, where even after his burial the Lord is known to have displayed miracles because of his merit. I add a few of these here, and so put an end to this work.

Chapter 22. A Certain Conversus Was Freed from a Fever at His Tomb

A long-lasting irksome fever troubled a certain *conversus*[46] of the same house, and there was no way he could find any remedy against his great distress. One night, in order to obtain health, he approached the tomb of the same father to spend the night there. While he was staying there, he slept. In his sleep, he saw a vision like this. It seemed to him that the middle of the cover of the tomb opened and a voice came from the top, proclaiming that he should leave there. It seemed that he answered that he would not budge from there until he had merited receiving his health from the loving father. The same voice ordered the same thing twice, and he twice gave the same answer to it. A third time the voice gave its command a little more sharply, thundering that he should leave, and when he gave the same response, it indicated that he had received his health. Strengthened, the man left

45. E. P. Sauvage, *Vita Vitalis*, 386n1, calls attention to the present tense of this verb and to Auvry, *Histoire*, who reported that Vitalis's body lay in the same spot until the destruction of the older church of Savigny in 1182.

46. *conversus*: Previously, *conversus* meant a man who came to religious life as an adult, a convert from secular life. By the time this *vita* was written it almost certainly meant a lay brother, a member of the monastery who was not literate, did not attend the divine office (which was in Latin), and usually engaged in manual work. Lay brothers had a very important part in the growth of the Cistercian Order in the twelfth century. See Burton and Kerr, *Cistercians*, 149–60.

there, took food, and, with the fever extinguished, grew stronger in the health he had received.

Chapter 23. A Brother Cured by Blessed Vitalis from an Illness in His Shinbone

A certain brother incurred in his shinbone a very grave illness that had gnawed away and consumed almost all of the bone. Since no application of bodily medicine aided or helped him in any way, he spurned the assistance of bodily medicine and turned all his hope toward Christ and entrusted the recovery of his health to Blessed Vitalis. When he had kept watch at Vitalis's tomb three times, by God's will and the help of Blessed Vitalis he gained the fruit of his hope through the speedy recovery of his health.

Chapter 24. A Brother Is Freed from Bodily Illness at His Tomb

Another *conversus* there, who exercised the office of gardener, labored under a grave bodily illness. When he had completed the vigils of one midday*[47] at the tomb of the blessed father, he was immediately made well.

unius meridianae vigilias

Chapter 25. A Raving Brother Freed from His Madness through Blessed Vitalis

An additional chapter will readily make clear how great were the power and virtue that the blessed man possessed from the Lord against the tyranny of the devil. The hidden judgment of God handed over a

---

47. This statement may mean that he stayed awake during a siesta period or simply that he kept watch at the tomb during the middle of the day.

*1 Cor 5:5

certain brother wearing the habit in a house of the Savigniac observance[48] to Satan for the destruction of his flesh.* All his perceptions were disturbed. He became frenzied in such an alienation and fearful insanity of mind that he could scarcely be restrained and controlled by the strongest and tightest chains, not to mention human strength. It was horrible to see him as he gnashed with his mouth, brought out things horrible to hear, and spat out saliva on the faces of these standing near. He twisted his head dizzily. By the movements of his whole body he made clear with surest indications the malevolence of the wicked inhabitant within him. Moreover, because those with whom he had entered community life had been wounded with that charity*[49] that knows how to weep with the weeping,* how to be weak with the weak, and how to be burned with the scandalized,* they knew no measure of sorrow and mercy, just as he knew no limit of suffering.

*Song 2:5
*Rom 12:15
*2 Cor 11:29

When for a considerable time they had entreated God with multiple prayers for the recovery of his health and were not heard, it became clear that the Lord had reserved the glory of his health to his confessor Vitalis. Meanwhile, a vision was shown to a certain devout monk of the same church. He saw Saint Vitalis on the edge of his tomb, clothed in white garments and saying to him, "Go and lead to me quickly the one who has deserted the service of the Lord." He repeated this three times. When with silent thoughts the monk pondered whether the one meant was the one who was suffering, blessed Vitalis responded to his

48. The sequel seems to indicate that the house was Savigny itself.

49. *Vulnerata caritate ego sum*, according to the Old Latin version. See Jean Leclercq, *Receuil d'études sur Saint Bernard et ses écrits* (Rome: Edizioni di Storia e Letteratura, 1962), 1:313; Bernard, *De diligendo Deo* 3.7 in *Sancti Bernardi Opera*, ed. J. Leclercq and H. Rochais (Rome: Editiones Cistercienses, 1963), 3:124, lines 18–19.

thought by saying, "He is the same one; he is the same one." When he had related this vision to the abbot, then by order of the abbot the man is led to the tomb of the blessed father, where together with some other brothers guarding him, he spent some nights. Already from that time by the merits and prayers of the blessed man he was completely returned to health and restored to the desired soundness.

Chapter 26. A Certain Foolish Monk Regains His Health at His Tomb

1. A certain man who had been a monk lost his senses and left the monastic life and became a spectacle to the world.* He wandered around here and there like a wretched fool. Once when he came to the place previously mentioned,[50] he had a conversation with the sacristan of the place. The man led him to the oratory and advised him to pray at the tomb of the holy man. Whenever the sacristan said anything, the man, acting out of stupidity, repeated the same things back to him. Finally left there alone, the man slept. On awakening he felt burdened by a very great weakness, but, as became clear, that pain was a medicinal pain. For when his delusion had been eliminated by weeping, his sense was restored to him. Cured, he took up the monastic life again and thereafter lived that life free of his affliction. He was accustomed to visit the same abbey each year and in memory of his cure wished to have something from it. But in all these things nothing else is shown except that, as it is written, "Precious in the sight of the Lord is the death of his holy ones."*

2. Behold, these are the things regarding the blessed man's virtues that we, stumbling because of our pedestrian style, have tried to commit to memory at the

*1 Cor 4:9

*Ps 115:15

50. This seems to be Savigny.

urging of your command. Thanks be to God who granted us to know them and deigned to grant speech of any kind to narrate them. So, at the end, let us ask for the mercy of almighty God so that he who, as we believe, conveyed his servant to the heavenly realms will by the intercession of his merits forgive us our faults. Bestowing his grace on us, may he grant that we live in such a holy way that we may be worthy to be among those he recognizes in the lot of the good. When we have been cleansed and purged of all vices, may we be given over to the company of the holy angels, where we will be able to see him face to face and, fully satisfied by his sight, be able to praise him without end. May he deign to grant this who lives and reigns, the true and only God through infinite ages of ages. Amen.

The end of the life of Saint Vitalis,
the first abbot of Savigny

The Life of Holy Godfrey, the Second Abbot of Savigny

Introduction to
The Life of Holy Godfrey, the Second Abbot of Savigny

Author and Audience

There are few clues about the author of Godfrey's *Vita*. E. P. Sauvage called attention to the few there are in his introduction to his edition of the *Vita*.[1] For example, the author of Godfrey's life was someone who could speak of Godfrey as "our father" (1) and so was very likely a monk of Savigny. Again, we do not know when he wrote the life, but his way of speaking about things in Godfrey's time as happening "then" suggests that he was writing at least some decades after Godfrey's death.[2] Additionally, the author seems to have been writing with his fellow monks in mind. For example, in the prologue he asks what good it does to praise those who have contempt for the world if by bad living we ourselves run away with their image impressed upon us. Elsewhere, he addresses his readers: "Brothers, let us . . . flee sin like a snake. . . . With our father, Blessed Godfrey, let us lay down every burden and sin" (7).

---

1. E. P. Sauvage, ed., *Vita Vitalis*, in *Vitae BB. Vitalis et Gaufridi, primi et secundi abbatum Saviniacensium in Normannia, Analecta Bollandiana* 1 (1882): 355–410, here 356 (hereafter cited as *Vita Vitalis*). References in parentheses are to chapters in the *Vita*.

2. Godfrey illumined the world in his time (*suo quidem tempore*: Prol.), Godfrey's father worshipped God in his time (chap. 1: *tempore suo*), and women wore wide sleeves at that time (chap. 2).

Aims and Purposes

The author returns several times to the notion of imitating saintly models. In the prologue he belabors the notion of imitating the saints. He praises Godfrey's brothers for their imitation of their parents' upright morals and thoughtful way of life (1). He reports that Godfrey transferred to Savigny in order to be formed by imitation of Vitalis's virtues, and once he had transferred, he humbly imitated Vitalis by following in his footsteps (10). Godfrey in his turn is a model for monks (11).

The author is very concerned about decorum, physical comportment, and appearance. He writes that Godfrey advanced in knowledge

> beyond all his contemporaries. . . . In what concerns the outer man, he radiated such beauty of face, such physical attractiveness and proper disposition of his limbs, that he appeared worthy of favor in the eyes of all who looked at him, because apart from any other merits, he won for himself their grace and favor. He had a beautiful face and a pleasing look, as one reads of Joseph, [Gen 39:6] and he was happy in his countenance and well ordered, gentle, and likeable in speech. . . . He lowered his neck, composed his eyebrows, arranged his face, controlled his eyes, held back excessive laughter, moderated his tongue, restrained his stomach, soothed his anger, and gave form to his gait. (4–5)

As abbot of Savigny,

> He was grave in his gait, eloquent in speech, pleasing to see, angelic in countenance, serene in appearance. He exhibited honor in every movement, gesture, or act of his body; he was mature in the fitting arrangement of all his members . . . remarkable in understanding, circumspect in advice. (11)

It is hard to read this description of monastic *bella figura* and not think of heroes of chivalric romances like Tristan, who

> was instructed in the seven arts. . . . He learned to play seven kinds of stringed instruments. . . . No one was more highly endowed than he in kindness of heart, generosity, and courtly conduct, in

intelligence, wise counsel, and valor. In good manners and distinguished deportment he did not have his equal.[3]

The author of Godfrey's *Vita* seems, then, to have been writing for monks. He presents Godfrey to them as a model of monastic sanctity and monastic decorum. He may, however, have had another purpose.

Date and Canonization Process

It is quite possible that Godfrey's *Vita* was written or revised around 1243, when the bodies of Savigny's five saints were solemnly transferred to the newly rebuilt abbey church. At that time there was an unsuccessful effort to secure the canonization of the abbey's saints. L. E. M. Walker has argued persuasively that not only was the abbey's *Liber de miraculis* written for that occasion but also that Hamo's *Vita* was edited to make it suitable as evidence for a canonization process that was proposed at that time. The same may be true of Godfrey's *Vita*.

The *Vita* contains three references to datable events in the congregation of Savigny: (a) the incorporation of the congregation of Savigny into the Cistercian Order (12), (b) its taking place under Abbot Serlo (14) in 1148; (c) the translation of Godfrey's body into the church of Savigny before the altar of Saint Nicholas (17) in 1243. E. P. Sauvage accepted the first of these in his edition of the *Vita* but thought that the other two were interpolations.[4] He thought that the *Vita* was written after 1148 but does not explain why he thought the reference to Abbot Serlo was interpolated. In any case, it is also possible that the entire life was not written until after 1243, and that both the second and the third references are part of the

---

3. *The Saga of Tristram and Ísönd*, trans. Paul Schach (Lincoln, NE: University of Nebraska Press, 1973), chaps. 17, 20. Around 1170, Bishop Stephen of Fougères, the author of the *Vita* of Vitalis, wrote a book of conduct for courtiers called *Le livre des manières*, ed. R. Anthony Lodge (Geneva: Droz, 1979). See David Crouch, *William Marshal: Knighthood, War, and Chivalry, 1147–1219*, 2nd ed. (New York: Longman, 2002), 191.

4. For (i) see Sauvage, *Vita Vitalis*, 403n1; for (ii) see Sauvage, *Vita Vitalis*, 405n1; for (iii) see Sauvage, *Vita Vitalis*, 409n1.

original text. If so, the *Vita* may have been written as part of the effort to secure official canonization of Savigny's saints.

What Did the Author of the *Vita* Know about Godfrey?

There is no certain answer to the question. Aside from praising Godfrey's sanctity in predictable terms, the author does not provide much concrete information. He says that Godfrey was a native of Bayeux. He gives the name of his father and indicates that Godfrey's parents were noble, devout, and wealthy. He says that Godfrey excelled at school and studied in Paris and that he was charming in appearance and bearing, so that people were drawn to him. He joined the abbey of Cerisy-la-Forêt and remained there for some time before then transferring to Savigny, where he imitated, assisted, and succeeded Vitalis. He was highly esteemed by King Henry I of England. He founded many monasteries, acted as their visitator, and instituted a General Chapter to be held at Savigny around the feast of the Holy Trinity. He died in 1138.

The author also tells of two very odd, miraculous happenings. One is the story that during a fire in Bayeux, relics that belonged to the Church of Saint Mary Magdalene flew to Godfrey's mother. Many years later, Godfrey obtained the relics from his father in Bayeux and brought them to Savigny. On another occasion, a beggar was saved from a rock that a philandering and intoxicated priest threw at him from the top of a tower in Bayeux that belonged to Godfrey's uncle. In addition, miracles occurred at Godfrey's tomb.

Some of this information is questionable. Left to create a family for Godfrey, a hagiographer would be inclined to say they were noble, devout, and wealthy. Godfrey instituted a General Chapter in 1132, and he surely visited the monasteries he founded, but we do not know exactly what was the relation between the abbeys and priories of the Savigniac lineage. Savigny seems to have related to the other houses in the congregation somewhat as Cluny related to its daughter houses, over which it had "total jurisdictional power."[5]

---

5. Mary Suydam, "Origins of the Savigniac Order: Savigny's Role within Twelfth-Century Monastic Reform," *Revue Bénédictine* 86 (1976): 94–108.

The story of the relics, told in chapters 2 and 15, frames the narrative of Godfrey's life and sounds like an effort to legitimate the transfer of relics from Bayeux to Savigny. Bayeaux was burned in 1106 when Henry I defeated his brother Robert Curthose. In order to succeed Vitalis in 1122, Godfrey had to have been born at least twenty years before 1106. Of course, it is possible that there had been a fire in Bayeux several decades before 1106, perhaps around the time that the new cathedral was dedicated in 1077.[6] Another possibility is that it was actually in 1106 that Godfrey's mother rescued the relics from the fire at Saint Mary Magdalene's Church in Bayeux and Godfrey was not in her womb but at her side as an adolescent or young man. In that case, Godfrey would have been born around 1090, entered Cerisy-la-Forêt not long after the fire, transferred to Savigny in 1113, and become abbot there in 1122 when he was in his early thirties.[7]

Godfrey, the Man and His Deeds

Godfrey is an elusive character. In his *History of the Congregation of Savigny*, Claude Auvry devotes hundreds of pages to Godfrey, but we learn very little about the man. Using information taken from the sources available to him, Auvry says that under Godfrey, Savigny changed qualitatively and quantitatively. He brought a stricter monastic discipline to Savigny, an effort that caught the attention of his contemporaries. When Vitalis died in 1122, Savigny had only two dependent priories, both near the abbey. But by the time of Godfrey's death, Savigny had founded more than fifteen abbeys, and some of them had founded still others. This expansion was made possible by two things: donations from many important persons and a large influx of recruits to Savigny and its dependencies, among whom enough had sufficient talent and training to lead the newly founded communities. To attract recruits and support

---

6. This problem was noted by Jean Hermant, *Histoire du diocese de Bayeux* (Caen [France]: Pierre F. Doublet, 1705), 1:186–89; Sauvage, *Vita Vitalis*, 392n2; and other authors since.

7. Hermant, *Histoire*, 186–89; Victor de Buck, *Acta Sanctorum*, October 8 (Brussels: A. Greuse, 1853), 1008–9.

on this scale, Godfrey himself and the discipline that he imposed on Vitalis's monastic family must have had great appeal. Godfrey's accomplishments and connections make it likely that he was in fact from a noble family, as the author of the *Vita* claims. They also suggest that the primness that his *Vita* ascribes to him may reflect the preferences of the author more than the reality of his subject, unless such strict decorousness was much more appealing in the first half of the twelfth century than it would be in the first half of the twenty-first century.

The Life of Holy Godfrey, the Second Abbot of Savigny

Prologue

As the lofty counsel of God has always willed to support those struggling faithfully, so it never ceased to propose examples of fruitful labor for those who are wickedly sluggish.[1] It does so that they may struggle more securely, that is, so that they will not falter as they labor or lazily not know what they are imitating. This divine providence mercifully counters mortals' weakness, so that when the deadly seedbeds of inactivity have been removed, they may have before their eyes the victories of those who share their lowly state and, having no hesitations about victory, may fight securely under their great Commander. To this end, the triumphs of the saints are frequently recounted to the ears of the church so that we who are delighted by the gentleness of his reign may not depart from this effort of following in their footsteps. For what profit is there in extolling with praises those who disdain the world if by living badly we run away from being stamped with their form?

Blessed Godfrey shines before the world for the imitation of the faithful. In his time he was a singular

---

1. This prologue is strikingly verbose. Its message is simple: God gives us the example of Godfrey and other saints to rouse us from our laziness and encourage us to follow their example by longing and living for heaven.

light. Burning with the interior love of piety, he spurned the pleasures of a worldly way of life. As an advocate of true religious life, he strove unceasingly to exercise the behavior that he espoused by his habit. Hence it was most fitting that he shone with many kinds of virtue, for no base desire chained his mind with pleasure. All of him longed for the heavenly realm. While still alive in the flesh, he enjoyed the company of the court on high. Therefore he showed to the world in a fitting way how much his way of life was worth to the Lord.

End of Prologue

☙ ☙ ☙

Chapter 1. *The Beginning of His Life*

Blessed Godfrey originated from a family illustrious in worldly dignity but worthier and nobler still in the piety of the Christian religion. His father is said to have been Alan, son of William, a man prudent and vigorous in arms, who was a member of an established and legitimate army. He had his own dwelling, a noble castle with a very strong tower, inside Bayeux near the northern gate. In his time he was a worshipper of God and held fast to justice. He was renowned for generosity and regarded with reverence by all the inhabitants. He struck no one; he defamed no one; he was content with his revenues by which he abounded in every good work. He served his temporal lords with his advice and arms in such a way that he did not neglect to render to his Lord what he owed.[2]

---

2. For a similar description of Vitalis, see above, "The Life of Blessed Vitalis of Savigny," chap. 5: Vitalis strove to please the will of his earthly lord in such a way that he did not displease his Creator.

His mother, praiseworthy no less for her mind than
for the nobility of her blood, also followed the apostolic rule in her state in life.*³ She was subject to her
husband and under him ruled her household according to the fear of the Lord. She was zealous in works
of mercy and nurtured her sons in every discipline.
The two parents lived together uprightly in conjugal
devotion.*⁴ By the generosity of God's gift, they bore
five sons for service to the Lord and for their own
support. Four, bound by oaths of allegiance, were
vigorous in arms and manfully*⁵ strove to imitate their
father's actions in upright behavior and prudent
living.⁶ The fifth, Godfrey by name, was dedicated to
the Lord before his birth because of a miracle, as will
be made clear below. When he was old enough, devoutly and effectively fulfilling their vow, the parents
handed him over to be instructed in the study of letters. He sped diligently through divine and human

in ordine suo

*in religione
conjugali*

*sacramentis
impliciti*

3. Some medieval historians focus on the division of medieval
society into three *ordines*—warriors, priests, and workers; for example see Georges Duby, *The Three Orders: Feudal Society Imagined*
(Chicago: University of Chicago Press, 1982). In medieval Latin
the word *ordo* had a wide range of meanings: a religious order,
the ordering of life within a religious community, rank, class, and
so forth; see J. F. Niermeyer, *Mediae latinitatis lexicon minus* (Leiden:
Brill, 1984), 745–47, which distinguishes twenty-six meanings. The
three *ordines* are about male roles primarily. When the author of
Godfrey's *Vita* writes of the "apostolic rule" and then in the next
sentence of Godfrey's mother as "being subject to her husband,"
he recalls the household codes in the New Testament epistles, for
example, Eph 5:21-22: "subject to each other in the fear of Christ
/ let women be subject to their men" (*subjecti invicem in timore
Christi / mulieres viris suis subditae sint*). Note the reference to "fear
of the Lord."

4. This could be translated as "their marital religious state."

5. This could possibly be translated as "sharing in the sacraments."

6. According to E. P. Sauvage, *Vitae*, 392n1, their names are
unknown except for William, who is mentioned in Matthew Paris,
Historia Anglorum, for the year 1138.

studies with marvelous speed; it is said that while he was still a boy he surpassed his teachers in knowledge. Heavenly grace, which foresaw that he was going to be a teacher of religion, had rendered him exceedingly docile and lovable in all things.

Chapter 2. The Miracle of the Relics

It happened that during the time his mother, a noble and devout woman, was carrying him in her womb, the city of Bayeux, with the cathedral church and other parish churches, as well as the suburb of Saint Vigor with its church, were burned down by the calamity of an unexpected fire, which the inhabitants called *ignis Droconis coillum.*[7] Amid the crowds of people weeping from grief and shouting pitiably in the midst of the great crisis and desolation, the woman just mentioned, feeling deep compassion, as though stunned left her tower in which she was staying. She went down to the river called Aure, devout and ready to administer what counsel and help she could to those working to put out the fire. As the fire grew stronger, it voraciously jumped to the Church of Saint

---

7. E. P. Sauvage, *Vita Vitalis*, makes no attempt to explain this phrase. According to Lewis and Short, *A Latin Dictionary* (Oxford: Clarendon, 1879), 364, *coillum* (a word taken from Greek) was the innermost part of a Roman house, where the household gods were kept. The only reference they give is Tertullian, *De spectaculis* 5 (see PL 1:711 and n27). If that is the meaning here, the phrase could mean something like "the inner chamber of Drogo's fire" or "the inner chamber of the dragon's fire," though what that would signify remains unclear. Another possibility is to emend the text to read *collum draconis ignis* ("neck of the dragon of fire") and see in it a reference to the legend about Saint Vigor mentioned below in note 17. It was suggested to me that perhaps the medieval French word *coilles* (testicles) lies behind the word *coillum* here, though what sense that might give is not clear. There are no contemporary mentions of the fire, which seems to have antedated the dedication of a new church in 1077. See Ordericus Vitalis, *Historia ecclesiae* 3.5.2 (PL 188:376C–377A), who mentions that many basilicas were consecrated in Normandy in that year.

Mary Magdalene, which was located at some distance from the other side of the river.

Marvelous to say, as it burned, by a wondrous working of divine grace a rather nice vessel containing relics of the Glorious Virgin, Blessed Mary Magdalene, Saint George the martyr, and many other saints departed the church through a glass window and flew down from above toward the River Aure to the place where the venerable lady was standing. It went into her wide sleeve, such as women at that time used, and as though it were seeking a refuge in her bosom, hid itself next to her belly, where she was carrying her boy. When relics so precious deigned to make their dwelling place with her in preference to all others, it was a clear judgment about the extent to which this woman kept the vessel of her body in purity and honor, not to mention what lay hidden within.*[8]   *Song 1:4

No less can we, not without just reason, presume that Godfrey was sanctified from the womb, as his deeds and the privilege of grace that he had in relation to God and humans clearly attest. Hence, what is said of Blessed Jeremiah—"Before you left the womb I sanctified you"*—can doubtlessly be said rightly of   *Jer 1:5
Blessed Godfrey. Moreover, it should not be passed over in silence but proclaimed with wonder that immediately after the relics had been received and hidden in the lap of that good lady, the intolerable heat of the fire so quieted down through the power of God and of the holy relics that it did not have the power to advance farther. And to make the holiness of Blessed Godfrey more widely known, the lavish abundance of divine kindness kept completely unharmed and safe from the misfortune of the raging fire the entire parish of Saint Patrick's, in which Blessed Godfrey was born.

---

8. *absque eo quod intrinsecus clausum latebat.* One could also translate this as "apart from what lay within," that is, she was a woman of great chastity but not a virgin, as she was carrying a child within her.

Chapter 3. Her Return Home

The venerable matron returned to her own house with unspeakable joy, both because of the precious treasure of relics that she had with her and because the fire had been put out. On the way, she met her husband, who was anxious for her return. He asked her where she was coming from. Wondering about a fragrance of unusual sweetness around her, he asked her what kinds of herbs she had eaten. She responded to him in a humble and submissive voice, "Now, amid so great desolation, it is not the time to use spices, because it is proper for the truly compassionate person to rejoice with those rejoicing and weep with those weeping."*[9] Then, speaking to her lord, she added, "Let us go up into our house, and I will reveal secretly to your prudence the cause of such a great fragrance." When they had gone up, she related to him everything that had happened to her, as it was recounted above. With fear and devotion she drew the precious vessel from her bosom and handed it into his hands. She said that on no account would she have dared to open it.

*Rom 12:15

Her husband accepted the vessel with reverence and honor and opened it with humble devotion. Seeing the precious pledges of the holy relics, he joyfully closed it with great honor and carefully secured it in a strong box in the safest place in his tower. Therefore the venerable man Alan, not ungrateful for such a great, divinely given favor, with devout generosity gave in perpetual alms to the aforementioned Church of Saint Mary Magdalene, as a perpetual remembrance of this miracle, two burgages[10] located on the near side of

9. Her "humble and *submissive* voice" is again a reference to the household codes mentioned in note 1. The author may feel the need to emphasize her submissiveness because she does not sound particularly submissive in this exchange.

10. A burgage was a rental property owned by a king or lord within a town (*burgh*).

the Aure River, in his own demesne.[11] Before that time the Church of Blessed Mary Magdalene had had no parochial possession beyond the river.

Chapter 4. His Excellence in Learning

The boy had good natural ability and a capacity for learning. He applied himself to letters and humbly obeyed his teacher with fear. Illumined by natural cleverness and divine grace, in an unimaginable and unheard of way he advanced beyond all his contemporaries among his people, so that it was commonly said that he progressed in learning as much in a week as his fellow students did in a year. All those who heard of these things were struck with shock and wonder. And no wonder, for it was obvious that he who teaches human beings knowledge was teaching him.* As he grew in age and grace,* the benevolent feeling of all toward him increased daily. In what concerns the outer man, he radiated such beauty of face, such physical attractiveness and proper disposition of his limbs, that he appeared worthy of favor in the eyes of all who looked at him, because apart from any other merits, he won for himself their grace and favor. He had a beautiful face and a pleasing look, as one reads of Joseph,* and he was happy in his countenance and well ordered, gentle, and likeable in speech. Thus one could fittingly say of him, "It was necessary that someone in whom God poured out such abundant grace be loved by all."

*Ps 93:10

*Luke 2:40

*Gen 39:6

Chapter 5. His Humble Courtesy and Graceful Eloquence

So great was his humble courtesy that he was regarded as a man of respected authority not only among poor and lesser folk but also among the rich

---

11. Demesne was land retained by the lord of a manor under his own management and for his own use and not leased to tenants.

and powerful. Hence deservedly he seems to fulfill this statement in Ecclesiasticus, "I am making you courteous in the gathering of the poor,"* because "humility pursues the proud man, and glory will receive the humble in spirit."* His speech was flavored with so much of the salt of wisdom that because of the sweetness of his speech, by which many were joined with Christ through his preaching and teaching, divine wisdom seemed to speak through his mouth. If any rich person came to him compelled by any reason, or any poor person, or any of middling estate, or if any noble or any undistinguished person came to him, whoever it was always left edified by a gentle word or a disciplined gesture, because he showed the kindness of his loving heart in the kindliness of his gentle speech, for he surrounded himself in discipline.

O, how ordered did discipline render the state of his whole body and the habit of his mind! He submitted his neck, lowered his eyebrows, arranged his face, bound his eyes, held back excessive laughter, moderated his tongue, restrained his stomach, soothed his anger, gave form to his gait. It is proper that the disciple of Christ be modestly adorned with such pearls. He so strengthened the souls of the faithful with sacred teachings by urging, beseeching, and rebuking with all patience and forbearance* that they thought they were already lying down in the green fields of Paradise, completely reclothed with the most splendid garment of immortality.* His conversation was so pleasing to all his listeners because of the honey-filled sweetness lying hidden under his tongue that there was a hint that the Lord himself had established a seat for himself in his mouth.

*Sir 4:7

*Prov 29:23

*2 Tim 4:2; see 2 Tim 3:16

*see 1 Cor 15:53-54

Chapter 6. His Custody of Heart

Among the other gifts that he received from the Giver of graces, one should not hide in fruitless silence that, taught by the discipline of the true Solomon, he shone more remarkably in the diligent custody of his heart by divine help than he did in his other graces. Desiring to keep a clean heart in himself, as much as he could he gathered himself within himself, fleeing the public and loving to be by himself. As much as human weakness allowed, he diligently devoted himself to reading, meditation, and prayer.[12] By his constant attention to these things, a truly great miracle occurred: he achieved such purity of heart[13] and steady

12. Guigo II (d. 1193), the ninth prior of the Grand Chartreuse, wrote a book called *Scala claustralium*, ed. and trans. Edmund Colledge and James Walsh, SCh 163 (Paris: Éditiones du Cerf, 1970); see also *The Ladder of the Monks*, CS 48 (Kalamazoo, MI: Cistercian Publications, 1981). Guigo distinguished a natural progression in the spiritual activities of the monk: reading, meditation, prayer, and contemplation. Such lists are common in twelfth-century writers, who sometimes expand them to include other elements, such as virtuous action, preaching, conversation, and compassion for others. Here are a few examples among many: Saint Anselm, *Orationes*, Prol., ed. F. S. Schmitt, *Opera omnia*, 6 vols. (Edinburgh: T. Nelson, 1938–61), 3:4, lines 2–12; Saint Anselm, *Epistola* 28, in *Opera omnia*, 3:136, lines 14–18; Hugh of Saint Victor, *Didascalicon* 3.10, ed. Charles Henry Buttimer, Studies in Medieval and Renaissance Latin, 10 (Washington, DC: The Catholic University of America Press, 1930), 59, lines 15–21; Hugh of Saint Victor, *Didascalicon*, trans. Jerome Taylor, Records of Western Civilization, 10 (New York: Columbia University Press, 1991), 92–93; for Hugh of Saint Victor, *Didascalicon* 5.9, see Buttimer, ed., 109–10, and Taylor, trans., 132–33. See also Richard of Saint Victor, *Apprehendet messis*, ed. B. Hauréau, *Notices et extraits de quelques manuscripts latins de la Bibliothèque Nationale*, 5 vols. (Paris: C. Klincksieck, 1890–93), 1:116–17: *Legendo et meditando metimus, orando et contemplando vindemiamus, operando et praedicando seminamus* ("By reading and meditating we reap, by prayer and contemplation we gather, by acting and preaching we sow").

13. This entire chapter is about purity of heart. This was an important concept, which Cassian used to translate Evagrius's *apatheia*. It meant discipline of one's mind (thoughts, feelings, and desire), a prerequisite for pure love and contemplative prayer. See, for example, Columba Stewart, introduction to Harriet Luckman

calmness of mind that he could pray a whole Psalter completely from habit without his mind wandering, so that for the whole space of time he thought only of God, of the things of God, and of the holy work of psalmody in which he was engaged. What does one find in these that is not profitable for salvation? The psalms put the demons to flight; they illumine the darkness; they accumulate virtues.

Chapter 7. Purity of the Flesh

From purity of heart it is necessary that there follow innocence of the body, which humility of mind is especially accustomed to acquire and preserve. Hence, according to Blessed Isidore, "As through pride of mind one goes toward the prostitution of lust, so the chastity of the flesh is kept safe through humility of mind."[14] It is not especially necessary for us to commend this virtue in Blessed Godfrey, which gave so many proofs of itself to all. For as it is believed, from the womb of his mother he remained a virgin in his body, sanctified before being born. When he was a youth he was completely intent on maintaining purity of mind and cleanness of heart.* Chosen a virgin by God, he remained a virgin forever.

*Matt 5:8

To keep this purity completely inviolate, he was so diligent in keeping vigils that it seemed that at every hour the judgment to come was present to him who was mindful of the saying of the Lord, "Be awake, because you do not know at what hour your Lord is

and Linda Kulzer, eds., in *Purity of Heart in Early Ascetic and Monastic Literature* (Collegeville, MN: Liturgical Press, 1999), 2–15. On Cassian, see also Columba Stewart, *Cassian the Monk*, Oxford Studies in Historical Theology (New York: Oxford University Press, 1998), 41–48.

14. Isidore, *Sententiae*, 2.39.1, http://www.thelatinlibrary.com /isidore/sententiae2.shtml, accessed July 16, 2014.

going to come."* For he was so conscientious in most   *Matt 24:42
devout prayers that unless he was occupied in prayer
or some other spiritual exercise, he believed the
tempter would be ever present. He feared that the
tempter would mock his fragile vessel with various
temptations and at the same time force his spirit to
waver in some way. In this he was mindful of the word
of the Lord, who says, "Stay awake and pray that you
not enter into temptation, for the spirit is indeed
willing, but the flesh is weak."* And in Ecclesiasticus,   *Matt 26:41
"A vigil of honor dissolves the flesh."*   *Sir 31:1

And by these three, namely, mortification of the
flesh, devout and continual prayer, and pure humility,
as "by spices of myrrh and frankincense and salves of
every powder," as one reads in the Canticle, the fire
of divine love is burned on the altar of the heart and
the smoke of virginal purity rises, spreading its scent
in the presence of the Lord on every side, wafting a
sweet odor to neighboring regions and both freeing
from and bringing confusion to every kind of
demon.*[15] Brothers, let us, breathed on by that most   *Song 3:6,
sweet odor, flee sin like a snake. Let us regard every   with the gloss
pleasure of the flesh as venom. Let us be continually
occupied in devout prayer, holy reading, and divine
meditation. Let no attack of the assailant cause us to
abandon our intimacy with penance, which is properly
the place of good things, just as pride is the place of
wicked things. With our father, Blessed Godfrey, let
us lay down every burden and sin that surrounds us,
following him "who for the joy set before him sus-
tained the cross, caring nothing for shame,"* and let   *Heb 12:2
us hurry through the struggle set before us, hastening
toward the prize* of our eternal calling.   *1 Cor 9:24

---

15. See *Glossa ordinaria*, pars 22: *In Canticum canticorum*, ed.
Mary Dove, CCCM 170 (Turnhout: Brepols, 1997), 206–9, especially n52; Gilbert of Hoyland, *In Cantica Sermo* 15.2–3 (PL 184:74–
76).

Chapter 8. His Zeal for Learning

As he was increasing in age, a burning desire to learn was increasing in him. So he came to Paris intent on vigilant study of the liberal arts. With a brief magisterial anointing he outshone those teaching him. When his understanding had been illumined for knowledge and comprehension of truth, through his disciplined learning of that knowledge he longed with dedicated desire for the saving doctrine of holy letters, for his feeling was inflamed by the fire of heavenly sweetness. Because with burning desire he longed to be intoxicated with the water of saving wisdom, that

John 3:8   interior teacher who breathes where he wills, opens
Rev 3:7   where he wills, and closes for whom he wills, he opened his mind to the understanding of the divine Scriptures so fully that afterward he could abundantly set before countless others subject to him the word of life to the honor of God and the edification of his hearers. For as secular wisdom is a leaking cistern that

Jer 2:13   cannot hold water and instead makes its wickedness
Jer 6:7   cold, so the wisdom that is from above, modest and
Jas 3:15, 17   peaceful, is an unfailing spring, a spring illuminating and warming heart and mind, a spring of water leap-
John 4:14   ing up into eternal life.

Chapter 9. His Entry into Religion at Cerisy[16]

For one who aspires to heavenly things, earthly things lack flavor. Once the Spirit is tasted, all flesh is without taste. So the man of God withdrew all his affections from these lowest things and fixed them

---

16. Legend has it that in the sixth century a wealthy man asked the hermit Saint Vigor of Bayeux to rid his territory of a dragon. Vigor put his stole on the neck of the dragon, which was then drowned in the sea. In gratitude, the wealthy man enabled Saint Vigor to erect a monastery in around 510 on a Roman road linking Coutances and Bayeux. The monastery declined after the Viking invasions in the eighth century. The abbey of Saint Vigor

exclusively on the love of the highest and unchange-
able good.[17] With Saint Paul, he forgot the things that
were behind and manfully strove toward those that
lay ahead.* Thinking about fleeing the world, which   *Phil 3:13
is placed in the hands of the evil one, he often considered in his heart that it is difficult to live in the world
and keep oneself spotless from the world.* He desired   *Jas 1:27
the monastic life, where he could give himself to God
alone after having left behind and excluded all other
things. He chose the abbey of Cerisy, in which God
arranged for him to receive the habit of religion, because at that time the constant discipline of regular
observance according to the Rule of Saint Benedict
was particularly flourishing there. Having become a
monk, he remained there for some time, serving God
in all humility.[18]

The grace of the Lord generated in him contempt
of the world, according to the vow of monastic profession. Why say more? Having laid aside the habit of a
secular way of life, having spurned the worldly haughtiness of nobility, having left the company of those
who love the world and of his relatives so that he could
freely serve Christ the true king,[19] he submitted his
whole self to heavenly teaching. Thereafter there was
in him a ready will for contempt of the world, a very

at Cerisy-la-Forêt was founded in 1032, by Robert, duke of Normandy, the father of William the Conqueror. This abbey pros-
pered quickly and erected a large and beautiful church, much of
which still remains.

17. John Scotus Eriugena, *Periphyseon* 3 (PL 122:621AB): *Nam
universalis boni prima sectio est in illud unum ac summum incommuta-
bile per se et substantiale bonum, ex quo omne bonum manat, et in illud
bonum quod participatione summi et incommutabilis boni bonum est.*

18. Sauvage, *Vita Vitalis*, 399n2, conjectures that Godfrey must
have remained at Cerisy for some time if, as several sources suggest, he became prior there.

19. RB Prol. 3; ed. Timothy Fry, *RB 80: The Rule of St. Benedict
in Latin and English* (Collegeville, MN: Liturgical Press, 1981),
156–57.

firm charity directed at the love of God, a dear brother-
liness toward love of neighbor, no difficulty in learning
thoroughly the order of regular observance, and ready
promptness in showing the good things of obedience
not just to the abbot but to all the brothers.[20] In him
there reigned a pure simplicity for giving to all the
example of a holy way of life.

It was no longer necessary that anyone instruct him
in regular observance, for a heavenly anointing taught
him about everything. So over time he began to shine
so perfectly in life and doctrine that in the house of
God he deserved to obtain the first and most excellent
place in the praise of all the faithful. He so pleased
God that he ascended through the various degrees of
humility to the height of monastic perfection,[21] so that
he seemed to excel no longer as one among others but
as foremost among the others and above all of them.
By divine gift he merited quickly to reach this humility
that merited such sublimity by the virtue of obedience,
continual compunction of heart, and bodily fatigue.

Chapter 10. His Coming to Savigny

The more intimately one comes near to God by the
merits of his life and the purity of his mind, the more
certain one is to sweetly sense the fragrance of fresh
spiritual aromas. One can certainly see this in Blessed
Godfrey, because the more the savor of internal sweetness grew in him, the more ardent in him was the
impulse to a higher way of life, to advance more fully
in the Lord. When he had heard the news of the sur-
passing holiness and religious life of Blessed Vitalis,
the first abbot of Savigny, with the permission of the
abbot of Cerisy he transferred to Savigny[22] in order to

---

20. RB 5.1; Fry, 186–87; RB 71.1; Fry, 292–93.

21. RB 7; Fry, 190–203.

22. Sauvage, *Vita Vitalis*, 400n1, says this occurred in 1113 or
the beginning of 1114.

merit to be imbued by the examples of such a great father, to be instructed by his teaching, to be advanced by his religious life, to be supported by his prayers, and to be formed for the better by imitation of his life and behavior. He came to the place mentioned, made his request with devout and mature humility, asked to be received, and persevered eagerly in his petition.[23] Blessed Vitalis, taking into account the fervor of his holy resolve and pondering no less the uprightness and prudence of his person, received[24] him gladly. So having changed from the black habit of his previous order, he was clothed in the habit of the monastery of Savigny, for there the monks used clothes of grey color.

How religiously he lived there the evident outcome demonstrated. In his way of life he had such humility that he perplexed the pride of all who looked upon him. His patience extinguished the anger of others. His obedience aroused the tepidity of others. His mildness softened the turbulent minds of others with the grace of consolation and edification. He strove to imitate humbly the footsteps of Blessed Vitalis; he began to be his diligent helper, as Blessed Maurus was for Blessed Benedict.[25]

Who was ever more ready than he for the work of God? Who more fervent in prayer? Who more careful about reading? Who keener in zeal for holy meditation?

23. RB 58.3; Fry, 266–67.

24. *suscepit: suscipere*, "to receive," is almost a technical term in the *Rule of Saint Benedict*, which uses it for receiving new members, guests, and the abbatial office. See the list of references in RB, Fry, 548–49.

25. Gregory the Great, *Dialogues*, 2.3.14; 4.2; 6.2; 7.1, 2, 3; 8.7, ed. Adalbert de Vogüé, trans. Paul Antin, SCh 260, 265 (Paris: Éditions du Cerf, 1979–80), 1:150, 152, 156–57, 164; see also *The Life of St. Benedict*, trans. Terrence Kardong (Collegeville, MN: 2009), 31–34, 42. Alcuin drew a similar parallel between himself and his student, Rhaban, to whom he gave the surname "Maur": Bruno Judic, "Grégoire le Grand, Alcuin, Raban et le surnom de Maur," in *Raban Maur et son temps*, ed. Philippe Depreux, et al., Collection Haut Moyen Âge 9 (Turnhout: Brepols, 2010), 31–48.

Who more pure in charity? Who more constant in temperance? Who more profuse in the amount of his weeping? Who more honorable in his body? Who more genuine in mind? Who meeker in anger? Who more forbearing in gentleness? Who more rarely given to the levity of laughter? Who more ardent in compunction? Who more mature in gravity? Who more cheerful in charity? Who more diligent in the exercise of the regular observances? Who more provident in giving advice? Who appeared more glorious in the eyes of powerful men?

Chapter 11. His Election as Abbot of Savigny

When Blessed Vitalis entered on the way of all flesh, the reputation of the holy way of life of Blessed Godfrey had spread far and wide; for this reason it was clear that the assembly of all his brothers chose him as abbot with unanimous agreement and an equal will. They judged that no one was more suitable by merit of life and wise teaching to take the place of such a great father and succeed him in the honor and the burden. Since Blessed Godfrey in every way detested all ambition and glory of the present life, he was more abducted by a kind of holy violence than elected. No wonder, for neither here nor elsewhere could anyone be found more ready for this office than Blessed Godfrey. So when elected, he pleads with them; when invited, he resists; when asked, he objects; when entreated, he trembles; when commanded, he acquiesces. Hence we give him praise, because the praiseworthy example of obedience overcame the principle of his objection.[26]

Once he had accepted the office of this holy dignity, he carried himself in such a way that he pleased God

---

26. This passage contains many legal terms, so we may imagine Godfrey arguing his case for refusing and then finally out of obedience acquiescing to the verdict of the election.

and the world—not the world placed under the evil
one, but the world reconciled to God the Father
through the blood of Christ. He was grave in his gait,
eloquent in speech, pleasing to see, angelic in countenance, serene in appearance. He exhibited honor in
every movement, gesture, or act of his body; he was
mature in the fitting arrangement of all his members;
he seemed acceptable to the eyes of all mortals, inasmuch as he was steadfast in faith, certain in hope, filled
with the twofold charity, distinguished in wisdom,
remarkable in understanding, circumspect in advice,
and a zealous cultivator of spiritual knowledge.*   *cf. Isa 11:2

Chapter 12. The Grace He Had in Relation to Princes

How much grace he found among princes and magnates, and especially with Henry the Elder, king of
England,[27] is evident from that fact that in his lifetime
by the gift of kings and princes he founded twenty-
nine abbeys and numerous daughter houses and
granddaughter houses.[28] For as popular report attests,
he deserved to obtain the grace of such intimacy with
King Henry that the king called him his father and
preferred him to all mortals. Whatever Godfrey asked
of him he easily took away with no objection.

It is no wonder that Godfrey was well received
among men, for he obtained such sanctity and grace
with God that with the help of divine providence he
was the father and founder of many great monasteries. In them (God be blessed today!) the fervor and
discipline of the Cistercian Order thrives and will
thrive until the end![29] For who can count the souls that

27. Henry I (1068/69–1135), who succeeded his brother William
Rufus as king of England in 1100.
28. See the genealogy in the *Acta Sanctorum*, October 8, 1022–23,
which lists twenty-nine houses founded between 1122 and 1137;
above pp. 18–19.
29. Sauvage, *Vita Vitalis*, 403n1, observes that this shows that
this life of Godfrey was not written before 1148 (actually, 1147 is

are already saved, are being saved daily, and will be saved in the future, who, had they remained in the world, would have been put in deadly peril. In these same places Christ Jesus the Lord is now served, vices are now resisted, the devil is now opposed, acceptable prayers are now offered to the Lord, more profuse tears are now abundantly poured out, the poor are now revived, acts of kindness are now mercifully shown to rich and middling, and from there other exercises of regular observance and works undertaken are abundantly fulfilled. Places that were once deserted and wild are now built up into places adapted and adorned for divine worship, consecrated and dedicated in honor of the blessed and glorious Virgin Mary, so that rightly what is written in Numbers can be sung with wonder by all those who see these places: "How delightful are your tabernacles, O Jacob, and your tents, O Israel. They are like shaded valleys, like

Num 24:5, 6   watered gardens near rivers."

*rigatione   *Chapter 13. Abbeys: Their Foundation and Watering*[*][30] *through Visitations*

Because the wise are not less conscientious in cultivating their vineyards and guarding them once they have been cultivated than they are in planting them, Blessed Godfrey strove to cultivate his with the hoe of discipline by pulling up vices, cutting off superfluities, removing things that would be harmful, and sowing plantings of virtues, cutting off occasions and opportunities for sins but doing so by the hand of the supreme high priest. For the mind that has not been diligently cultivated by the hoe of discipline contracts many blemishes, according to this saying, "The vessel

---

a more correct date), when the congregation of Savigny was joined to the Cistercian Order.

30. This odd word choice seems to be an effort to echo the "watered" (*irrigui*) of the previous sentence.

that lacks a cover and the sack without a drawstring are open to many impurities."* But as the Holy One says, "We are a vineyard, planted by the Lord's hand, redeemed by his blood, watered by his word, propagated by grace, made fertile through the spirit."*

As we said, Godfrey himself planted the vineyard and watered it, even visited it, preaching that on the Day of Judgment those clothed with inappropriate garments would be separated from those clothed with a nuptial vestment and cast out, bound hand and foot, into the outer darkness.* For he planted in the humility and poverty of religion those he had uprooted from the empty show of the world, according to the voice of the prophet who says, "If we have been coplanted in the likeness of his death, we will also be sharers in his resurrection."* For one who is uprooted from the muddy and earthly filth of vices as though waking from death is transplanted into the greenness of the virtues as into excellent soil, which yields fruit a hundredfold to the laboring farmer.

He watered with the teaching of holy preaching so that by watering souls he would make into fruitful sprouts of virtue and fruits of good work those whom he had planted in the aridity of religious life as in a deserted, trackless, and waterless land,* lest growing parched amid the unfamiliar severities of religious life without the moisture of the teaching of the word of God they would not only remain unfruitful but also not even root in the soil and so die and rot.[31] Therefore he strove to fatten* the minds of his subjects with the

*Num 19:15

*see, e.g., Ps 79:9, 15; Isa 5:1-7; Jer 2:21

*Matt 21:33-41; 22:1-14

*Rom 6:5

*Ps 62:3

*inpinguare

---

31. Sauvage, *Vita Vitalis*, 404n2, comments that according to the *Chronicle of Savigny* Godfrey imposed customs more demanding than the early Savigniac observances. Ordericus Vitalis, *Ecclesiasticae historiae* 8.26 (PL 188:644B), writes, "After [Vitalis's] death, Godfrey of Bayeux, a monk of Cerisy, succeeded him. [Godfrey] was zealous for immoderate innovations and added a heavy yoke on the necks of his disciples" (*Quo defuncto, Bajocensis Goisfredus, ac Cersiacensis monachus, successit; qui et ipse immoderatis adinventionibus studuit, durumque jugum super cervices discipulorum aggregavit*).

dew of preaching in order to fatten them with the
sweetness of humility and the rich wine[32] of the other
virtues.

For as without the sustenance of food the body becomes thin and listless, so the human mind without
the spiritual nourishment of heavenly sustenance
grows weak in strength of virtue. In making visitations and corrections, he adhered to the greatest caution and diligence so that he could stir the souls of his
subjects to hatred of vices, to love of virtues, and to a
stricter keeping of discipline. He strove, according to
Jer 1:10 the saying of Jeremiah, to pull up vices by the roots,
to destroy sins, to remove occasions for transgression,
to disperse harmful and suspicious familiarities, to
edify each and all with his way of life and teaching, to
plant seedbeds of virtues in their hearts, to incline
them to love and reverence for their prelates, and to
inflame them to greater love of God and neighbor.

Chapter 14. The General Chapter that He Instituted

Although this holy man always glorified the Lord
in all his works, he is especially venerated for this: so
that the discipline and rigor of the Order would continue to be observed more fervently and conscientiously in the abbeys that through the grace of God
he had founded, he arranged that a General Chapter
be held at Savigny on the feast of the Holy Trinity for
three consecutive days. To it each and every abbot of
the whole family descending from Savigny was annually to convene. All pretexts and excuses were disal-
lowed. They were to discuss and promote the salvation
of the souls of their subjects, the good of obedience,
and the regular observances and the progress of their
order. This was conscientiously observed throughout

---

32. *pinguedine saginaret: pinguis* means fat, but also "rich wine."
Here it is interpreted as the latter.

his time and afterward until the time of Blessed Serlo, abbot of this place, who submitted with all his contemporaries to Blessed Bernard, the first abbot of Clairvaux, and received the habit, observances, and institutions of the Cistercian Order.[33]

Chapter 15. *The Translation of the Relics of Savigny*

With the passage of time, while Blessed Godfrey by the disposition of divine grace governed the abbey of Savigny solicitously with ever-watchful care, once it happened that there were reasons for him to go to the city of Bayeux. He recalled the incomparable treasure that was kept in the house of his father, namely, the holy relics that we mentioned earlier. While he was still enclosed in his mother's womb, at the time of the fire in the town, they miraculously flew into his mother's lap. He thought to ask his father for them and transfer them to Savigny. His father gladly complied. Taking the vessel with the sacred relics, he handed it over to him, saying, "Dearest son, accept this precious treasure and take it to the house of Savigny with honor and reverence. Strive diligently to conform your life to this great grace, so that the power of the miracle that occurred may obtain as its effect the holiness in your religious way of life." Blessed Godfrey received the gift he desired and carried it to the abbey of Savigny with spiritual joy and due reverence. There

33. Sauvage, *Vita Vitalis*, 405n1, unnecessarily it seems, thinks that the reference to Serlo and the Cistercians may have been an interpolation. Blessed Serlo was Godfrey's companion at Cerisy and transferred with him to Savigny. He died at Clairvaux. At Savigny he received the same honor as Vitalis, Godfrey, Peter, and Hamo. It does not seem, however, that a *Vita* was ever written for him. In Latin, this chapter consists of two lengthy sentences. The word *generatio* occurs twice. In these two instances, it is translated as "family descending from" and "his contemporaries." In chap. 17, it is translated as "progeny."

to this day it is kept with honor, as a witness to the miracle previously noted.

Chapter 16. A Certain Miracle

It happened that in the city of Bayeux a certain priest of a less honorable way of life than was proper, in the dusk of day's end, in the darkness and murkiness of night no less of mind than of body, had a banquet prepared for himself. It is a shame to say that he shamelessly arranged that there be invited to it along with him a certain woman decked out as a prostitute, to mislead souls, in order to enjoy illicit embraces with her in an effort to fulfill the insatiable desire of his flesh. While they passed time in eating and drinking, in tales and silly talk, the priest, overcome by intoxication and drunkenness, as usually happens to gluttons, fell asleep during the feast. The woman, who did not find his company at all acceptable, secretly left and so eluded his villainous hands that night.

Therefore when the priest woke up he perceived himself mocked and altogether robbed of his hope. This led to his being goaded by the poisoned arrows of the devil; as if mad, he followed his sordid prey. He went up a certain tower, which belonged to a great man, noble and powerful, who was an uncle of Blessed Godfrey. He ran through the corners and hidden places of this tower but did not find what he had lost. Looking around through the windows carefully, he heard a certain poor man lying on the ground next to the tower, gravely ill. He thought the woman whom he sought was lying there in disguise. The priest, as though prompted by an evil spirit, raised a large stone from the window and threw it with all his might at the poor man lying there. The poor man, terrified both by the horror of the rock mercilessly coming down on him and by the fear of death, began to cry out over and over in a loud voice, "Saint Godfrey, Saint Godfrey, help me. Do not let the rock loosened from the house of your uncle kill me." The priest, hearing the pitiable shouting of the poor man and fearing he had committed murder, departed in confusion, fleeing with hurried step, and almost broke his foot.

Why say more? Divine loving-kindness knows how mercifully to free the devout from temptation and the innocent not only from tribulation but also from death. It customarily punishes the wicked and evil living with the rigor of justice as they deserve. For example, in the furnace in Babylon, it kept the three innocent boys completely unharmed from the burning fire and turned the power of the fire on those stoking the furnace.* So, through the merits of Blessed God-frey, the invocation of his name miraculously kept the poor man untouched from every injury, and through the misfortune of a paralyzing illness it suspended the priest, who lost the use of his hands and feet, from the service of the altar. Thus, as is fitting, it turned the punishment on the perpetrator.

*Dan 3:19-26

Chapter 17. The Death of the Blessed Man

After the venerable Father Godfrey, under the rule of the Holy Spirit, had founded many monasteries in France, Normandy, Maine, Touraine, Anjou, Brittany, England, Ireland, and Wales, he saw with his bodily eyes the sons of his spiritual sons to the third and fourth generations. Now worn out by a prolonged old age, he wanted "to be dissolved and to be with Christ."* He was thankful that the house of Savigny, which by God's dispensation he had ruled with vigor, flourished like a vine all over the land, and its daughters were everywhere like new olive shoots.* Never-theless, he feared to leave the new plantings, which he had planted in the Lord while God had given the in-crease,* lest perhaps after his departure ravenous wolves should invade his flock. Therefore, hesitating between hope and love, with groaning and tears he said in his prayers, "Lord, now it is enough that I have

*Phil 1:23

*Pss 127:3;
143:12

*1 Cor 3:6

fought to this point, but as you command, I will fight.
But if you spare old age, it is good to me. Please guard
these for whom I fear."

When the time of his summons approaches, he has
been perfected by a fullness of many virtues and most
perfect merits. Already he has been made most beloved to God and all his saints. With the monastic
affairs well arranged and in very good order, with his
subjects situated in deepest peace through the wisdom
given him by God and joined to each other with the
kindness of mutual love, the renowned shepherd is
seized with a fever and placed on that noble funeral
bed adorned and decorated most properly with ashes
and a rough covering for the humility of his soul. He
most devoutly commended his sheep to the Lord. His
sons, abbots and monks, rushed to him from all sides
to bid farewell to their most beloved father. They
breathed sighs from deep in their breasts and poured
out tears with gasps, although they knew that instead
they should be rejoicing, if the force of their sorrow
would answer to reason. It was a devout thing to rejoice for Godfrey, and it was a devout act to weep over
Godfrey. His body was burdened with weakness, but
his spirit, because it had always ruled his own limbs
well, vividly turned to God and the things of God and
did not allow his heart or mouth or hands to stop
praying.

And so the most blessed father, strengthened by the
sacraments of the church while the abbots and monks
correctly celebrated around him the proper offices
of the dead, in the year of the Lord 1139, on the eighth
day of the Ides of July,[34] taking leave of his noble
progeny, amid words of prayer, with happy peace and
blessed rest, happily and blessedly handed over his
precious soul to the Giver of spirits and the Creator
of all creatures. He was made a companion of all the
saints while the angels rejoiced. He was granted joyous

---

34. July 7. See above, Introduction, n69.

entrance into the palace of heaven and received the rewards acquired by his devout labors.[35] His most holy body was buried with honor in a stone tomb worthy of the burial of so great a father and later was placed with all honor in the church of Savigny before the altar of Blessed Nicholas, bishop and confessor. At his holy tomb the blind receive sight, the paralyzed are raised up, the deaf receive hearing, and those with dysentery and fevers are returned to good health. This our Lord Jesus Christ grants, who lives and reigns with the Father and the Holy Spirit, God through all ages of ages. Amen.

The End of the Life of Saint Godfrey

/3 /3 /3

[Appendix:] Likewise a Few of the Miracles of the Saints of Savigny[36]

In the city of Avranches there was a girl, Thomassa by name, daughter of a certain noble citizen of the same city. . . . Throughout her body she was punctured by ulcerous spots, that is, in her body were

---

35. Sauvage, *Vita Vitalis*, 409n1, suggests that the next two sentences are an interpolation from the thirteenth century. The translation of Godfrey's body to the chapel of Saint Nicholas occurred in 1243 during the abbacy of Stephen of Lexington.

36. All these miracles can be found in the *Liber de miraculis sanctorum Savigniacensium*, ed. Léopold Delisle, in *Recueil des historiens des Gaules et de la France*, 23:587–605. The footnotes below contain references to the corresponding places in Delisle. Delisle usually abbreviates the entries, breaking off before the cure takes place. There are other slight differences between the present text and the accounts in his edition of the *Liber de miraculis*; here the cures are attributed not to Godfrey alone but to the relics of the saints of Savigny collectively. We have not been able to pin down two topographical locations, *Plessiaco* and *Villeriis*. It seems possible, even likely, that *Plessiaco* is modern-day Le Plessis-Robinson. As for *Villeriis*, our best guess is that it is modern-day Villiers (*Département* of Indre), but there are other Villiers that are possible.

visible more than fifty openings from which pus flowed out. She was brought by her parents to Savigny and in a few days was healed through the merits of the saints.[37]

A noble girl of twenty-two years, Alicia by name, was deaf and mute from birth. Her mother, Gervasia, commended her to the saints and brought her to Savigny. Through the suffrages of the saints the tie on her tongue was loosed and her ears were opened.[38]

Dionysia of Barneville was badly troubled by a demon. She was brought to Savigny bound with iron handcuffs and shackles. Through the merits of the saints she returned home well and sound.[39]

Laurentia of Plessiac had a hand that was crippled from birth. She was brought to Savigny. At the touch of the holy relics, she opened the hand that had been closed all her life long. From then on it was fit to do everything.[40]

Guillot Burnet had been lying paralyzed for six years on a pallet. Through the merits of the saints he was raised up and healed.[41]

Aliz, of Villery, was mute for a long time. Her friends commended her to the saint, and immediately the tie on her tongue was loosed.[42]

Alicia, a widow, had an only son named Walter. He died while his mother was away. When she heard this, the mother, acceding to the counsel of her neighbors, commended the boy to the saints, and by their merits he was called back to life.[43]

William Mansel, of the diocese of Avranches, had on the back of his neck a disease that was awful to

37. Delisle, *Recueil*, 23:589GH.
38. Delisle, *Recueil*, 23:590D.
39. Delisle, *Recueil*, 23:592J.
40. Delisle, *Recueil*, 23:593A.
41. Delisle, *Recueil*, 23:593B.
42. Delisle, *Recueil*, 23:593H, 601D.
43. Delisle, *Recueil*, 23:594KL, 595AB.

look at. There were nine openings, and vapor seemed to go out of them. When he was close to death, the man commended himself to Blessed Vitalis and his companions and obtained complete health.[44]

44. Delisle, *Recueil*, 23:597C.

The Life of Blessed Peter of Avranches, Monk of Savigny

Introduction to
The Life of Blessed Peter of Avranches, Monk of Savigny

THE *VITA* OF PETER OF AVRANCHES, monk of Savigny, is brief, comprising fifteen modest chapters in all. The anonymous author of the *Vita* was surely a monk of the same congregation, writing chiefly for his confreres, to honor the memory of their former brother and to give them a model of saintly life. He probably knew both Peter and Hamo, for he records conversations and interactions between the two, although these could have been invented as edifying examples. The writer concentrates on Peter's virtues and his devotion to spiritual life but neglects to give his date of birth or death or details of his activities before he became a monk. At the outset of the biography the writer summarily reports that Peter came from Avranches, attended school and progressed in his studies, and loved the "diversions of the world." As a solitary example, the author notes that the young man was charmed by musical instruments, and through practice and use he became adept at playing the fiddle (*viella*).

The *Vita* of Peter is found in the same two Parisian manuscripts that include the *Vitae* of Vitalis and Godfrey. The editor, E. P. Sauvage, was aware of a third manuscript containing Peter's *Vita*, which dated from the eleventh to the twelfth century; it had formerly belonged to Clermont College, but Sauvage had no access to it.[1]

---

1. E. P. Sauvage, ed., "Vitae B. Petri Abrincensis et B. Hamonis monachorum coenobii saviniacensis," *Analecta Bollandiana* 2 (1883): 475–560, here 476.

Since an incident reported in chapter 10 happened in the time of Henry II, who became king of England in December of 1154, and since Hamo, who died in April of 1173, survived Peter, the events recorded in his *Vita* must have occurred between those years. Although the date of Blessed Peter's death remains uncertain, Sauvage suggested 1172, perhaps on December 24, for that day was assigned to his commemoration in Savigny martyrologies.[2]

A didactic purpose is evident in the *Vita* of Peter of Avranches, as is common to saints' lives. When the author describes the character of his subject's spiritual life and admirable qualities, he then summons his "dearest Brothers" to imitation of Peter's holy ways, or he offers instruction on a particular virtue. For example, he devotes short chapters to a call for repentance (chap. 10), the benefits of prayer (chap. 12), and humility (chap. 13). In places he admonishes the brothers (*fratres*) to avoid wanton speech (chap. 5) or idle curiosity (chap. 7). Moreover, he employs scriptural quotations or cites church fathers, including Augustine and Jerome, to illustrate Peter's conformity to doctrine and to the will of God.

The most extensive example of didacticism in the *Vita* occurs in chapters 10 and 11, where the writer, in recording a revelation granted to a certain gravely ill knight, provides vivid, detailed descriptions of hell and heaven, both amply supported by scriptural references. He invokes the lurid punishments of hell as a warning to unrepentant sinners while presenting celestial bliss as an inducement to prayer and the practice of a good life modeled on that of Peter, for in his vision the knight saw a monk dressed in white conversing familiarly with Christ in heaven. After the knight recovered his health and sought that unknown monk, he found him at Savigny: Peter of Avranches.

Another example of the writer's didactic intention appears in his contrast between Peter's "strict severity of spirited charity" and Hamo's "abounding kindness of prudent charity." Although the writer reports that these two monastic friends were bound by mutual love and that in fact Hamo was Peter's confessor, they evidenced very different temperaments and pursued paths of holiness that were quite dissimilar. Peter was known for strictness of

---

2. Sauvage, "Vitae B. Petri Abrincensis et B. Hamonis," 498.

discipline, observance of silence, and avoidance of conversation. The author of his *Vita* declares that he was "never remembered to have laughed openly" (chap. 6), while descriptions of Hamo reveal an outgoing, affable person known for his kindness to all. The comparison of the two men leads to a lesson about the diversity of graces mentioned in 1 Corinthians 12:4 and culminates in the following verses:

> Peter of Avranches, who sheared sins like a sword;
> Hamo, dovelike, pious and patient, and like a sheep.

From the short *Vita* of Peter of Avranches, we learn that he was a monk of stern bearing and strict conscience. In fact, the author notes that his frequency of confession sometimes irked his confessors. We know that he "especially loved" Hamo, yet when his friend brought to him the greetings of King Henry II, he rudely rebuffed him. Peter so nourished the virtue of humility that he asked to be assigned to lowly tasks and vile exercises that others in the community tried to avoid, including the washing of soiled cautery rags. The author considered it miraculous that Blessed Peter never became ill or infected from handling such putrefaction and that he overcame his abhorrence of this foul office. Indeed he lived a long life, suffered the afflictions of old age, and eventually became so feeble as to require the support of a stick to walk. He died peacefully, "surrounded by the presence of angels" and "the community of chanting brothers" (15). The anonymous author records that Blessed Peter was buried "not in the common cemetery of the monks, but in a suitable marked place." On May 1, 1243, his remains were translated to the rebuilt abbey church at Savigny.

The Life of Blessed Peter of Avranches, Monk of Savigny

Here Begins the Life of Blessed Peter of Avranches, Monk of Savigny, Order of Cistercians

Chapter 1. How He Was Converted into a Different Man

Blessed Peter originated from the city of Avranches. When he was still a little boy, he was handed over to the study of letters by his parents and, applying himself to his school exercises, attained sufficiency in the appropriate literature. And when the ardor of youth grew strong in him, as is the custom for many at such an age, he began to love the diversions of the world and to be charmed by musical instruments, especially in handling the fiddle, knowledge of which he gained for himself by practice and use. Moreover, with the mercy of the Holy Spirit (which breathes when and where it wishes) blowing upon him,* our kind and merciful Lord touched his innermost heart, exposed the vanity of the world to which he had determined to devote himself, set before his mind's eye the horrible punishment of hell, his past conduct, and the dreadful Judgment, and recalled to his memory the joys of the blessedness to come. And so, mercifully enlightened, humbled internally, and also feeling remorse within himself in all the depths of his innermost parts, he was suddenly changed into a different man.

*John 3:8

137

Chapter 2. That He Received the Monastic Habit at Savigny

Therefore, seeing that it would not be safe for him to dwell together with the Serpent any longer, Peter began to think about flight from the world. Moreover, reflecting and deliberating with himself where he might more securely and more fittingly bring to completion the good that he had conceived, he chose the abbey of Savigny for this purpose, because this place, which appeared to illuminate not a little the whole country through its religious ardor and the fragrance of its good reputation, was also a model of holiness. For this reason he went to Savigny; he sought diligently, and he found; he asked earnestly, and he received; he knocked perseveringly, and the door to grace was opened for him;* and so in that same place he was admitted to the monastic state.

*Matt 7:7-8; Luke 11:9-10

Chapter 3. How He Devoted Himself to Perfection and to Guarding His Soul

In truth, since Blessed Peter bore in mind that opposites are cured by opposites, he was determined to heal the wounds of his past worldly frivolity through great seriousness and gravity, and to this purpose he applied himself wholly. For this reason, although he devoted himself to the practice of virtues, to the constant observance of religious life, and to advances in goodness, yet he especially kept ever-watchful care in guarding his soul, in the discipline of his senses, and in the salutary zeal for prayer. In these he decided to complete his days.

Chapter 4. Concerning His Tenderness of Conscience and Diligence of Confession

In truth, how ardent a longing he had for that gospel beatitude ("Blessed are the pure of heart," *et cetera*)*

*Matt 5:8

is clear from the fact that the delicate tenderness of his conscience could not bear the gnawing recollection of a mortal sin, nor indeed of a perceptible venial sin, but, seizing the opportunity of confession, at once rushed back to that salutary remedy. The frequency of this holy importunity was thus sometimes a bit irksome to the confessors of the house of Savigny. But, solicitous of his own salvation, he gave little heed to this fact, knowing that "since confession is truly a good ornament of the soul, it purifies sinners and renders the just more pure."[1] In truth, Augustine says, "The more anyone confesses the foulness of his sin in hope of pardon, so much the more easily does he obtain the grace of remission."[2]

Chapter 5. How Much He Strove for Silence, and How He Shunned Common Conversations as Much as He Could

And so, diligently heeding that saying of James ("If anyone thinks himself to be religious, not bridling his tongue," *et cetera*),* and again ("One who does not offend in word, he is a perfect man"),* he strove to shun the common conversations of religious and laymen, and also their fellowship, as much as the observances of the Order, the integrity of fraternal peace, and obedience to his teachers permitted. For indeed, idle speeches in the mouth of others are blasphemies in the mouth of a priest, and much more so in the mouth of monks; thus a mouth consecrated to prayer and to divine discourses ought to be closed to idle speeches and fables.[3] Wherefore Blessed Peter took

*Jas 1:26
*Jas 3:2

1. Nicholas of Clairvaux, *Sermo in Festo Sancti Andreae* 12 (PL 184:1055A).
2. Pseudo-Augustine, *De vera et falsa penitentia* 10.25, in *Sancti Aurelii Augustini Opera Omnia* (Paris: Gaume, 1837), 1634D.
3. Bernard of Clairvaux, *De Consideratione* 2.13.22, ed. Jean Leclercq and H. M. Rochais, *S. Bernardi Opera: Tractatus et opuscula* (Rome: Editiones Cistercienses, 1963), 3:429; Bernard of Clairvaux, *Five Books on Consideration: Advice to a Pope*, trans. John D.

care to fulfill effectually that saying of the Rule, "Vulgar words and those leading to laughter we condemn in all places with an everlasting prohibition."[4]

Dearest Brothers, why in Jerusalem do we want to speak in the Egyptian language? Why do we who ought to speak wholly in the Jewish language venture to speak half in the tongue of Azotus?* Therefore let us who are men of the gospel speak entirely in the language of the gospel. Let our speech be redolent of the law, the prophets, and the apostles; let us sharpen our tongue with their words. Let a weight of lead, according to the word of Zechariah,* not be cast upon our mouth. For a leaden mouth is that which says nothing refined, nothing acute, nothing about things above but is wholly slack, wholly dull, wholly concerned about the lowest things and perhaps about unjust things. For assuredly injustice sits upon a talent of lead.[5] Therefore let us remember that our mouth is consecrated to celestial kisses and divine declarations; let us consider it a sacrilege if our mouth gives utterance to something not sweet, not divine, not edifying, not about Sacred Scripture. Let these words briefly suffice for our admonition.

*2 Esdr 13:24

*Zech 5:8

Chapter 6. Concerning the Outward Strictness of His Discipline

But since a fool is recognized by his laughter, and a simpleton raises his voice in laughter,* Blessed Peter considered laughter a fault, and to worldly joy he said: "Why are you vainly deceived?"* For mourning takes hold of the end of such joy, which then never receives consolation.* Thus he kept his countenance in such

*Sir 21:23

*Sir 2:2

*Prov 14:13

Anderson and Elizabeth T. Kennan, CF 37 (Kalamazoo, MI: Cistercian Publications, 1976), 76–77 (hereafter CF 37).

4. RB 6.2.

5. A Grecian unit of weight, usually used of silver or gold; lead would be of less value.

great strictness of discipline that he is not remembered ever to have laughed perceptibly in religious life. Indeed, this strictness was of greater virtue in that way of life in comparison to how much in the world he used to delight in music and song.

Therefore, dearest Brothers, do not be so foolish as to judge the one who laughs to be joyful. Believe me, true joy is a serious matter. For truly, to embrace voluntary poverty, to keep desires in check, to meditate on the endurance of afflictions—one who reflects on these has great joy inside but not very visibly outside. Solid therefore is the joy of a good and holy person, since it comes from internal and eternal sources; it is destroyed by no cause, no adversity, no misfortune. Such a one is cheerful and tranquil always and everywhere. In fact, such people do not depend on another or await favor from without, for their own happiness is within, in the good state of their conscience, where no one sees.

Chapter 7. Concerning a Certain Sin of Curiosity, Which He then Anxiously Repented

How concerned Blessed Peter was about restraining curiosity of the senses and avoiding loss of time can be observed from that which follows. For once when he was appointed to be over the abbey's fishpond for a certain reason, he saw that class of birds that are called ducks. With some curiosity, he watched them swimming here and there; he was not mindful of his accustomed rigor in guarding his mind and in disciplining his senses. When he returned to himself inwardly, his conscience reproached him severely, and with ardent sorrow, as if he had committed a grievous crime, he hurriedly proceeded to Blessed Hamo, who was one of the confessors assigned to hearing confessions in the monastery, humbly confessing the aforementioned offense and saying with very great contrition in his heart, "Ah, wretched me! I've wasted my time in empty and idle pursuits; through my curiosity of seeing and careless guarding of my mind, I've negligently lost my spirituality." In fact, he had made a covenant with his *Job 31:1   own eyes* that he would not look at any delightful earthly thing too carefully and curiously, knowing that the mind is infected by excessive and intent looking and that depraved and sordid thoughts are engendered in so doing.

Thus Gregory wrote, "It is not permitted to consider by looking (namely, by intent, careful looking) at what is not permitted to be desired."[6] And in Prov- *Prov 16:17   erbs we read, "An intent eye is detestable to the Lord."* Let those who are wandering and culpably incautious about guarding their sight heed this warning, and let them recall to mind that the raven first attacks the eye of a dead farm animal and through the eye draws out the brain. So also does the ancient enemy: indeed, his instigation, if he has found an approach, enters secretly and spreads itself deceitfully and creeps like a cancer,[7] to take possession of the whole person and to tear away all the inner good. For that reason Jerome wrote, "Let wickedness be crushed in the seed. While the enemy is small, kill him,"[8] for we must not wait for the one to grow who ought to be feared when he is small; nor should the one be allowed to enter who, when he is shut out, still does not cease to assail the internal peace of the heart "by going about just as a *1 Pet 5:8   roaring lion."*

---

6. Gregory, *Moralia in Job* 21.2.4, ed. M. Adriaen, CCSL 143A (Turnhout: Brepols, 1979), 1066:38–39; trans. as *Morals on the Book of Job*, Library of the Fathers (Oxford: Henry Parker, 1845), 2:571.

7. The phrasing here echoes Ovid, *Metamorphoses* 2:825 (*solet cancer serpere*), ed. and trans. F. J. Miller (Cambridge, MA: Harvard University Press, 1960), 1:118.

8. *Epistola 22 ad Eustochium* 6.5, ed. and trans. F. A. Wright, *Select Letters of St. Jerome* (Cambridge, MA: Harvard University Press, 1975), 66–67.

Chapter 8. How He Scorned the Empty Applause of Men and Lightly Esteemed Royal Greetings

And so, choosing to be always lowly in God's house as much as it was in his power, and to be humbled more with the meek than to divide spoils with the proud,* Blessed Peter strove to avoid every honor and empty favor of the world as the worst poison. Thus when Blessed Hamo, returning from court, one time greeted him devoutly on behalf of King Henry, inasmuch as Peter was a man renowned and recognized in the court of the aforementioned king for the firmness of his sanctity and the earnestness of his praying, he responded with a certain severity to the aforementioned Hamo, whom he especially loved, "I do not care about the greetings of kings, who can die; my attention is directed elsewhere." Thus he sometimes used to rebuke even the aforesaid holy man, as a familiar friend in Christ, more harshly than he did the others regarding the immoderate favor of powerful people, and with the ardor of righteous zeal. But without doubt it was a charitable error. For there are diversities of graces,* and the Disposer of the universe, distributing his gifts to each one, so governs all that when he raises up someone through his grace, he also subdues another through a rather different grace. Thus we sing truly about individual confessors, "There is not found one like unto him," *et cetera*.[9] If indeed Blessed Hamo was eminently endowed with the abounding kindness of prudent charity, Blessed Peter was surely possessed of the strict severity of spirited charity and integrity. Thus although by a different path of graces, they ran toward the one prize of a heavenly vocation,* like impetuous boxers and indefatigable soldiers.

*Prov 16:19

*1 Cor 12:4

*Heb 3:1

9. This antiphon and responsory was used in the Common for Confessors.

For this reason, when in the Lord we remember the holy severity of Blessed Peter and the most gentle charity of Blessed Hamo, that story, commendable and worthy of recollection that is written in the *Life of the Holy Fathers*[10] about Saints Arsenius and Moses, abbots, deservedly comes to mind. A certain brother came from distant parts with the desire of seeing Blessed Arsenius, and when the brothers staying there exhorted him to refresh himself a bit, he responded to them, "I shall not taste bread unless I have been worthy to see Abbot Arsenius." Then one of the fathers took him to the forenamed old man, and after they knocked on the door of his cell, they were received by him, and, after a prayer was said, they sat down together with him. When Blessed Arsenius remained silent in his accustomed way, however, that one who had taken the visiting brother to him said, "I am leaving." Likewise also, the brother who had come with such great longing, sitting in silence out of reverence, responded, "I am going back with you, Father." And so both left. Again the brother asked to be taken to Abbot Moses; they were kindly received by him in charity, and afterward they went back.

Therefore the one who had led him to both of the fathers said, "Behold, you have seen those whom you requested; which of the two pleases you more?" And he responded: "This one who received us so kindly seems better to me." When they heard about this conversation throughout the cells, one of the brothers entreated the Lord, saying, "Make this matter known to me, I pray. On account of your name, one man avoids seeing and speaking to people, but another, on account of your name, is affable to people." And behold, two ships were shown to him in ecstasy. In one

10. *Verba seniorum* (trans. Paschasius, PL 73:1040); *The Sayings of the Desert Fathers, The Alphabetical Collection*, trans. Benedicta Ward, rev. ed., CS 59 (Kalamazoo, MI: Cistercian Publications, 1984), 17–18 (#38).

he saw Abbot Arsenius in repose sailing in silence, but
in the other he saw Abbot Moses and holy angels offering a honeycomb to his mouth and teeth. By this
revelation the Lord certainly showed that he approved
of each saint with joy, and he willingly accepted the
manner of each—though dissimilar in the sight of
humans, yet not unequal in goodness in the eyes of
the angels. Indeed, Jacob blessed his separate sons with
their own blessings.* Let everyone thus beware of
passing judgment rashly about the merits of saints
until that time has arrived in which the Lord himself
will judge justices.* Indeed, of Blessed Hamo and
Peter it was aptly written:

> Peter of Avranches, who sheared sins like a sword;
> Hamo, dovelike, pious and patient, and like a sheep.

*Gen 49:28

*Ps 74:3

Chapter 9. How He Fled from the External Comforts of the Body

Indeed since the first proof of an orderly mind is
to be able to be steadfast and to restrain itself (for
harmony of the mind stands firm as a virtue), Blessed
Peter took care to keep his stability solid, and he did
not agree to accept external comforts as remedy for
the tedium of the cloister. Certainly he refused to accept heights of preferment, outside occupations, and
useless expeditions, which many seek. But yet, by begging humbly and by not resisting haughtily, the earnestness of his humility prevailed, on the one hand
preserving in him through devout obedience, just as
it should, peace, and the favor of his pastors, and on
the other hand guarding him against peril and providing for purity. Because although Martha merited the
fullness of divine grace by most dutifully ministering
to our Lord Jesus Christ, yet Mary chose the best and
sweeter part, who, while sitting at the feet of the Lord,
was fed by him with heavenly feasts.*

*Luke 10:38-42

Chapter 10. Concerning a Glorious Revelation Brought about for a Knight of Britain

In the time of Louis and Henry, illustrious kings of France and England, a certain knight in Britain, vigorous at arms and noble of birth, became infirm even to approaching death. And so, with his distress bestowing understanding, returning to his senses,[11] and strictly examining his prior way of life, he ardently felt remorse and truly confessed; determining to make satisfaction worthily and perseveringly, he earnestly sought the sacraments of the church, believed in them faithfully, and received them humbly. But after these were completed, no longer withstanding the distressing torments of his sickness, he began to suffer at the point of death, so that he lost feeling and movement entirely, with the life in his body carrying out the sole function of inhaling and exhaling. And so, with the Lord exalting mercy above judgment,* this knight was caught up in spirit and led away by two angels who showed him the punishments of hell, which he feared, and then the joys of heaven, to which he ardently aspired in the depths of his soul.

*Jas 2:13

Indeed he saw the dreadful region of hell, where the one who torments is not provoked and the one who is tormented does not die. In spirit he saw the fire that is not quenched and the frost of cold that is never dissolved by the shining sun, according to that saying of Job, "They will pass from waters of snow to excessive heat."* He saw the gnawing worms, never sleeping or ever dying, about which Ecclesiasticus says, "Vengeance on the ungodly flesh is fire and worms."* And again Job says, "Those who eat me up do not sleep."* In fact, Isaiah says at the end, "Their worm shall not die, and the sulphurous fire shall not be

*Job 24:19

*Sir 7:19

*Job 30:7

11. *Ad cor rediens* is a common expression in medieval spiritual writers that seems to derive from Isaiah 46:8, *Redite, praevaricatores, cor.*

quenched." * The knight also observed the dreadful *Isa 66:24
darkness about which the gospel says, "Cast him into
the outer darkness," * and Exodus, "For three days" *Matt 22:13
(that is, while the Blessed Trinity shines for the saved
in heaven) "no one saw his brother." * He was damned *Exod 10:23
in hell, clearly so that he might receive some consolation from such a vision. Also, the knight contemplated
and greatly feared the enormity of the scourges, their
continuation and countless variety, about which Prov-
erbs says, "Judgments are prepared for scoffers, and
striking hammers for the bodies of fools." * *Prov 19:29

Also, he observed there the most foul stench—
rotting, spoiling, and utterly unbearable—about which
Ezekiel says, "Assur is there, and all his strengths; his
graves are round about him." * Also he saw there so *Ezek 32:22
many kinds of burning fetters and fiery chains that
there is no counting them; about these the Psalmist
says, "Sitting in darkness and the shadow of death,
bound in beggary and in iron," * and again, "To bind *Ps 106:10
their kings in shackles, and their nobles in manacles
of iron." * And the Lord in the gospel says, "With *Ps 149:8
hands and feet bound, cast. . . ." * Also, he saw there *Matt 22:13
the frightful and misshapen forms of demons about
whom Job says, "Terrible ones will go and come upon
him." * He also saw all around an infinite multitude *Job 20:25
of souls in pain, horribly tormented, weeping, gnashing, crying out, and wailing constantly in the misery
described, in misfortune, in everlasting fire, about
which Matthew says, "Go, you cursed, into everlasting
fire, which was prepared not only for the devil but also
for his angels," * that is, for all his servants: namely, *Matt 25:41
those who, forsaking the ways of life and the paths of
justice, commit mortal sins and do not worthily repent
before death.

How great a sorrow, how great a grief and how
great a distress, how great a fear, how great a dread
assailed the aforementioned knight in his vision cannot be written with a pen, cannot be even partly stated
by the tongue. Indeed hell is wide without measure,

deep without bottom, full of incomparable fire, full
of unbearable stench, full of unspeakable sorrow;
there is misery, there is darkness, there is no order,
there is eternal dread, there is no hope of good, no
hope for the end of evil. Everyone who is in hell hates
himself and all others. There are all kinds of torments,
the least of which is greater than all the torments,
whatever ones there can be, in this world; there are
weeping and gnashing of teeth, there is a passing from
the cold of snows to the heat of fires, and both unbearable; there all are burned by fire and gnawed by worms
and are not consumed; there is no word except Woe,

Rev 8:3   Woe, and echoes of Woe.

Woe they have, and Woe they cry out. Tormentors,
the devils, torment and are tormented; there will
never be an end of torments there, or relief. Such is
hell, and a thousand times worse. And so, dearest
Brothers, let us call back before the eyes of our mind
the sins that we have committed and the forenamed
punishments of hell that we have deserved by sinning,
so that in comparison with these that we escape by
truly repenting, we may beneficially consider all the
evils that we suffer now to be sweet delights.

*Chapter 11. Concerning the Glory of Heaven and Its
Citizens*

Indeed, since our gentle Lord brings calm after a
storm and imparts exultation after weeping and wailing, the two angels showed the aforementioned
knight, after the kinds of punishments to be inflicted
on those condemned, the joys of heaven promised to
those living rightly. And so he was led by them into
the celestial regions, where he observed, insofar as he
could, that ineffable majesty of the indivisible Trinity,
without beginning and end, that dwells in inaccessible

1 Tim 6:16   light. That brightness and that beauty truly surpass
all perception and all understanding. Yet for a little

while he looked upon our Lord Jesus Christ, God and
Man, sitting at the right hand of God the Father, that
is, in eternal life reigning over all creation, ineffably
beautiful, so that even the angels desire insatiably to
gaze upon him,* yet gloriously having in his body the   *1 Pet 1:12
marks of the sufferings by which he redeemed us and
standing before the Father as an advocate for us.

He saw also the glorious Virgin Mary, Mother of
God, sitting next to him on a wondrous throne, exalted above all the angels and saints, interceding with
her own blessed son for us and pitying whom she
wishes. He saw the most holy ranks of blessed spirits
who stand continuously before God. Also, no person
is capable of clearly contemplating, much less describing, the praises that they render to the Creator. He
saw the assembly of patriarchs who had happily ex-
changed the weariness of long waiting for the everlasting joy received. He saw the apostles sitting on
thrones, ready to judge all tribes and tongues. He saw
a countless host of holy martyrs wondrously crowned
with glory and honor. He saw a glorious multitude of
confessors who had fortified the holy church with
their teachings; they shine like the sun and like the
stars for everlasting eternities. He saw there holy
monks and anchorites occupying vast palaces even
brighter than the sun in place of cramped cloisters
and narrow cells; from their eyes God wiped away
every tear,* and they see the King of Glory in his   *Rev 21:4
comeliness. He saw also the choir of virgins whose
glory, splendor, and song no human eloquence is capable of describing worthily; indeed, they were chanting "a new canticle which no other could say," as we
read in the Apocalypse.*   *Rev 14:3

Therefore, in the course of this glorious revelation,
with reverence and humility, as far as the knight was
able, while he was contemplating our Lord Jesus
Christ sitting on that starry seat, on that throne of his
glory, he saw next to the throne a certain monk
clothed in white, kneeling, with hands raised, with all

his soul and the whole disposition of his body intent upon the King of glory, the Ruler of the universe, and, as an anxious suppliant, he was humbly telling him, in his ear, as it were, those things that he had in his heart. In fact, as it seemed to the knight, the Lord himself kindly inclined his ear to the aforementioned monk, and he received the words and wishes of this monk with such great grace of good will that he seemed to pay attention to the monk alone, as if with the rest passed over, so to speak.

Wondering earnestly about him and carefully considering the monk's countenance and condition, because he had not seen him before, the knight humbly inquired of the two angels, his guides, who he was whom the Lord deemed worthy of such a great favor of familiarity. One of the angels said to him, "A certain monk of Savigny, humble and devout, especially attentive to meditation and prayer, whose prayers are so pleasing and acceptable in the Lord's sight that the gracious Lord delights in them just as in certain celestial delights, who said through Solomon, "My delights are to be with the sons of men."*

*Prov 8:31

And so, after seeing and hearing these things at the direction of the divine will, the knight recovered consciousness and began to gain strength little by little, having now learned through the angelic escort with how great a vigilance of anxious care he ought to avoid the punishments of hell and desire the blessed joys of heaven. For indeed in celestial glory nothing is wanting, nothing is a hindrance, nothing is superfluous, nothing ceases, nothing exists outside that is sought, nothing exists within that is scorned. There are incorruptible health and invincible strength, there are inestimable delights and endless riches, there are the most agreeable sweetness, the safest security, the most pleasing purity, the most splendid serenity—a universe of good things. There are delectable repose, imperturbable peace, and indissoluble harmony. There are a sociable friendship of the saints, a desirable presence of the beloved one, and perpetual joy in him and from him.

There are the light of truth, the manna of charity, unfailing glory, and undying life. There are every order, every honor, every virtue, everything that pleases, everything that is fitting, everything that is useful, everything that suffices. There are everlasting power, which will not be taken away, and the reign of charity, which will not be corrupted. There are perfect knowledge, full rejoicing, the utmost pleasantness, every beauty, and eternal blessedness of such a kind and extent that eye has not seen nor ear heard, nor has it entered into the heart of mortal man.* How anxious the wishes, how great the longings he would have had, how deep the sighs he would have brought forth for reaching the aforementioned felicity, the often-named knight knew so much the more surely as he recognized the joys of the aforementioned blessedness, the more fully by experiencing them, although in part, yet to some degree.

*Isa 64:4; 1 Cor 2:9

And so, with his former health restored to him through God's pity, the knight determined in his mind to go to the abbey of Savigny and to search diligently for and respectfully visit that monk to whom the Lord, as he himself saw, kindly wished to show the mercy of such great grace. Therefore, arriving at Savigny, he asked to speak with the prior, and from him he requested that the favor be granted to him of seeing the community in the parlor. But to the prior, who refused and said that this was not accustomed to happen in the house of Savigny without a very reasonable cause except in the choir and the chapter, the beforementioned knight, with anxiety of conscience, humbly made known his previously described revelation. To him the prior said, "Since you have never entered this house nor seen the community, will you know how to recognize among the others the monk about whom you speak?" But the knight answered, "I know him perfectly well."

Thus, the prior called the community, which was in the choir, into the parlor before the knight, but the knight did not find among them the monk whom he sought. Likewise, after the feeble monks from the infirmary came together before him at the order of the prior, he did not find the one whom he longed to see. And so, remembering Blessed Peter and his religious way of life, the prior learned that he was absent when the rest presented themselves. For, now weakened very much by the daily severity of his abstinence, impaired by the affliction of old age, entirely dried up, as it were, by the exercises of holy religion, and in a certain manner drained of strength, he was not able to join the community, but, remaining in the infirmary, he used to proceed toward God through his meditation and eagerness, and, though declining in his bodily condition, yet with an ardent spirit he was always ascending to more exalted heights.

Hence he loved solitude and frequented a solitary place as much as obedience and the customs of the Order permitted, knowing that a crowd makes noise but the sight of God longs for a solitary place. Indeed, to tarry very often in a crowd is known to be harmful to good morals, because there one goes more easily toward many things. Thus a wise man said, "Let the one who wishes to live innocently love a solitary place in the cloister, or solitude." And again, "Toil and hidden recesses and voluntary poverty: these are the marks of monks; they regularly ennoble their monastic life." [12]

Therefore Blessed Peter was summoned by the prior, and he appeared without delay, supporting the feebleness of his body with a staff, in the manner of

---

12. Saint Bernard, *Ep. 42 ad Henricum Senonensem Archiepiscopum*, 37, SBOp 7:130; Bernard of Clairvaux, *On Baptism and the Office of Bishops*, trans. Pauline Matarasso, CS 67 (Kalamazoo, MI: Cistercian Publications, 2004), 81.

old people. He was seen by the knight and recognized by him, since clearly he was the one whom he sought. Hence, immediately falling prostrate at his feet, with great devotion in his heart, he said, "Blessed be God! Now I have found what I longed for. You are that monk whom I happily saw next to God's throne, the one whose prayers the Lord accepted, the one to whom so great a majesty inclined his ear so courteously that he seemed not to pay attention to the rest." And then raising up the knight with great astonishment, Blessed Peter wanted to depart from him immediately, but remaining out of respect for the prior, after he heard about the blessed vision from the knight, he departed directly, rejoicing in the Lord. And since he especially shunned the vanities and false favors of men, he asked the knight not to tell anyone that he had seen so wondrous a vision about him. And so, after these matters were settled, the knight, edified, as he truly ought to be, returned to his own home.

Chapter 12. Concerning the Benefit of Prayer and the Commendation of the Same

Therefore, dearest Brothers, let us consider how great the benefit of prayer is, and of what sort the monastic office truly is. For, just as the saint says, "The end and perfection of every monk is directed toward continual and unbroken steadfastness in prayer, and, as much as is granted to human frailty, he strives toward immovable serenity of mind and perpetual purity." [13] On account of this we tirelessly seek and continually practice toil of the body as much as contrition of the spirit. For indeed the edifice of virtues will

---

13. This is a slightly altered citation of Cassian, *Conférences* 9.2.1, ed. E. Pichery, SCh 54 (Paris: Éditions du Cerf, 1958), 40; *Ancient Christian Writers* 57, trans. Boniface Ramsey (New York: Paulist Press, 1997), 329.

*1 Thess 5:7

in no way be able to remain solid and stable unless it has been fastened to a pillar of prayer. For that reason the apostle says, "Pray without ceasing,"* and the saint says, "In every action, trust more in the power of prayer than in your own diligence or toil. For we believe that the holy angels assist those who pray to offer to God the entreaties and wishes of men when they have seen pure hands raised up yet without anger

*1 Tim 2:8

or dispute."*[14]

Wherefore, so that prayer can be sent forth with this fervor and purity that is suitable, first, all vices ought to be entirely driven out and renounced, then unshaken foundations of deep humility must be laid, and afterward the spirit must be restrained from running about and from unsteady straying. For according to Augustine, "Undefiled prayer appears before God like a certain person with legal rights and executes a contract with him, where weak flesh cannot reach."[15]

Therefore a person entering upon prayer ought to think of nothing other than the fact that he is about to approach that heavenly city in which the King of Kings sits upon his starry seat, with a numberless and unutterable host of blessed spirits surrounding him. And so with how much reverence, how much trembling, how much humility ought a worthless little frog, going forth and creeping from this lake of misery and this mire of impurity, approach that place? Indeed, a worthless little human ought to stand in the sight of the angels, in the council and congregation of the saints, trembling exceedingly and begging submissively, very humble and anxious and intent with his whole mind upon the majesty of Jesus' glory.

And so much vigilance is needed in all actions, but particularly in prayer. For although we may always be seen by God in truth, we especially present ourselves to him in prayer and show ourselves to him face to

---

14. See Bernard, *De consideratione* 4.4.12, SBOp 3:458; CF 37:125.
15. *Persona, intrat,* and *mandatum* all have legal senses here.

face, as it were, speaking with him as with our lord or with our friend or with our betrothed. But although God may be everywhere, yet he must be prayed to in heaven, and at the time of prayer he must be imagined there, according to that Scripture, "Our Father, who art in heaven."* For by a certain special claim, heaven is called the seat or throne of God because, according to the comparison by which the souls of the elect and the holy angels see God in heaven, we wretched ones, we mortals and wayfarers on earth, are scarcely able to have hold of just the name. Indeed, we do not reach the state of pure prayer through contemplation of an image, or through a succession of words, but after the mind is ignited by our intention to pray, we discover the spirit with inexplicable joy through inexpressible ecstasy. With truth it may be written, "Prayer is the pious disposition of the mind toward God,"[16] a disposition that, lest it be slack, bursts into speech; however, through a more liberal acceptation of this word, as Rhabanus says, prayers are not only dispositions of speech but also all the good things that we do: for whatever is done with fear and love of God is a prayer and a scent of sweetness to the Lord.*

*Matt 6:9

*Sir 35:8

Therefore, Brothers, let us love the constant practice of prayer from the very depths of our soul, for great is its fruit and great its virtue, if only the spirit of the one praying is devout, honorable, and humble. Truly, the constant prayer of a just person avails much.* Thus the Lord says to his disciples in the gospel, "If

*Jas 5:16

---

16. This definition of prayer (*Oratio est pius animi affectus in Deum*) is found in the work *De spiritu et anima* 50 (PL 40:816), sometimes attributed to Alcher of Clairvaux. The author seems to have drawn the definition from Hugh of Saint Victor, *De virtute orandi*, 5, ed. Hugh Feiss, *L'oeuvre de Hugues de Saint-Victor*, 1, Sous le Regle de Saint Augustin, 1 (Turnhout: Brepols, 1997), 152: *Nihil ergo alius est oratio quam mentis devotio, id est, conversio in Deum per pium et humilem affectum* ("Therefore, prayer is nothing else than devotion of the mind, that is, turning toward God with a loving and humble feeling").

*John 16:23

you ask the Father anything in my name, he will give it to you."* Indeed, about Blessed Martin it is written that in the time of the Arian falsehood and its most savage persecution, the prayer of Martin benefitted the church as much as the disputation of Hilary.

Chapter 13. Concerning the Cautery Rags that He Was Accustomed to Wash, and a Double Miracle

And so, fleeing as if avoiding like the plague every claim to earthly loftiness, Blessed Peter, for the nurturing of his own humility, strove in allowable ways to occupy himself, insofar as he could, with vile exercises that others were sometimes accustomed to abhor. Hence he asked and obtained from his superiors that the duty be assigned to him of washing those rags or vile bindings that monks frequently use for ailments; they are called *cauteries* by the common folk. And so, when he had carried out the work described for a long while with humility of mind and body, at a certain time, through the evil machination of the malevolent demon who does not cease to plot against the deeds of the good, the holy man began to consider on the one hand the whole rags, stinking and stained with bloody matter, and on the other hand the impurities of the washings, most foul and unpleasant to see, and he shuddered so much at the aforementioned stains of poisonous corruption and then conceived so great an abhorrence that he could scarcely restrain himself from vomiting, and he began to be somewhat weak. And so, almost overcome by the force of this temptation, he began to yield and to study in his mind how he could secure from his superiors a release from so abhorrent an office.

But since the Lord is faithful, he who does not permit his own to be tempted beyond that which they are able to bear but causes something beneficial to arise with the temptation,* he filled the heart of his servant with the radiant light of his grace and disclosed the

*1 Cor 10:13

sinuous deceptions of the crooked serpent.* And thus, *Isa 27:1
returning to his senses and putting forth tearful sobs
from the depths of his innermost parts, Blessed Peter
began with great anxiety to ponder how great and
what sorts of punishments he might demand of himself for the aforementioned offense. And so, taking up
with an ardent spirit a vessel filled with abhorrent and
stinking wash water, he put it to his own mouth and
quickly drank it with eagerness, as if it were the best
drink. What was left he poured over his own head, as
a man totally inflamed by faith and devotion. Thus
the stench and bloody matter of these washings
flowed on all sides over his neck down to his lowest
limbs. A wondrous thing, and one to be commended
readily to the minds of good men! Certainly the Lord
is compassionate* who doubled the spirit of Elijah in *Sir 3:13
him when Elisha asked;* with regard to Blessed Peter, *2 Kgs 2:9-10
he mercifully produced two miracles in the aforementioned deed, for he kept him entirely unharmed from
the infection of most foul and poisonous putrefaction,
and likewise he banished from him completely all abhorrence, so that not only did he not shudder to fulfill
his aforementioned office, but he was very often
drenched in inestimable sweetness and spiritual fragrance and happily refreshed when he was allowed to
carry out the oft-mentioned task.

Dearest Brothers, let us diligently pay attention to
such blessed examples of the saints and, fleeing lofty
places for the name of Christ, let us devote ourselves
to vile exercises with a willing spirit. They impress on
our minds the virtue of humility pleasing to God; they
nourish and preserve it. Therefore, when lowly tasks
are ordered for us by our superiors or imposed on us
by our confessors, let us not shun them, let us not
grumble, let us not consider them unworthy. For it is
difficult, or I should rather say impossible, that anyone
who delights in present and future honors, or is first
in both, may appear glorious in heaven and on earth.
Indeed, humility is a certain good and first foundation

of the virtues; if it totters, the assembly of the others is not exempt. In fact, we are never more easily overcome by the ancient foe than when we follow him by being proud, and we never overthrow him more forcefully than when we imitate the Lord with humility.

Chapter 14. *That He Had the Grace of Tears*

Moreover, how great were the visitations of the Holy Spirit that Blessed Peter had, how great the internal consolations, how pleasing the refreshments of mind in unutterable joy and ecstasy can be so much more surely apparent as he more fully abounded in the grace of tears. For in this he was in a certain way another Arsenius, about whom we read that he kept a piece of cloth on his chest because of the tears that used to fall frequently from his eyes by reason of his longing for eternal life.[17] Truly, Truth itself, which, just as it cannot be deceived knows not how to deceive, says, "Blessed are those who mourn, for they shall be comforted."* And again the psalmist says, "According to the multitude of my sorrows in my heart, your consolations have gladdened my soul."* Hence the Lord said to King Hezekiah, "I have heard your prayer, and I have seen your tears."*

Therefore, concerning the commendation of tears, Jerome said, "O tear! Power is yours, the kingdom is

*Matt 5:5

*Ps 93:19

*2 Kgs 20:5

---

17. For this saying about Arsenius, a Desert Father who had served as tutor under Emperor Theodosius to the princes Acadius and Honorius, see *Les apophtegmes des pères, Collection systematique* 1, ed. Jean-Claude Guy, SCh 387 (Paris: Éditions du Cerf, 1993), 150–51; Benedicta Ward, trans., *The Desert Fathers: Sayings of the Early Christian Monks* (New York: Penguin, 2003), 12 (#3). A similar saying is found in *Sayings of the Desert Fathers, Alphabetical Collection*, 19 (#41). In keeping with the previous story about Peter's willingness to work in filth, a saying has it that Arsenius changed the water in which he prepared palm leaves only once a year, as a penance for the perfumes he used before his conversion: *Sayings of the Desert Fathers, Alphabetical Collection*, 11 (#18).

yours. You do not fear the judge's tribunal; you impose
silence on the accusers of your friends; sometimes you
snatch a decision from the mouth of the judge. There
is no one who forbids you to approach; if you enter
alone, you never return alone or empty. Why say more?
You conquer the unconquerable, you bind the omni-
potent." [18] And so, Brothers, let us wash the couch of
our conscience for our separate sins, flooding the bed
of our soul* with tears of repentance; for us, let tears   *see Ps 6:7
be the bread of consolation day and night,* because   *Ps 80:5
prayer appeases the Lord, but a tear compels him.

Chapter 15. Concerning His Passing Away

As that time was now approaching when Blessed
Peter was about to depart from the world, Blessed
Hamo, who was bound to him by a very strong bond
of love, went to him with tearful devotion, adding
words of this sort, "Brother Peter, as I estimate, we
are at the doorway that you will pass through from
this wretched, mortal life to that compassionate Lord
whom you have sought, whom you have always desired. Now, therefore, because of that very powerful
love with which we have loved one another in Christ,
do three things for me. The first is that when you will
have been happily presented in the sight of the Most
High, you will greet him humbly and devoutly on the
part of Brother Hamo, his humble and unworthy little
servant. The second is that you will assure me of the
blessedness of your state, your colleague and friend,
such as he is, since in my heart and mind I have wished
for your good as much as my own. The third is that
you will inform me about the mercy of the divine

18. The author attributes this quotation to Jerome. It is found
in Ludolph of Saxony, *Vita Jesu Christi* (Rome, 1865), 1:541, where
it is attributed to Saint Bernard. The passage from "O tear" to
"return alone or empty" is found in Peter of Celle (d. 1183), *Liber
de panibus*, chap. 12 (PL 202:983–84).

permission concerning the insufficiency and unworthiness of my servitude, how it is regarded in the sight of God." To him Blessed Peter replied, "Although these things that you request are not placed in human power, yet if the benevolence of the Almighty is willing to grant them, I shall do what you ask."

Without delay, soon after these events, the aforementioned Blessed Peter, armed with the firmness of faith, invigorated by the confidence of hope, strengthened by the sweetness of charity, fortified by the sacraments of the church, and surrounded by the presence of angels, with the community of chanting brothers standing around him, happily commended his spirit to God. And so, after his funeral rites were celebrated according to custom, the brothers, presuming their own greater good from his sanctity, devoutly delivered that blessed lump of his holy body for burial, not in the common cemetery of the monks, but in a suitable, marked place.

And the Lord did not allow the brothers of Savigny to be deceived in their hope on this point regarding their greater good, nor to be in suspense for long by being uncertain. For when Blessed Hamo was devoutly and fervently attending to prayer in the chapel of Blessed Katherine, with eyes and hands intent on heaven according to his custom, suddenly so great a light beaming down from heaven illuminated the whole place that he could not fix his eyes of flesh on it, and he did not even have the capacity to cast them on it very briefly. In the midst of it he saw and recognized Blessed Peter shining with indescribable radiance. Very much strengthened in the Lord by this vision, he thus addressed him in a friendly manner, saying, "Blessings!" Blessed Peter certainly responded in a friendly manner, "The Lord be blessed."

Blessed Hamo said to him, "Are you my brother and special friend, Peter of Avranches?" And he said, "Truly, I am. The most merciful Lord has sent me here to console you and to satisfy your wish. First, you

should know that he who commands the salvation of
Jacob* commands salvation for you. Likewise, concerning your status, you should know most surely that
our heavenly Father, who prepares mansions in
heaven,* in procuring dwellers for the mansions has
prepared through the mercy of his compassion a
greater glory for you than for me among the splendors
of the saints." Then Blessed Hamo said, "To you, Lord
Jesus Christ, be praise and honor forever! Concerning
the third request, Brother Peter, there is no need for
you to answer me, for, as an eyewitness, I already estimate that it goes well with you." Blessed Peter said
to him, "It is true. Blessed is the God and Father of
mercies, who does not forsake those trusting in him."

Then Blessed Hamo said, "Tell me, dearest Brother,
how and why have you attained in heavenly glory the
great radiance in which I see you wondrously shining
forth?" Then he said, "How great a tenderness of conscience I always had in religious life, God well knows,
from whom nothing hidden lies concealed, and you
yourself have known in part; for I could not to any
extent bear not only mortal but also even noteworthy
venial sins; not enduring the pricks and bites of a devout conscience, I used to run back immediately to
the remedy of holy confession. Therefore, because of
my excessive frequency of confession, as it was
thought, I was very often not a little burdensome to
you and other confessors. And so, on account of the
serenity and security of mind that from the time I
entered religious life I did not cease always to desire
fervently, I earned and received, with divine grace assisting me, the honor of such great radiance." After
these words were spoken and he bade farewell to
Blessed Hamo, Saint Peter disappeared and returned
to heaven, where he reigns forever with Christ.

Dearest Brothers, let us turn our attention carefully
to such examples of our holy fathers; let us faithfully
frequent the good gift of confession, for confession
of guilt is the doorway to forgiveness. Indeed, the

*Ps 43:5

*John 14:2

foremost and first beauty of soul proceeds from confession. Hence the psalmist says, "You have put on the
confession of guilt first, then the beauty of grace;
finally, you are clothed in glory with light like a garment." *

*Ps 103:1

Here ends the Life of Blessed Peter of Avranches,
Monk of Savigny

The Life of Blessed Hamo, Monk of the Monastery of Savigny

Introduction to
The Life of Blessed Hamo, Monk of the Monastery of Savigny

THE *VITA* OF BLESSED HAMO was composed soon after Hamo's death on April 30, 1173, and surely before that of England's King Henry II in 1189, for the *Vita* speaks of Henry as still alive and well. The anonymous author was a confrere of Hamo's at Savigny, for in words borrowed from the gospel (John 3:11) he affirms in chapter 18, "We declare this that we know, and we assert this that we have seen." Moreover, the author of the *Vita* records in chapter 33 that he once accompanied Blessed Hamo on a journey and says that sometimes his source was "private disclosure" (*secreta reseratione*) by Hamo himself. In a prologue to the *Vita*, the writer also thanks a "Holy Father" (*Pater Sancte*) for wresting information from a certain monk of Savigny, information that he has included in his account; in chapter 22, in what is clearly a resumption of his work, the author acknowledges the wish of this "Reverend Father" (*Venerande Pater*) that he write about the holy man's ways and works. Comprising fifty-eight chapters and spanning some sixty pages of the Latin text, the *Vita* of Hamo is the longest of those on the Savigny saints.

The editor of the *Vita B. Hamonis* collated seven manuscripts containing the work.[1] The earliest of these is British Library MS Cotton

---

1. E. P. Sauvage, "Vitae B. Petri Abrincensis et B. Hamonis," *Analecta Bollandiana* 2 (1883): 475–77.

Nero A XVI, dating from the twelfth century, most likely between 1170 and 1190. It may even be the original text, according to Professor Lorna E. M. Walker, who has pointed out that the Cotton MS is the only one that includes passages revealing a distinctive, familiar friendship between Blessed Hamo and King Henry II.[2]

The author of the *Vita* was writing to uphold an example of outstanding holiness and to instruct his brothers in the ideals of monastic life. The prologue clearly affirms this didactic purpose when the writer declares that saints are placed in this "open sea of the world" like lamps to guide us amid the darkness and the swelling billows to our desired port. In every chapter, he offers lessons based on the exemplary words and deeds of Blessed Hamo or admonitions to imitate his virtuous ways. For example, after describing in the first chapter the saint's persistence in prayer and his struggles to overcome weariness, he reminds his fellow monks that heavenly beatitude does not await "the sleeping and slothful," and he encourages "the lazy and languid" to fulfill God's commands with vigor. The author seems never to neglect an opportunity to provide uplifting examples of monastic virtue in his subject's life "for the benefit of those hearing them" (*ad utilitatem audientium*), as he repeatedly acknowledges.

The *Vita* of Hamo is generous in detailing Hamo's personal qualities and appearance. We learn that he was a native of Brittany and that he entered religious life at Savigny after rejecting "the pomp of the world." He remained ambitious, however, and while still "a neophyte" he was desirous of advancement toward a prelacy. The Lord curbed this longing in him through a rumor that he was leprous, and since he was not allowed to receive the monastic habit, nor did he wish to return to secular life, he asked for the assignment of caring for two leprous monks in the community. Through this office his humility was restored, and when the rumor of his leprosy proved unfounded, he received monastic status and was later ordained to the priesthood. In the celebration of Mass he often went into ecstasy and experienced visions that are related in his *Vita*. Also, in his ministry he exercised his gift of discernment and led many sinners to confession and penance. In the words of Pro-

2. Lorna E. M. Walker, "Hamo of Savigny and His Companions: Failed Saints?" *Journal of Medieval History* 30 (2004): 45–60, here 47.

fessor Walker, "It was as a confessor and searcher of hearts that he excelled."

Hamo had great devotion to saints. He collected and dispensed relics, and through these and his own merits, numerous miracles were granted to him. The author records many of them to illustrate Hamo's sanctity and "to embellish the series in our narrative." One charming example is that told in chapter 17 of a widow named Reneldis, who bought a little lamb with coins given to her by Hamo. One day a wolf carried off the lamb, but on the next morning it was found unharmed in her yard. The writer declares that the miraculous rescue of the little beast made the holy man even more devout, the "poor little woman" glad, and those hearing the story overcome with wonder.

Several chapters of the *Vita* record Blessed Hamo's interactions with powerful figures of the nobility. His persistent intervention and counsel persuaded the count of Boulogne to spare the property of the nuns at Mortain Abbey (chap. 25); he admonished Empress Matilda and recalled her "from the coils of the devil and the death of sin" (chap. 41); and he advised King Louis VII of France in the matter of an heir (chap. 21). The author calls Hamo the "familiar friend" (*familiaris*) of Henry II of England in chapter 20, and he records several encounters between the saint and the king. In fact, we learn that Hamo occasionally heard the king's confession, counseled him, and won from him concessions and pardons for prisoners. Their relationship was confirmed in visions that the saint experienced, including one (chap. 35) that before Henry became king and before Hamo had ever seen him in person foreshadowed their friendship. The *Vita* several times underscores the mutual familiarity that developed between the two men, and the writer openly states (chap. 35) that "King Henry became accustomed to embrace him [Hamo] particularly . . . before all other mortal men."

Blessed Hamo surely had an attractive personality, a charisma reflected in genial ways and generous kindness. His "abounding kindness of prudent charity" was hailed in the *Vita* of his friend Peter of Avranches, and his own biographer described him (chap. 36) as "a simple man and one divinely adorned with a certain innate and natural gentleness and goodness." He affirmed that Blessed Hamo's face shone with a serene expression and that he was thought to have been sent as an "exemplar of angelic purity." In physical appearance, Hamo had a pleasing countenance, a somewhat long face, a straight nose, a slender mouth, a thin beard, and black hair mingled with gray, but scant baldness on the sides of his forehead. He was so thin, says the writer, that he had scarcely any flesh and resembled "a collection of bones."

Although Hamo had "many antagonists and detractors" of his works, even among members of his own house and order (chap. 33), he was undoubtedly an admired figure, a spiritual father to communities of nuns, a counselor to nobles, and a benefactor to lowly folk. As Professor Walker observed: "No one who has read the *Vita Hamonis* could question the reality of Hamo's sanctity in the eyes of contemporaries."[3]

3. Walker, "Hamo of Savigny," 50.

The Life of Blessed Hamo, Monk of the Monastery of Savigny

Here Begins the Prologue to the Life of Hamo, a Monk, a Man of Great Holiness

To commit to memory examples of the most out-standing men is known to confer very much humility. For when their way of life and their actions are recognized, usually their strengths are attributed to the weakness of little ones, the devout are made more devout and active in God's work, and those who falter in faith are rendered more firm. Indeed, who might be so made of stone that his heart would not tremble when he heard of their virtues? Or who would not rejoice to be occupied with good works when, taught by their examples, he recognizes that the way to the kingdom of heaven is open to such men? In fact, they are placed in this open sea of the world like certain great lamps,* by whose light the little boat of those sailing amid darkness and billowing swells might be able to reach port unharmed. For just as sailors cleaving the blue surface of the sea are attentive to the course of the stars so that they can reach the desired port and avoid the dreadful whirlpools of Charybdis, so is it necessary for us, if we wish to come by the right path to our homeland, always to place the actions and examples of the fathers who have gone before us carefully before the eyes of our mind and to retrace their footsteps with the watchful execution of our

*Gen 1:16

deeds. For while they are going the way of all flesh, thus do we recognize their way of life.

Hence in the law it is written, "If, while walking along the way, you should find a nest in a tree or on the ground, and the mother sitting upon chicks or eggs, you shall not take her with her young, but allow her to go, keeping the young that you have caught, so that it may be well with you and you may live a long time."* Indeed we walk along the way when we read Sacred Scripture; truly we find a bird's nest when we recognize there the life of holy ones. But we permit the bird to go away, because holy men are raised up to heaven when the burden of flesh has been put aside. We keep the captured chicks, however, since we have their way of life and path for living well included in the Scriptures. If we cling to these, it is well with us and we live a long time, because we trample vices that bring evil and we pursue virtues, and with the burden of flesh put aside, happily crowned, we shall have life without end in heaven.

*Deut 22:6-7

Hence, Holy Father, thanks to your relating them, we have taken care, at your request and in whatever style, to insert in our book for the benefit of those hearing them a few things that we were able to learn from a certain spiritual monk of the church of Savigny (which you wrested from him), beseeching the Lord's mercy so that for this he might pay us the reward we seek and lead us with all the saints to the sight of himself.

The Prologue Ends

The Life Begins

Chapter 1

And so this man about whom we have undertaken to speak was born in Brittany, in a town that is called Landecop. Certainly he was not of the lowest family and not insufficiently instructed in the knowledge of letters; rejecting the pomp of the world, he received the habit of holy religion in the forenamed monastery. Moreover, when he was living as a novice in the house of novices, he used to apply himself to divine Scripture, and he stored up very useful maxims in the box of his memory. While doing these things, however, he decided that he was one who could now help many and who would be worthy to gain the peak of prelacy. Burning with this desire, he was empty of Scripture;[1] still a neophyte, he did not perceive that such an intention was improper. But the Lord, knowing what is advantageous for each one, did not permit him to be vexed for long by such an ardent desire, and he eradicated this itching from his mind when he applied a cautery of tribulation.

Indeed a rumor began to fly[2] that he was leprous, and it spread in the mouth of those inside and outside. And when it had now flown swiftly through the

1. This seems to be the sense, although *Scripturae vacat* can mean open to, i.e., receptive to Scripture.
2. This phrase echoes Virgil, *Aeneid* 4:173.

mouths of many for some time, at last this rumor about him was reported to him. What would the soldier of Christ do? Where would the new spiritual athlete turn? To seek again the world that he had abandoned is not his purpose: he is not allowed to receive the habit of a monk, with many abhorring such an infirmity. And so he found a sufficiently salutary plan, one exceedingly suitable for preserving humility.

In this same abbey, there were two monks beset by leprosy; they were set apart in a house assigned to such sick ones. And so he asked to be sent to them, and he was granted his request. After he had obtained it, his mind began to grow cold toward his former passion for prelacy; he began to return more properly to the knowledge of himself; he began to turn the anchor of his heart more purely toward God; he began to subject body to spirit. Indeed, he used to apply himself to prayer, to wear down his body with fasting, to keep his mouth from useless and superfluous speech, and to strive for silence, which is the pursuit of justice;* he zealously served the lepers with whom he lived; not cursing their stench, he used to wash their feet at different times; he used to stay awake for holy vigils and psalms. For example, often when they had given over their limbs to sleep, he would go forth secretly and prostrate himself in prayer in the chapel that was nearby.

*Isa 32:17

Let the lazy and slothful hear, let the idle and languid hear, let them hear and blush, and when they have heard, let them drive sluggishness far from themselves, knowing without doubt that heavenly beatitude is granted not to the sleeping and slothful but to those who strenuously fulfill God's commands. Indeed, when Hamo grew tired from bending his knees and his body almost gave out, he used to take off his clothes and, naked, would persist in forcing his weary limbs to serve his spirit. Moreover, when he had remained for some time with the lepers, intent on such labor, and no sign of infirmity in him corresponded to the rumor that was being spread about him, the Lord turned the hearts of the monks toward compassion for him, and, withdrawn from that house, he received the status of monk, which he strongly desired. Then, after a little time intervened, he was advanced to the office of subdeacon and deacon in one day, and he who had humbly endured such great abasement began to be visited by the Lord's grace. For after not much time had passed, he was advanced to the office of priesthood, although trembling with fear, and at his ordination so great an overflowing of the Spirit filled him that often he instilled in Hamo a forgetfulness of bodily foods, and nothing that delights the flesh tasted sweet to him, as he himself bore witness. Yet as a man, he used to eat but for the support of life and not for the pleasure of the palate.

Chapter 2

Moreover, this was astonishing about him: he received such great grace of discernment through the gift of the Holy Spirit that he would scarcely look upon anyone whom mortal sin engulfed who could evade his penetrating percipience. Hence he led back to the way of confession many whom he delivered from abominable wickedness, and placing a basket of dung (that is, the humility of penance) at the root of their heart, he taught them to bring forth fruit to God.* In *Rom 7:4 fact kings and powerful men of the world used to defer to him, and he was held in such great reverence by them that they revealed the secrets of their hearts to him without fear, and through his counsel they received a knowledge of their healing after the deadly rubble of their vices was taken away, and they used to do many good deeds. Indeed he made known to all the things that were suited to salvation, and he did not stroke their faults with flattery, as is the custom of certain people, but he used to rebuke them with unrestrained speech, as seemed suited to each one. Moreover, they did not spurn him but embraced his correction with loving arms, and he found such great humility in them that he used to complain about the obstinacy of certain religious in comparison to them.

Chapter 3

In fact this man, a monk in his way of life, a priest in office, because he was often exceedingly terrified while offering the host of the holy sacrifice because of the enormity of his own past sins (for he had been worldly and very carnal), and he feared that the service of the holy altar, which is life for all who act purely, would become everlasting death for him, approached the sacrifice with trembling limbs as often as he celebrated it. God had mercy on him. From that for which he used to be afraid to incur blame he received from our good God, from our kind Jesus, a most amazing and astonishing confidence in divine mercy.

For on a certain day, while celebrating the sacred rites, when he came to those awe-inspiring words of the holy canon in which power especially resides, namely, "Who, on the day before he suffered, took bread," after he took bread, looking upward he saw the heavens open and Jesus standing with his face turned toward the east and looking gently at him with his body bent forward through a spirit of compassion and cheering his heart and conscience through the anointing of his mercy, thoroughly filling the innermost parts of his soul with indescribable joy and inestimable sweetness. And the Spirit in him was speaking, saying, "This is the Son of God, and he has condescended to appear to you on account of your grace of consolation."

While he delighted in such a great fullness of grace, he was bathed in immense light, refreshed by pleasant sweetness. Made altogether senseless, he went out of his flesh, not leaving the dwelling place of the flesh, but sensing no evidence of the flesh, or, just as the apostle says of himself, "Whether in the body or out of the body, I know not."* He was aware of nothing earthly, nothing corporeal; he did not sense the presence of any person; he did not see the chalice or the altar before which he was standing; alone with the Alone, he was joyful; a man was contemplating God, but in a man; a priest was feasting with a priest. After the joy of such amicable rejoicing had at last been celebrated, however, he returned to himself, he who had been out of himself yet remaining always in himself, who did not act regarding himself because he could not act on his own.

*2 Cor 12:2

For he whose presence wondrously employed wondrous power worked his good pleasure regarding him. And having returned to himself after the magnitude of so great a vision, when he had opened his eyes, it seemed to him as if the day had then begun to dawn, although at the time when the vision appeared, the third hour had passed in the convent, after whose completion it is the custom in the summer season to celebrate the solemn sacrifice of the Mass. Hence it is right to observe that, returning to us after seeing that inner light and its supreme splendor, he considered the splendor of our days passing away in time, however great this temporal splendor, like a gloomy night in comparison with that light. And so, after he had been restored to himself, he continued the celebration of the sacred mystery.

Moreover, coming to the subsequent consecration of the Lord's blood, he saw a right hand stretched over the holy chalice, a substitute for his own hand to be stretched forth, sanctifying the chalice according to our custom and making the sign of the holy cross over the sacred mysteries with its extended tracing; he saw the mighty hand, he saw the beautiful hand, he saw the glorious hand, and along with the hand, he saw an arm stretched out from the elbow over the holy altar. He saw and he rejoiced, and he proceeded with his office. And both men there were refreshed by so great a sweetness of exotic fragrance that, as often as they recalled this wondrous fragrance, so often did they also feel that they had experienced[3] the presence of the life-giving fragrance of which he had had a fore-taste. And this was very remarkable and commend-able, that this man, indeed a noble priest, returned to himself and to his brothers as he did after so great a vision: not stunned, not amazed, but in a sound mind, a pious life, with usual conversation, not sighing, not weeping, not moaning openly, not speculative, not solitary, not judging others, preferring himself to no one, but always sociable and living without complaint and without reproach.

Chapter 4

Also in the same monastery but on another day, when he was celebrating the divine service in a similar manner, at those sacred words "Humbly we implore You, Almighty God, bid these offerings to be brought by the hands of your holy angel to your altar on high,"[4] while bending forward according to custom and hum-bly imploring God, he saw angels standing around the altar, cheerful and congenial and clothed in stoles of wondrous beauty. Among them one appeared promi-nent, more eminent in form, and more charming in countenance, and he alone before the rest was taking the sacred host from the altar, alone raising it upward, and alone offering it to the divine presence, and he appeared more joyful than the rest, exulting more in the service of his oblation. In fact, the rest who were

3. Literally, "tasted" (*degustare*).

4. From the Roman Canon (First Eucharistic Prayer). This and the following quotations from the Roman Canon in chapters 5 and 10 form the text that follows words of consecration.

standing by were congratulating that angel to such an extent that it seemed as if each would take the host if he gave it, if he offered it. With his eyes turned back to where Mass was being celebrated, the priest found and took up the consecrated sacrament sanctifying him, and so, filled with joy, he finished what needed to be done.[5]

Chapter 5

In fact, while Hamo was standing at the holy altar for the celebration of Mass on a certain day, he came to that prayer whose beginning is "Deign to look upon them with a gracious and tranquil countenance." When he had spoken these words—"Just as you deigned to accept the offerings of your just servant, Abel, and the sacrifice of our father, Abraham, and that which your high priest, Melchizedek, offered up to you, a holy sacrifice, a spotless victim"[6]—with his eyes lifted up to heaven, he saw the three oblations of the forenamed saints like three very bright beams of light being borne on high, and his own oblation following after theirs. Indeed, it seemed to him to have less brightness, but the High Priest gratefully accepted it. That it is said to differ in brightness from the others, however, must not be applied to the virtue of the sacrament, but this statement should be understood in the disparity of their merits. No one should doubt that Hamo had been exceedingly nourished by this vision. But he did not emit groans or sighs by which the ministers standing near him could learn that he had seen a vision.

So, so, Christ, you restore those whom you will; so when it pleases you, you gladden the minds of your friends with an abundance of your sweetness! Indeed,

5. The last line of this chapter is obscure in the Latin, owing (apparently) to omitted words and variant readings.
6. From the Roman Canon (First Eucharistic Prayer).

you have the power to illuminate whom you will and to nourish them with the unfailing gift of your grace. Who, hearing these things, is not inflamed? Whose heart is not strengthened in faith, with every doubt put aside? For truly we believe that in the consecration of so great a mystery the heavens are opened and holy angels offer our gifts to God. Hence Blessed Gregory said, "For who among the faithful could doubt that at the voice of the priest in that hour of sacrifice the heavens are opened, the choir of angels is present at that mystery of Jesus Christ, the lowest things are united to the highest, earthly ones are joined to celestial ones, and one thing comes to be from the visible and invisible?"[7]

Chapter 6

And another similar vision followed after this one. While the same man was celebrating another Mass on a certain day, he was worthy to be comforted by divine consolation. For when he had said this prayer, "Holy Lord, Almighty Father, Eternal God, grant that I may so receive this most holy body and blood of your Son, our Lord Jesus Christ, that I may through this deserve to gain remission of my sins and to be filled with your Holy Spirit,"[8] while saying this last word he saw tongues of fire, as it were, shining before him, and he rejoiced that he was worthy to obtain the outcome of his prayer. God deigned to impart the Holy Spirit to him in tongues of fire just as to the apostles. He alone saw them, he alone recognized them; no one of those standing near deserved to see this or to discover it. O, would that with the palate of the heart we might experience the sweetness that man had in his heart

---

7. Gregory, *Dialogues*, 4.60.3, ed. Adalbert de Vogüé, SCh 65 (Paris: Éditions du Cerf, 1980), 202.
8. From the Roman Canon.

when he received the grace of so great a vision! But he alone knew it who perceived it; he alone knew it who had the power of perceiving. And since Scripture says, "The Holy Spirit of discipline will flee from the false,"* confident of his humility, we dare to say that he was free from all feigning, in whom the grace of the Holy Spirit so clearly willed to flow.

*Wis 1:5

But amid these considerations it is pleasing to turn back the eyes of the mind toward ourselves and to weep for our imperfection with a sighing spirit. Surely we who are puffed up by pride, infected by envy, weakened by vainglory, and blackened by unsuitable and fickle thoughts are presumptuous to approach so great a mystery as do those who have a good conscience— or, to speak more expressly, we blush with shame not to frequent Mass. We approach the Mass, I say, more out of habit than desire, more out of custom than devotion, more out of duty than merit. But woe to us if the same Spirit should not be a petitioner for us! Woe to us if the Lord should consider our merits! Woe to us, I say, if he should not grant us his grace! "For he who eats unworthily, eats and drinks judgment to himself."* Whose heart is so hard as stone that it does not greatly fear these words? Whose mind is so made of iron that it does not become soft at these words?

*1 Cor 11:29

Therefore let our eyes bring forth tears; let us cleanse the stains on our conscience with weeping; let our twisted thoughts be dissipated; let our perverse actions be utterly expelled. Let us confess our sins, and let us vomit up the fungus of our vices so that we might not share in so great a sacrament to our judgment, as we cannot say without groaning. Let us invoke the grace of the same Spirit with zeal; let us implore the divine mercy with heartfelt sighs, so that the same Spirit who blows where he wills and through whom remission of sins is granted and who imparted his grace to this man as he wished may deign to penetrate our hearts and refresh us inwardly with the consolation of his visitation.

Chapter 7

In the aforementioned abbey there live not only monks but also laymen whom they call *conversi* and who serve God in the habit of religion.[9] A certain monk, however, who is known to be renowned for his teaching of wisdom and his preeminence in religion, is put in charge of these. In fact, sometimes this man, Hamo, instructed these men, and he watched out for their salvation with zeal. But since it is written, "Unless the Lord guards the city, he who guards it watches in vain,"* while he had charge of these men, many of them, abandoning their way of life, returned to the world; imitating Lot's wife;* they let go of the plough handle that they had seemed to hold. Hence it happened that this same man was greatly tormented and distressed by internal anguish of heart. For fearing that this was happening on account of his own sin, he blushed with shame before the eyes of God. But also he dreaded the judgment of people, lest their departure should be attributed to his negligence. Indeed, he used to confess humbly his own imperfection.

*Ps 126:1

*Gen 19:26;
Luke 17:32

But when Hamo was being vexed by such anxiety and his mind was cold in its spiritual zeal, he was appointed the week's priest on duty for the daily Mass for the dead. Moreover, on the sixth day of the same week, he went as usual to offer sacrifice to God and to pray for the dead. He was anxious, however, to know in what way God might deign to show him if those men were departing on account of his guilt. Therefore, when he was holding that life-giving body in his hands before receiving it, he saw a thin rod, as it were, brandished before his eyes; at this brandishing, he closed his eyes. With his eyes of flesh thus closed

9. E. P. Sauvage, "Vitae B. Petri Abrincensis et B. Hamonis," *Analecta Bollandiana* 2 (1883): 511n1, notes that in addition to choir monks, there were two groups of lay members of the congregation at Savigny: *conversi* and *donati*.

and the eyes of his heart open, he saw Jesus, alive, hanging on the cross and keeping his head inclined to the right side. He saw, I say, he saw him as a most beautiful young man, adorned with a rosy complexion and assuredly differentiated from the rest of mortal men by such great beauty. And deservedly, for about him it is written, "Beautiful in appearance before the sons of men."*

And Hamo received an answer through divine inspiration: "If, undeserving, I have suffered so much for you, it is right that you not consider it a hardship to endure distress on my account." Moreover, a very great sweetness immediately entered Hamo's heart; this drove out all anguish, and he truly believed that so great a vision had appeared to him for the sake of relieving his sorrow. He perceived that the departure of those men did not come to pass on account of his guilt. Furthermore, neither was he able to report, nor are we able to narrate, what sweetness, what devotion, what delight, what love he received. We can, however, assert this: whatever soothes the bodily senses, whatever tastes sweet to the flesh, yields in comparison to this refreshment. These are wondrous things that we have woven; let those things that we weave below remain wonderful so that, from a most beautiful order of narration, as if through a most becoming distinction of colors, we may be able to put together the tapestry of Hamo's visions.

Chapter 8

This venerable man was full of anxiety sometimes for the souls of his own father and mother, and to a certain extent he was unsure about their salvation. Moreover, with the revolving of the year, a day arrived on which his father, departing from the world, discharged his debt to nature. Therefore, on that very day, during a certain interval when Hamo was at prayer before a certain altar and was with the greatest emotion imploring the Lord for absolution for his father, he saw on high a path extended like a shining ray of the sun, yet surrounded on this side and that by a certain darkness. But he saw the souls of his father and mother go forth from that darkness and enter the same path of light. Thus strengthened by better hope, he understood that the Lord had deigned to show him in this vision that his parents would obtain salvation, a thing that he had desired. And so he rose up from prayer happier and put aside the uncertainty that he had had before.

Chapter 9

Sometimes when the monks of this same monastery were keeping solemn vigils for God, this blessed man was present. And since he intended to offer sacrifice to God on this very day for the absolution of his father's soul, he began to turn over in his mind whether he ought to offer the collect for him singly or in the plural.[10] And when he was hesitating because of this uncertainty, he perceived the soul of his father on high, and behind it he saw many other souls. Instructed by this vision, he learned that a good work extended to all can be more beneficial than a good work offered singly for one person. In fact, from that day on it was his custom always to say collects at Masses in the plural, unless the deceased were present, believing that God found this practice more acceptable. Indeed, a spiritual good work applied to many people is not diminished, nor is any loss suffered by this bestowal, but it is known to shine more brightly.

---

10. The collect prayer occurs near the beginning of the Mass. There were several choices of collect prayers for Masses offered on behalf of the dead. Hamo chose a prayer for the (many) dead, not just for one deceased (his father).

Nevertheless, this monk used to say truly that he did not fully know whether this last vision had appeared to him while he was sleeping or awake.

Chapter 10

Since the Lenten season has been very recently completed, a time in which, desisting from the activity of composing, we devote our attention to the observance of the holy season as the Lord has deigned to allow, let us add to what was set down earlier something that attests to the resurrection, whose delightful season we have celebrated.

While very devoutly celebrating the most holy mysteries, the forenamed servant of God uttered those most sacred words, "Mindful, therefore, Lord, of the blessed passion of Christ, your Son, we your servants, as also your holy people." [11] Having said them, he went into ecstasy; he saw Jesus as a most illustrious young man hanging on the cross. Moreover, while adding "And of his resurrection from the dead," he saw the same Jesus coming from the dead accompanied by a vast multitude of souls exulting with the greatest joy. Furthermore, Jesus seemed to be clothed in a snow-white garment, as if all of silk, and he held in his right hand a cross shining with snowy splendor.

After Hamo saw this, he returned to himself, but again rapt beyond himself, he deserved to see still more wondrous sights. For while adding, "But also of his glorious ascension into heaven," he again went into ecstasy; he saw a host of angels coming toward his Lord in heaven and rushing with unutterable joy to meet him. Also, he was intoxicated with such great sweetness by these visions that he used to say that he would be exceedingly blessed if it were granted to him

---

11. Roman Canon (First Eucharistic Prayer).

to enjoy so great a blessedness of delight in the kingdom of heaven. He saw these visions not once but frequently; he deserved often to be given access to these matters for contemplation. In fact, when he had servers assisting him in whose devotion he had confidence, permitting him to linger over those aforementioned words without their becoming weary, he was often carried away in ecstasy while uttering them, as he used to say, and very often this good contemplator was given access to such visions.

Hence he reflected much on these words and consented to linger over them, to have the sharp point of his mind fixed on contemplating them, because it can happen that in the contemplation of these words the Holy Spirit deigns to grant his grace to the soul that is contemplating and to pour the dew of his visitation into the heart that is intent on such words. When he had assistants in whose devotion he did not have confidence, however, and in whom he was afraid to produce loathing[12] if he were to linger over these words, he was not refreshed by such great joy in a vision when, complying with the custom of his ministers, he did not pause at these words.

Hence I must now accost with a few words these helpers who come to the celebrations of Masses lukewarmly and with no ardor, or little. Why is this, soldiers of Christ? Why is it that you do not run to them with lively ardor of mind? Why is it that you do not willingly present yourselves? Why is it that you do not rejoice to stand in the presence of the Lord and his angels? Or do you not know that you are sharers in these? Does the priest not intervene on your behalf? For so he says, "Be mindful, Lord, of your servants and handmaids, and all who stand here present." For what reason, therefore, do you not assist attentively

---

12. Used by our author several times in this chapter, *fastidium* means "squeamishness" or "nausea."

at these so that you might have a share in so great a
gift? Do you not come to this to serve God? Do you
not come to this to render obedience to one another?* *RB 71–72
Do you not know that the fruit of obedience is lost
when one does not obey from the heart? Finally, what
do you now have to do with the world, you who have
decided to live for Christ? But where does this loathing
of yours come from except that you do not love
Christ?

This is supreme starvation![13] For truly is it said that
a soul is swiftly detached from prayer and forsakes it
that . . . does not love Christ.[14] For behold, we see
certain people applying themselves to prayer slug-
gishly; behold, we see many going about the cloister
curiously, and they believe that they have found a certain solace, as it were, when they can turn their attention freely to such things. But then they are held tight
by certain chains, as it were, when they are occupied
in ministry of the divine office. You see their faces
downcast by sadness, as it were; you see their eyes
turned here and there by curiosity. If it happens, however, that they are invited to a conversation, they run,
they become cheerful, they rejoice, they exult, and if
it happens that they hear what soothes their ears, they
dance with their whole heart. And those who suffered
themselves to be present at the sacred mysteries for
scarcely a little hour, and this in fact with loathing, are
willingly engrossed in conversations and sometimes
harmful ones,[15] and for those who were languid in
prayer for a brief hour, a day seems not to suffice for
conversing together with people, if leave is given.
They seek out rumors, they chat about kings, they
very often engage in conversations about battles, so

---

13. *Inedulitas* means "fasting," "abstinence," or even "starvation."

14. There is a lacuna in this line of the text.

15. *Inutilis*, "useless," can also mean "harmful," which it seems
the author intends here.

*2 Tim 4:4

that in them that saying of the apostle seems to be fulfilled, "And indeed they will turn their hearing away from the truth, but will be turned to fables."*

Behold, we have brought forth these words for the admonition of the fainthearted, to recall them from such things to divine love and to restrain them from pursuing harmful curiosity. And perhaps not without cause, for, God willing, it could happen that someone who is afflicted with such a vice, hearing these words, might recover from this plague and be roused more ardently toward divine love after his spirit has been chastised, knowing that a heart for which this life is still sweet departs far from God and that nothing among the things below ought to delight the one who has an inheritance in heaven, since it is written, "One who wishes to be a friend of this world is made an enemy of God."* We learned these things that we have reported from that man who wrested them from him with difficulty; we have taken care to write them down at his request and for love of him, seeing that he is a most veracious man.

*Jas 4:4

Since I decided to comply with his holy requests once, it remains that the following discourse should strive to make known what he was able to learn from the narration of the holy man.

Chapter 11

And so Hamo, ardently inflamed with love of God and the saints, sometimes collected relics of many saints, and by his dispensing of them, God enriched the poverty of many churches through him. Since there are many, however, I omit some things that the Lord did at that time through him for the glory of his own name and the honor of the saints. I direct my pen to a few that happened when he was present, imploring the power of the Holy Spirit to grant me speech that may suffice to set them forth worthily.

And so, on a certain night, in the house of a certain *conversus* who lived apart from men because he was a leper, when Hamo was separating relics into parts to distribute them but was in no way able to arrange them according to his wish because the candles were shining very dimly, he began to be troubled in his own thoughts and to be very uneasy, fearing that perhaps God was not pleased because he dared to touch holy relics of such a kind and so great with his hands. But the Lord alleviated this fear of his with a visible miracle, and with swift mercy he strengthened his mind. For one of the candles, removing itself from the candlestick, settled on the wooden base made for it in the manner of a little wheel, and casting very bright light, it remained there with the same light and, through divine power, without any support, until Hamo finished the whole task. Moreover, that same *conversus* was present there at that time; he saw these events, as he reported, while marveling at them with him. O the unutterable mercy of God! O the ever-venerable blessings of the Highest Majesty, which comes to its servants as it wills and, coming to them, makes them most glad!

Chapter 12

Further, let another miracle of light be added to embellish the series in our narrative. On a certain night when Hamo had finished similar work in the aforementioned house and was returning to the monks' dormitory, the torch leading the way was put out by the severity of the winds, and while the same *conversus* went back to his house, Hamo was left alone in the midst of the darkness. But the Lord did not allow him to remain in the midst of the darkness or to suffer a collision because of the hideous gloom of night. For a light sent by divine providence appeared to him, leading him with abundant light all the way to the intended place. Behold, the true Israelite* is not abandoned in darkness! Behold, one who is vigilant in his love of God and the saints is made glad by a gleaming light, and through such great gladness he is rendered more devout to remain vigilant.

Chapter 13

Moreover, on a certain day, while Hamo was occupied in the same task, the same aforementioned *conversus* was there assisting; however, his left hand was weakened by a powerful infirmity; with its fingers constricted, it was really capable of no work and was to him more of a burden than a thing that confers honor.[16] But in order that he might more readily do what he wished, the holy man held out to him relics of Saint Benedict, which he took with his weakened hand. O the boundless power of God! O the praiseworthy attentiveness of the man of faith! O the venerable merits of the saints! Immediately the hand of the *conversus* grew warm; immediately that man clearly sensed the Lord's blessing. Indeed, his hand got back its former shape, with the fingers straightened, and recovered strength for use in working, strength that he had long lacked. Not only was that hand restored to its former use but also the whole left side of his body, which had been feeble, as he himself attested, was improved.

Moreover, Hamo used to say that he handled these holy relics with so much trembling and judged himself so unworthy for so great a task that while so doing he feared either to be struck with blindness or punished by some injury to his limbs. Hence he was also often disposed to remove himself from such work. But lest he should do this, God always comforted him by some

16. The author's pun on *oneri quam honori* is lost in English translation.

showing of a miracle. For when he understood that either hearing or seeing or the impaired health of other faculties is restored by the power of saints, and, what is more, the souls of many long dead because of terrible sins are revived by oral confession and penance, he was made happier and returned to this work.

Chapter 14

With the greatest longing, however, Hamo wished to understand this: that the Lord might deign to show him in some way how long he wanted him[17] to persist in such a task. Moreover, the Lord did not deprive him of so holy a longing, as the following miracle teaches. For at a certain time, while he had before him the most holy relics unwrapped on a certain linen cloth, suddenly the cloth is turned upside down by a divine hand, and the lower part is made the higher, and the relics that were on it are covered. When he saw this, Hamo, to whom the Lord deigned to show so clear a miracle, understood that he ought to cease from this task.

Chapter 15

Moreover, by no means do we think that this should be passed over: that Hamo learned that many relics had increased in size through divine power. For when he had at different times put back such little relics that nothing seemed to remain that could be divided, when he returned to them, he found them increased to such an extent that the size sufficed abundantly for division.

---

17. Reading *eum* in the text, not *cum* as in the edition.

Chapter 16

It is worthwhile to insert another similar miracle into this text. What we have said concerning relics is also well known to have been done with respect to coins. For abounding with a heart of mercy in his sustenance of the poor, Hamo faithfully disbursed coins received from rich men able to find no other steward so faithful in this matter. A great multitude of the poor flocked to him from all the neighboring districts on every side to hear the word of salvation from his mouth. For their support, either in food, in clothing, or in other necessities, he knew that the coins had often been very abundant. But when he believed that he had now disbursed almost all, he found that he was still disbursing abundantly, and in his own thoughts he wondered greatly at this. Sometimes also when he put his hand in his pouch, he drew out of it just as many coins as he was determined to disburse at one time, not more, not fewer. It is no wonder if that one who in his own hands multiplied five loaves for the refreshment of five thousand people multiplied money in the hands of his servant for the restoration of the needy. For indeed the Truth himself made this promise to his faithful ones, saying, "He who believes in me will do the works that I myself do, and even *John 14:12   greater will he do."* Truly, with pious affection Hamo strove to succor the needs of lepers, widows, and other poor people; hence he was also embraced with loving arms by all who could recognize him. Therefore, so that faith might be accorded to our words, we ought not by our silence omit a certain miracle that we have recently learned was done.

Chapter 17

A certain widow named Reneldis used to live in the neighborhood. After she received coins from Hamo, she bought three little sheep with his assent, along with a certain lamb, with his prayer also supporting her in such a purchase. While she was watching these sheep carelessly, a wolf came and seized the lamb, and carrying it off, the wolf sought the trackless ways of the fields and the dense parts of the forest. But, wonderful to say, the one who had the liberty of seizing did not have the power of harming.[18] For on the following day, the same lamb is found unharmed under the open sky next to the house of the forenamed widow; it is altogether unknown whether the same wolf returned it or how it was brought back. No one, however, ought to doubt that this was done by the power of God, who alone could restrain the rapacious maw of a wolf and rescue a weak little beast from its greedy jaws; by its rescue he gave the holy man confidence in entreating, and by its recovery he gladdened the heart of the poor little woman and lifted up the spirits of those hearing it to an astonishing degree. Through this deed the holy man is rendered more devout, not more exalted, the poor little woman is revived by gladness, and those hearing it are overcome with astonishment.

Chapter 18

Let this also be inserted in our page, which I believe to be very beneficial, if it is properly heeded, for the instruction of the humble and the depression of the presumptuous. For we declare this that we know, and we assert this that we have seen.* The monks of a *John 3:11 certain abbey, deprived of their own father, in a general council chose this holy man to be in charge of them, but they did not obtain a favorable result in their request, for he chose rather to have a place of subjection, following the Highest Master, than to ascend to

18. The author displays a nice rhetorical parallelism here, as elsewhere in the *Vita*.

the summit of prelacy. O, with what mighty entreaties did they persist! O, with what great supplication and even prostration of bodies did they humble themselves before their abbot in his presence! But they were not able to obtain what they were seeking.

Also, in the abbey of Savigny, where he had been professed, they once wanted to establish him as subprior, but he strove to decline by fleeing this place. But what is this small recollection? Solicited very often even for a bishopric both by the king and by the clergy, he refused to accept the office, truly striving with ready reflection of mind to acknowledge his own lowness; for he knew that it is safer to lead a life in peace than to be subject to public tumult. Because even if the management of temporal affairs for the love of God is good, it can scarcely or never be without a stumbling block. Because, as Blessed Gregory says, "Those who preside over the managing of earthly affairs are widely exposed to the darts of a hidden enemy, and, while they remain steadfast in the battle line, it is difficult to escape without a wound." [19] I say this also about those who look after themselves with the greatest care.

Hence I grieve for certain ones who, though they linger in the lowest places while living lukewarmly, do not fear to seize the summit of prelacy if it is offered, as if conscious of their own sanctity; rather, to speak more truly, they eagerly aspire to what is not offered. O grief! How does one who is unable to direct oneself wish to command others? Or with what rashness does one aspire to a place of command whom a life of sanctity does not commend? Or with what audacity does one who does not know how to teach oneself presume to instruct others? Now let those who are such be cured of their presumption by humbly being

---

19. *Moralia in Job* 2.48.75 (commenting on Job 1:17), ed. R. Gillet, SCh 32 *bis* (Paris: Éditions du Cerf, 1989), 364.

prudent in imitation of this man, but those who are humble, let them be rendered even more humble and become pursuers of poverty through his example. For both can find in this man a source from which to make progress, if the former endeavor to give up the pride of their presumption and the latter love the most secure place of submission while seeking the depths of humility. But for us who have made this little digression, it remains to return to our purpose and to insert now in this page an example of his humility.

Chapter 19

At a certain time, the wickedness of robbers gained strength after peace was disturbed, and they wrongfully plundered the possessions of others. Hamo, however, was made a swineherd and was pasturing the pigs lest the robbers should plunder the property of the aforementioned abbey. But while performing this duty, he used to persist in fasting until evening every day, except the Lord's Day. For he did not love the belly's gormandizing but always used to strive after the severity of parsimony. But should we think that, engaged in such service, he devoted his attention to searching out fables and rumors? Not at all! In fact, carrying with him books of divine Scripture, he used to attend to reading and meditation, and he was busy refreshing his mind with such food. O how many there are who glory in the name of monk, if they employ such boldness, who might be engaged for a short time in work of this kind but who would more willingly be occupied with idle and useless matters, or more willing at times to be engaged with harmful ones.

In fact, at night Hamo did not yield to dozing and drowsiness, but he used to devote himself vigilantly to solitary prayer, as he himself attested. Thus he gave over each time, day and night, to divine offices. Moreover, it happened that at this very time the pigs that he was pasturing in a certain desolate grove situated in Brittany were plundered by robbers and carried off in different directions after being divided. Following these robbers not on horseback but on foot, the holy man at last overtook a certain one of them who seemed to be the leader among them. As he looked at the holy man, the whole of this robber shuddered, and cold fear ran through his bones.[20] What more shall I say? Not only were the pigs that were being led away by him released but also all the others that had been led away in different directions; wonderful to tell, they were restored together in their entire number! Furthermore, by so evident a miracle the Lord gladdened Hamo's mind; more and more he strengthened him and made him more devout in his holy purpose. But since we have shown how great a humility that man had in himself, it remains for us to demonstrate by this next example how great was the authority he had among the powerful men of this age.

Chapter 20

In the year of our Lord's incarnation 1167, Henry II, king of England, was spending time in the region of Brittany[21] and was striving to place the rebellious necks of that nation in their savage state under the yoke of his rule. While he was doing so, the vigil of the feast day of the blessed apostles Peter and Paul was approaching, and the king had arranged to send his army to ravage this land on that very day. As soon

20. This line is a clear echo of Virgil, *Aeneid*, 2:120.

21. Henry Plantagenet, duke of Normandy, became king of England at the age of twenty-one in December 1154. Known for a keen mind, administrative efficiency, and a volatile temperament, he reigned until his death in 1189. The editor of Hamo's life notes that Robert of Torigni, *Auctarium Savigneiense*, chap. 1, 367, dates this expedition to August 1167.

as the holy man, who was by chance present then, heard this, he went to the king about this matter as his familiar friend and admonished him to show respect for so great a day out of reverence for the blessed apostles, promising that if he would do so, God would make him very glad in that same year through the merits of the saints. Obedient to this counsel, the king was eager to do what Hamo had advised, and he held back his barons and knights from their ravaging out of reverence for the blessed apostles.

Learning this act and remembering the promise that he had made to so great a man, the holy man began to be extremely agitated and to entreat the holy apostles with urgent prayer that what he had promised might be fulfilled through their merits, both through themselves and through others. What more need I say? Indeed, his promise was fulfilled in the same year. For that nation was completely subjected to the king and given over to the domain of his son. Moreover, the king of France,[22] who had formerly had discord with Henry for a long time, was allied to him along with his barons in the restoration of peace, and by this covenant the disturbance of the kingdoms was put to rest. And so, after this was done, the king of the English was made exceedingly glad; he used to listen to Hamo willingly, and he used to do many things after he had heard Hamo; he even used to reveal the wounds of his soul to him without fear, knowing that Hamo was a just man and holy.

Chapter 21

Also, Louis, the king of France, knew of Hamo's sanctity, not only by reputation but also by experience. For this king, clinging to the conjugal embrace for a

22. *Gallia*, literally "Gaul."

long time, had no heir of the male gender.[23] Very anxious over this matter, he revealed the sorrow in his heart to Hamo, and from his heart he drew sound counsel. For Hamo counseled him to go to the Church of Blessed Denis, where the bodies of the holy martyrs, Eustace and his companions, rest and there with the queen to pour forth prayer with a faithful heart for the attainment of his desire and to hear Mass celebrated there. He promised the king that through the intervention of the blessed martyrs he would obtain his wish, unless God in his providence should want France to be afflicted through the lack of a royal male child.

Putting faith in his words, the king undertook to do what he had counseled, and not a long time after this was done, the queen conceived and brought forth a son.[24] And thus fulfilling the promise of his faithful one, God not only cheered the king through the receipt of a desired offspring but also brought great gladness to his kingdom. O man faithful through all! O man eminent in justice and counsel! When he counseled from the heart that veneration be shown to the saints because of their merits, he did not believe that what was requested would be without result.

Indeed, the memory of this man is deservedly passed on in written records, whose faith and holiness were shown to be renowned to such a degree through the sure proof of events. Moreover, I beseech all who will read these words to pray to the most merciful Lord for me, a sinner and the least of all men, so that

---

23. Sauvage, "Vitae B. Petri Abrincensis et B. Hamonis," 524n3, notes that King Louis VII was married to Eleanor of Aquitaine from 1137 to 1152 and had two daughters by her before their marriage was annulled. He married Constantia, daughter of the king of Spain, in 1154 and also had a daughter by her. After her death, he married the daughter of Count Theobald of Campania in 1160 and by her had a son, Philip Augustus, on August 21, 1165.

24. Philip Augustus.

through their prayers, sins might be forgiven me, a sinner, who does not have confidence in my own justice. And let them not complain about my unembellished prayer, and let them believe that I have written nothing except what was ascertained most truly. Otherwise, I would prefer to have placed my finger on my mouth rather than to have inserted something false; as God is my witness, I say this.

Chapter 22

I used to think, Reverend Father, that I had already satisfied your wishes and desires with so many and such great things set forth about the holy man, but I was mistaken. Indeed, the ardor of your heart and the zeal of your love toward him impressed on my mind to compel me to add still other things about him, I who have decided as much as possible not to neglect your wish. Therefore I shall undertake what remains, so that our service, of whatever kind, might thus satisfy you.

And so, sometimes a vision of this kind was shown to this man in a dream: indeed, it seemed to him that he was celebrating Mass, and in the midst of the celebration, after the gospel, a certain exceedingly handsome person appeared to him, who, as it seemed to him, was offering him a certain talent of gold; when he had freed his hands, after he had handed the offering over to his server and turned back and looked again, it seemed to him that the person who had offered the talent to him was the Son of God.

Then there was at this time a certain master among scholars named William,[25] a man of great renown,

25. Sauvage, "Vitae B. Petri Abrincensis et B. Hamonis," 526–27n2, argues that Hamo's *Vita* was written during the lifetime of William of Toulouse, a native of Caen, who was briefly abbot of Savigny before being elected abbot of Cîteaux. Citing the history of the abbots of Fontaines, however, he contends that William of

originating from the town of Caen. When a short time had passed after Hamo saw the vision, this man came to Savigny. He conversed with the holy man, since he had previously been a friend of his. Moreover, when they were conversing together, the vision shown before came to Hamo's mind, and his mind perceived that this master was the gift that seemed to be offered to him by the Son of God. Why should I linger over many details? Hamo incited him to contempt for the world, to taking up the light yoke of Christ,* to trampling on the fleeting honors of the world, to following the footsteps of the Lord. And to make William more eager for this change, he reported the aforementioned vision to him. What more shall I say? Drenched in tears, that man placed himself in Hamo's hands, and scorning the pomp of the world, he solemnly promised his conversion in that place.

*Matt 11:30

But since he had been occupied with many cares in the world, cares that he was unable to abandon without making arrangements, as it seemed to him, after brief delays of a short time had been approved, he still wanted to return to Caen to dispose of these himself. The abbot of Clairvaux[26] and others who happened to be present at his deliberation, along with some monks of the same house, opposed his plan, since they were very much afraid that if he departed from there, he would not return. But although they strove to their

---

Toulouse was abbot of Savigny twice, 1161–63/64 (between abbots Alexander and Joscelin) and again in 1178–79. Since the author of Hamo's *Vita* makes no mention of William's election as abbot of Cîteaux, that had probably not occurred when he wrote the life. Moreover, it is hard to see how the author could say that an abbot who reigned only one year is known to have done many good things for the monastery. Regarding an earlier abbot of Savigny named William, Sauvage notes that the *Chronicle* of Robert Torigni mentions no abbot between Serlo and Richard; in fact, the author of the *Historia Saviniacensis* denied that there was any. Two charters indicate, however, that there was an abbot William who held office briefly after Serlo and before Richard.

26. His name was Godfrey.

utmost to convince him of this, while he was adducing sufficient reasons for returning, as it were, they were disappointed, in spite of their every effort. And perhaps God did not will this delay to happen through them, since he reserved it for Hamo.

Therefore, after William had refused all of them, Hamo appeared and easily accomplished what they had been unable to do. Holding William back, Hamo promised that he would go in his place to Caen and dispatch his affairs for him. When he had accomplished this goal, his sanctity became more clearly known to the aforementioned abbots, and therefore these men were able to receive instruction in their way of life. And so in such a way that master was held back and made a novice, and after a year of probation was completed, he was consecrated a monk, and a little while after, through God's will he was chosen abbot of the same abbey; through him, as we understand, God is known to have done many good things for the same house. For, as we believe, he was the offering that seemed to have been offered to Hamo by the Son of God. For he was a man of the highest devotion, an energetic follower and lover of Christian poverty.

Chapter 23

Moreover, that venerable man Hamo, a meritorious soldier of the Eternal King, was revered like a father by the nuns who lived near the town of Mortain; he loved them as special daughters on account of the zeal for religion and chastity that he knew to be burning principally in them. Thus it happened on a certain day when he was present there that the wife of Robert, whose surname was Bouquerell, came there with a baby boy to whom she had recently given birth. (Her husband had discharged the duty of constable in the forenamed town, but the king of the English, moved by the tears of the wretched people from whom that man had by guile taken away property, had deposed him.) And when the servant of God had sat down with her, along with some sisters, the infant's nurse, who was present as well, gave a certain ripe fruit to the little boy to suck on.

But in fact a certain small piece of this fruit suddenly got stuck in the baby's throat, and he began to tremble with anxiety; turning black like coal, he now became almost totally lifeless. And so his nurse, expending every care and concern that she could, put the nipples of her breasts in his mouth, which, as if they were made of stone, he not only did not take hold of but also did not feel. And when the boy's mother became frantic, as it were, and was gripped by excessive grief and lamentation, and the sisters were also agitated beyond measure, a certain one of them suggested to the blessed man that he take the relics of the glorious martyr Blaise and immerse them in water and pour this water into the boy's mouth.[27]

Indeed the man of God swiftly carried out the advice of that sister; pouring water into a cup, he put the relics into it, and he touched the infant's mouth with this same water. When he had done this, the boy, suddenly recalled from the utmost point of death, immediately burst into laughter, and so he restored to his mother and the rest of the sisters a cause for incomparable joy. Certainly in this miracle the virtue of the blessed man is rightly believed to have worked together with the relics of the saints; there is no doubt that through his power the same little infant had received salvation and safety.

Chapter 24

Another woman, distinguished as much for the nobility of her family as for the wealth of her possessions, was bound to the aforementioned nuns by a

27. A story about Saint Blaise in the *Legenda Aurea* tells how he cured a boy who was choking on a fish bone.

strong attachment of friendship. Therefore, when this woman was approaching childbirth, as the suitable time was arriving, and, already laboring for a long time in this birth, she could not deliver herself, she directed her messenger to the nuns, asking that they deign to send her something from the relics of the saints, through whose effect she might be released from the distress of such great danger. And so a certain one of the nuns sent to her in place of a sacred relic a certain belt that she had received from the blessed man and that she preserved with great care for love of him, instructing her to what extent she ought to gird herself with it. When that woman had done this, she was immediately freed from the distress by which she was burdened, as the birth went forward, through the merits of the servant of Christ, with divine mercy aiding it.

Chapter 25

Moreover, how much trust or how much efficacy he had if he decided to ask anything of the powerful men of this world can be shown from the following. Since the count of Boulogne,[28] after the death of his father, Stephen, king of the English, had received from the venerable King Henry (who succeeded this Stephen in the kingdom) the land of his father with this condition and permission, that he might regain it for himself from all places, religious or secular, without hindrance by anyone, he was endeavoring to take away from the same nuns their dwellings as well as other property that they had received as alms from King Stephen and to add these to his own dominion.

---

28. William of Warenne (d. 1159), son of King Stephen of England, was count of Boulogne and Mortain after 1153, when the settlement at the end of the civil war made Henry of Anjou (the son of the empress Matilda) successor to King Stephen; in 1154 Henry succeeded as Henry II.

When the blessed man Hamo had learned this, although uneasy, he sought out the count, who was staying in the castle of Mortain, to petition him humbly about this matter.

And when the count scarcely deigned to look at him, much less deigned to listen to him, the servant of Christ, returning sad and troubled to the abbey of the nuns, with sighs and groans made known to them the count's obstinacy and his heart hardened by malice.[29] And at the same time he urged them in so great a matter to implore the aid of blessed Paul, whose conversion was being celebrated on that day, so that, just as he was considered most effectual in every respect in the court of the Eternal King, in this need he might aid and assist them. And when all the nuns had devoted themselves to prayer for a long time, with Hamo praying as well, at last, relying on the Lord's help, he returned in haste to the court of the forenamed count. And when he had been received by him this time with respect and addressed courteously, the man of God understood that his journey had been blessed by the Lord.

So after the matter for which he had come had been concealed for the time being, he requested of the same count that he would deign to go as far as the nuns' abbey, saying that if he departed across the sea with the nuns not visited in this time of trouble, he would have given to his justices or sergeants a reason for injuring or accusing them by abandoning them in inconsolable grief. Assenting gladly to his request, the count, hastening to the abbey of the nuns, along with the countess, the blessed man, and many people in attendance with him, said along the way with great intimacy to the blessed servant of God that thereafter he could in no way resist his requests. And so when the count arrived at the abbey with his companions

---

29. *Cor induratum* echoes the description of Pharaoh's hard heart in Exodus 7:13.

and had entered their chapter, the nuns fell prostrate at his feet with their faces on the ground (just as they had been instructed beforehand by Roger, the prior of Savigny,[30] who was there at that time) and implored his mercy.

When they had raised themselves up from the ground at blessed Hamo's bidding, the count, moved to mercy in his innermost parts by their very great humbling and supplication, and all who were with him, began to weep most bitterly. What more need I say? In this same place, the count immediately gave to them and conceded to them all that he had wanted to take away or what they were asking of him, with the charters and privileges of these same donations besides. Without doubt all these things are known to have come to fruition principally through the merits and foresight of the blessed man, as is clear from what was said before.

Chapter 26

Employed at a certain time on a journey with William, the prior of Savigny,[31] Hamo had with him relics of Saint Martin the bishop and other saints, which he was carrying with great reverence. When they had come to a certain very large stream and were utterly unable to cross over with the horses at any spot on account of the overwhelming force of the water, dismounting from the horses, they came to a plank. When, however, the blessed man had approached the edge of the river next to the plank, seeing the violent, rushing surge of water flowing below, he was very much afraid and terrified. But taking steadfast hope

30. Sauvage finds evidence in a charter that this was Roger de Alneto, who was prior of Savigny in 1157.

31. Sauvage finds evidence for a Prior William in charters from 1163, 1171, 1174, and 1178 but does not think this was the prior referred to here.

entirely in divine mercy and the intercession of the saints whose relics he was carrying with him, he said to himself, "Even if I can fall into this stream, yet carrying so many relics of Christ's saints with me, I cannot be wholly drowned or perish." A wondrous thing to say, and proven completely by very few saints! Indeed, when he had placed his first foot on the plank, he marveled greatly that he was seized and transported to the other bank of the river by divine power, since the prior, his companion, although more vigorous in body and more agile, could scarcely cross over to the same place supported by the help of two men.

Chapter 27

When Hamo had been invited at a certain time by Henry, king of the English, he went as far as Barfleur to meet him; at last, when the journey was completed, he arrived there on a Saturday. But on the following night, when he had given over his little body, worn out by the journey, to nocturnal sleep, a vision of this kind appeared to him: truly it seemed to him that he and a certain other person together were supporting between them a certain very large crucifix holding a dead man. And when they were grasping it by the arms on each side, suddenly the same crucified man, reviving, attained the character of a living human and was healed. Arising from sleep after this vision, Hamo began to be agitated inwardly by different anxious thoughts as to what so terrifying and so unusual a vision might portend. And on the following day, which was Sunday, the king summoned Hamo privately in a certain church, together with Lord Rotrocus, a wholly religious man who was then indeed a bishop but later became archbishop of Rouen.[32] The king confessed

32. Sauvage, "Vitae B. Petri Abrincensis et B. Hamonis," 532n1, citing *Gallia Christiana* 11.575, 48, says that Rotrocus, son of the

to these two all the sins that he had committed from his earliest age, whatever ones he could remember. And thus, according to the vision of the blessed man of God, by confessing and doing penance the king was recalled from the death of sin to true life. In addition to imposing a suitable penance on him, which should not be kept silent, they commanded among other things that he clothe three hundred poor people, a task that he devoutly fulfilled.

Chapter 28

At another time, when Hamo had gone to sleep on a certain day, he saw the husband of a certain sister of his coming to him and kissing his hands affectionately, weeping bitterly and wailing. Troubled by the man's sorrow and wishing to search with more certainty into the cause of the matter, Hamo arose immediately from sleep and thought that he found the man on bent knees before him. Indeed, while Hamo, still situated in the world, had frequented the schools, this man, along with Hamo's sister, had bestowed great comfort of kindness and assistance on the man of God. In truth, at the time when he appeared to Hamo, the man had recently died, although the man of God was utterly ignorant of this fact.

When a little time intervened after this vision, when Hamo had learned for certain from people reporting it that his sister's husband was dead, the man of God understood without doubt that in that apparition in which the man had shown himself to Hamo in his sleep, the man, subject to punishments, was requesting the support of spiritual benefits from him; these Hamo kindly and mercifully hastened to bestow on him.

---

earl of Warwick, was ordained in 1139 and became archbishop of Rouen in 1165.

Chapter 29

Among the other signs of miraculous powers, the blessed man used to experience this especially: if he sensed that people were bound inwardly by a serious sin of excess, he would not only rouse them with frequent words of exhortation to correction of their fault but also, what is greater, he was moved to ask the Lord with much urgent prayer for their liberation. And so when he was standing in church on a certain day, he devoutly prayed to the Lord (following the example of blessed Stephen) for a certain brother who he greatly feared was encumbered by serious bonds of sin and who often used to disparage the blessed man's actions without Hamo's knowing it. Suddenly, rapt in ecstasy and looking upward, he saw a certain shadowy darkness and, standing in the midst of those shadows, the very brother for whom he was imploring the Lord's mercy: hideous, pale, and unsightly, more resembling a man dead than one living. But above that darkness he saw an abundant light of pleasing brightness, and at the same time through the Holy Spirit a voice of this kind arose in his heart, saying, "This man whom you see does not have the grace of God in him, but he is proud and envious and also seeking vainglory, and he is a revealer of others' secrets." Having returned to himself after the vision, the blessed man recognized through sure proofs that that monk delighted in the aforementioned vices, and he remained in them.

Chapter 30

Also, at another time when he was on a journey and had turned aside at a suitable opportunity to the abbey of nuns, it happened at that time that a certain one of them, Borgognia by name, was suffering from an extreme and very serious bodily infirmity. When the blessed man had gone to her for the sake of hearing her confession and imparting consolation, a little afterward, with the exigency of his journey pressing upon him, he began to pursue his intention of leaving. But when the aforementioned sister learned of his sudden departure, she began to bear with great regret the fact that he was attempting to leave so quickly. Observing the anxiety of her grief, the man of such great compassion, trusting in the compassion of the Lord, spoke thus to her, "Wait for me, and you will not die until I return," he said. But, oh indeed, the wondrous power of the man of God, even against the universal inevitability of the death of all mortals! For lying at the utmost brink of life, so to speak, while obeying the commands of the man of God, she waited in her body until he should return to that place. But lest perchance some unbeliever might wish to apply such great intervals of delay more to chance than to the holiness of the man of God, the following outcome of the matter refutes him. For when he had returned after some days, as soon as he visited the aforementioned sister, as if his command of obedience had been carried out and she had been made fearless by the presence of the man of God, she departed forthwith to the Lord.

Chapter 31

Finally, for a fuller commendation of the deeds of that man, one can estimate from the following miracle with how incomparable a simplicity of devotion and purity the mind of that blessed man was united to his own Advocate, who had been accustomed to punish affronts to and rejection of his servant with so swift an act of vengeance.[33] For it happened at a certain time that Henry, king of the English, ordered a certain knight, who was accused of having wickedly conspired to kill him, to be shut up in the dungeon in Domfront

33. See chap. 25 above.

Castle under the strictest watch. And when the aforementioned knight, tormented in the same dungeon
for two years, had awaited the lamentable sentence of
a dreadful fate with fear and trembling, at last, after
the king had held an inquest with his nobles about the
man and a sentence was rendered, he ordered the
aforementioned knight, after his eyes had been gouged
out, to be deprived of his manly parts, too.

When this order had become known to the blessed
man, at the suggestion of certain noblemen he sought
out Henry, king of England, who at that time was
staying at Ger in the forest of Lande-Pourrie, to beg
for the deliverance of the aforementioned knight.[34]
And when the king had received him with respect, as
he had always been accustomed to do, then the servant of Christ makes known[35] to the king the matter
for which he had undertaken the journey to him. And
so the blessed man begs strenuously that the king re-
voke the cruel sentence of vengeance imposed on the
aforementioned knight, saying that it is very unjust
and impious, and that to presume insolently is contrary to the word of the Lord, which says, "Vengeance
is mine, and I shall repay," * if by avenging his own
injuries the king should force someone to imperil his
own salvation. What more need I say? The king, as he
was clever and cunning, while mocking and refusing
the blessed man's request with carefully chosen words
and not without bitter resentment in his heart, allowed the servant of God to return to Savigny.

But the justice of the Lord compensated for the
rejection of his servant in this way with a swift gain
and compound interest. For although the man of the
Lord in departing from the king had left him healthy
and in good condition, by the will of God, within a

*Rom 2:19;
Deut 32:35

34. Ger was located between Domfront and Mortain.
35. Here, as elsewhere, the author uses the historical present
tense to suggest urgency.

quarter of a day he was laid low by so great an affliction of illness that for fear of death, which he thought
was most surely threatening him, he sent messengers
and summoned the aforementioned servant of Christ
to him with utmost haste. Indeed, while hearing the
king's confession and at the same time seeing that an
opportune time had been provided by the Lord for his
request, among other salutary counsels that he gave
him, the servant of Christ asked and admonished the
king to allow all the bound and imprisoned men who
were being held in his entire realm to go free and
unharmed.

In fact, the king most willingly granted this request
at the first suggestion of the blessed man, and according to Hamo's word he ordered all to be released and
dismissed. Thus, with divine providence cooperating,
what the king at first refused to do for Christ's servant
in one case, after a short time he very readily fulfilled
at the man of God's first request concerning a thousand or even more who were being held throughout
the different territories of his realm. Besides these, he
bestowed on countless people other vast and manifold
benefits, which, since it is a long task to recount them
individually, we have decided to pass over in silence
rather than to describe them in a careless manner.

Chapter 32

But how the same king triumphed over the devil
during the same illness through the gift of the Holy
Spirit and the counsel of the blessed man should be
placed next, I think. For when the king had suffered
grievously, beyond measure, because of this same illness, later, as he was convalescing, while he was keeping vigil, a certain voice sent from heaven brought
these words to him as follows, saying, "This is the
death of your enfeebled enemy." Moreover, when the
same king had revealed these words privately to

Christ's servant, the man of the Lord asked him what he thought they meant for him. And the king explained the aforementioned revelation to him in this way: "This health is the death of my enfeebled enemy, that is, the devil, who is enfeebled by our good works, and he does not dare to approach us, but through our evil works he rules us and does not fear to attack us." Furthermore, the outcome of the matter showed that the explanation of the divine word had been completely true, since, as was said above on the occasion of this illness, the king performed such great good works and so wondrous that if all were recounted and recalled to mind one by one in writing they might seem to be almost beyond belief.

Chapter 33

Now I think that we should by no means pass over in silence the fact that this servant of Christ bore with many antagonists and detractors of his works, following even in this the footsteps of our Lord, whom when he expelled demons and performed other remarkable works of divine power the Pharisees, moved by a spirit of envy, wickedly used to accuse that he did these *Matt 12:24; Luke 11:15* through Beelzebub.* Moreover, he endured this abuse not only from strangers but also, what is more painful, very often from members of his own house and men of his own order. For when he used to receive alms, which he obtained by entreaty from kings and princes and other powerful men of this world as a faithful steward of his Lord, he carefully expended them on erecting churches, building chapels from their foundation,[36] constructing bridges, feeding and clothing the poor, and carrying out other works of mercy.

Ps 56:5 Especially on this account some used to equip their tongues with swords* against him, because from these

36. See chap. 52 below.

alms he would leave not enough, or really nothing, for himself or these with whom he was living the common life. And so, according to the apostle, he was for them the odor of life unto death.* Finally, after he had built many churches[37] in honor of Christ and his saints, as we have said, he was persuaded that, with his full support expended, he should help rebuild the church of the lepers of Saint James de Beuron, which, formerly constructed in honor of the Blessed Virgin Mary, had fallen down after its walls were impaired, as they were made not of concrete but of clay.[38]

*2 Cor 2:16

As is the weakness of human frailty, however, he was affected by a certain weariness of spirit on account of the stupefying complaints of those who were grumbling, as we have already said, about his almsgiving; he refused supplies for the aforementioned work, yet he decided within himself to invoke the will of the Lord over the matter with unceasing prayer. In fact, it happened that at that time he was in haste to undertake a sociable journey to Mortain, to the abbey of nuns, and I along with him. While I was returning sooner, however, he remained there for a few days, and in that place he celebrated the birth of the Blessed Mother of God, which was at hand then. And so, having entered the church on the day of the same celebration, when he had sought out a certain crypt with a certain altar that was on the right-hand side of this church for the sake of praying more privately, seeking pardon repeatedly with genuflections, he began to beseech the Lord's mercy, so that if it were the Lord's will that he should devote his attention to building the aforementioned church, the Lord might deign to reveal this to him in whatever way he might please.

---

37. *Basilica*, used here, often refers in later Latin to a cathedral or metropolitan church.

38. According to sources cited by Sauvage, "Vitae B. Petri Abrincensis et B. Hamonis," 537n1, in 1696 this was called the chapel of Saint-Hermel or hospital (*maladerie*) of Saint-James de Beuvron.

And when he persisted in prayer with his whole mind on this reflection and with eagerness of purpose, as we have said, so that he might be able to perceive the Lord's will for the aforementioned work, suddenly there stood before him a beam of boundless brightness and greatness sent from heaven, not down in a straight line, as is the manner of a sunbeam, but extended upward from earth high into the air. Meanwhile, however, when the man of the Lord had fixed his sight for a long time on this same beam standing before him, he was filled with indescribable delight[39] through the presence of the Holy Spirit, who had come, no doubt, with this very beam. Finally, after his consolation had been divinely carried out, the same beam receded through the roof of the church into heaven whence it had come. But rendering deserved thanks to God for the visitation from heaven granted to him, and made most certain (through the inspiration of the Holy Spirit) concerning the Lord's will in that which he had sought, he began immediately, after spurning the derision of slanderers, to build the church in honor of the Blessed Virgin Mary with the greatest disposition of devotion, and to pursue the works of piety that he had been accustomed to pursue before, as a most zealous emulator of all virtues.

Chapter 34

*1 Tim 3:6

Moreover, lest anyone appearing ungrateful to the One who acts should fall into the judgment of the devil,* I think it proper to bring forth as an example for readers a certain memorable response of blessed Hamo that he gave a certain monk, a man equally religious in every way and perfect in his fear of God, namely, Ralph of Nigella. Indeed, to him before all men the man of the Lord made known the secrets of

---

39. *Suavitatis dulcedine*, literally "delight of sweetness."

his own soul, in solitary confession as well as in private conversation, and he did not at all conceal from Ralph anything of which he was aware, whatever Ralph asked him. Truly, lest the reader should incur loathing from my wordiness, I refrain from telling in what way this venerable man, Ralph, obtained this favor of familiarity with Hamo, and how on the occasion of a very serious sickness into which Hamo, the servant of Christ, had fallen, Ralph was able then and thereafter to come to the knowledge of Hamo's secrets, by terrifying him in many ways with frightening reminders of divine judgments.

Therefore, to return to what was said before: once when this same Ralph, amid other discussions in friendly conversation, thought that the servant of Christ should be reproved for the imprudent excess of his fasting—for he had a body so meager and thin that it was believed barely to cling to his bones—this same servant of Christ spoke to him thus: "See," he said, "I admit to you what I have confessed to no one before, and so you may know most surely that, if I wished, as far as what pertains to the condition of the body, I would be fat and robust, and made up of a vigorous stoutness of limbs."

Indeed I have decided to bring this response of Hamo's before the community so that perhaps by his example we might remind ourselves, we who are encompassed by frail flesh, whose whole life on earth is a temptation, in the struggle of combat we have undertaken, with how great an exertion of caution we must refrain from an excessive appetite for food and drink. Affording a remedy for pleasure, Hamo without a doubt attributed the abundance of such things to the ancient tempter as a means of gaining access to us. If through the inflexible severity of fasting this man strove to subdue the flesh to the spirit with tireless and continuous zeal, the bounty of the Highest Divinity smiled on him with so many and almost unheard of distinctions of miracles.

Chapter 35

Now it remains for us to make known very carefully, with complete trust, how the man of the Lord foresaw long before in spirit, with the Lord revealing it, the acquaintance and familiarity that before all men he had with Henry, king of England. For when the same Henry, while only a duke,[40] was not yet at the helm of his kingdom and was not known at all to the venerable servant of Christ, who had never laid eyes on him, the same man of the Lord, divinely inspired, with a prescient mind received from the Lord a vision of Duke Henry as follows, surely a presage of things to come. Indeed, he saw himself together with the same duke standing apart in a certain place, and around himself and the duke a countless crowd in a populous multitude were standing on every side, positioned at a distance. But the same duke, standing utterly naked except for his breeches and stretching his arms on both sides over the shoulders of the blessed man, placed his arms around Hamo's neck; the man of the Lord was so burdened by their pressure or weight that he felt his knees trembling because of the excess of weight. But at last the aforementioned duke fell forward on bent knees before him, nor did he raise himself up from there afterward.

Moreover, no one who has become fully acquainted with the mutual familiarity and favor of both men is believed not to know how this vision agrees in every way, through suitable parallels, with the future outcomes of events at that time. For the fact that Hamo foresaw himself standing apart with the duke suitably indicates the singular and especially inseparable preference of love and harmony with which King Henry became accustomed to embrace him, particularly, as

40. As noted above (n. 21), Henry of Anjou was duke of Normandy from 1151 through 1154, when he became king of England as well.

it is thought, before all other mortal men. In fact, the crowd standing on every side and looking toward them indicates the admiration of lay people. Because of this, people used to proclaim far and wide their most intimate oneness by being struck with amazement. Furthermore, the extending of the duke's hands and the placing of them over Hamo's shoulders makes known more clearly than light that most loyal faith of the king, through which he entrusted himself to the prayers and counsel of the blessed man in many, even countless, acts of his own.

Also, the fact that, after falling forward on bent knees before the man of the Lord, he did not raise himself up from there afterward not only indicates the submissiveness of humility in which he used to subject himself chiefly to Christ's servant, but it no less presages most effectively the steadfast constancy of his devotion, because of which he never recoiled later from his love after the friendship was once begun. Next, that nakedness that he exposed before Hamo undoubtedly shows that not only in private conversation but also in solitary confession he laid bare before him, by revealing in pure and simple narrative, all the sins that he had committed that he could remember from the beginning of his life.

Now the fact that he was stripped of all other garments and had only breeches signifies his special claim of chastity. Although in many ways, as is the custom of laymen and especially of noblemen, he lived stripped of the garment of justice through the fault of a perverse action, yet in the virtue of continence, which is wont to be a friend very rarely to kings especially, he shone so brightly (although it was thought otherwise of him by many who were ignorant of the inward and hidden secret of his soul before God) that if we were to make known by the use of our pen these actions that Christ's servant, the faithful and knowing witness of his deeds, learned from the same king through his most truthful testimony, just as we heard these same things from him in private disclosure, perhaps they would seem unbelievable and insupportable to those who devote less diligence to preserving continence. Since, however, we have decided to write in this work not so much about commendations of kings as the virtues and merits of Christ's servant[41] for the benefit of our readers, with these commendations omitted for now, let us, with Christ aiding us, direct our writing principally toward him.

Chapter 36

*see Deut 33:29

*Num 21:22

*Num 21:22

*Rom 1:30

Thus, relying on the Lord's strength and favor, and treading upon* the necks of powerful and eminent men by the authority of his unrestrained censure, according to the decree of the law, by walking the royal road* this man neither turned aside to the right* in extolling their good works through shameless acclamation, no matter what they were, nor inclined to the left by falsely keeping silent about their deeds through fearful dissimulation. Therefore he used to say things more salutary than pleasing, more needed than agreeable, thrusting forth the sword of his tongue against individuals as seemed useful for each one, a sword fortified by the sharp point of harsh invective more than smeared with the perverse flattery of fawning adulation, like honey, and hateful to God.* And so he used to exhort the cruel to mercy, the savage to peace and patience, those in conflict to concord, the envious to good will, the greedy and grasping to kindness, the haughty and wanton to humility and chastity, and all to the law of the Lord and to the perfection of evangelical strictness that must be followed.

And although he was so fervent in spirit and faith, as we have said, that he did not in the least hold back

---

41. *Merita* can also mean "miracles"; *servus* literally means "slave."

the necessary invective of righteous censure from anyone, especially of the rich and of the noble when the
facts and occasion required, yet no less did he strive
with great care and concern to become, according to
his ability, a father of the poor,* a defense of the op-   *Job 29:16
pressed, a consoler of the grieving,* a support of the   *Job 29:25
sick, a helper of the needy, a ready intercessor and
effective liberator of those put in prison, and finally a
vigorous executor of all piety and mercy. And since
he was a simple man and one divinely adorned with
a certain innate and natural gentleness and goodness,
there used to shine on his face, so to say briefly, a
certain serene expression of complete virtue and grace,
so that he was believed to have been provided from
heaven by the Lord as a certain divine exemplar of
angelic purity for directing and rightly ordering the
crookedness of human life.

Moreover, to say something about the features that
pertain to the outer appearance of the body, this same
man of the Lord had a simple, pleasing countenance,
a face somewhat long and moderately sharp, a straight
nose, a slender mouth, a beard unbroken but thin, hair
black and a little intermixed with gray, revealing an
agreeable but scant baldness on both sides of his forehead, with hair lying in the middle. He had a body
weakened and very slim, so much that he was believed
to have scarcely any flesh beyond a collection of
bones,[42] indeed one whom a plentiful taking of food
or drink did not revive, since he had learned more to
taste or to nibble food than to eat of it and to refresh
himself.

But now what shall I say about the nature of that
inner man, especially since he always had such zeal,
as much as was in him, that he preferred to conceal
rather than to proclaim his own virtues? But since this
is a rule of perfect justice that the more it wishes to

42. *Copula*, literally "a binding."

*Matt 5:15

*Luke 1:79;
see also Pss 87:7;
106:10

be hidden from view the more clearly it becomes known, the very concealment is a discovery; according to the Savior's command, his lighted lamp could not be concealed under a bushel,*[43] but from the abundant fullness of his inner virtues, though unwilling on account of his conscience, he very often, even repeatedly, used to send forth the rays of his own light to illuminate those who were sitting in darkness and the shadow of death.* And so, living as a tireless follower of contemplative life, he was continually striving to gaze upon his Maker's face,[44] fleeing for love of him all things by which he could be diverted from this effort and making all his thoughts and every hope depend on delight in it.

Chapter 37

Hamo used to devote himself incessantly to holy meditation on Sacred Scripture. Examining his whole self as reflected in these, just as in a shining mirror, he set right whatever he found to be unseemly in himself; he perfected what he found honorable. Removing himself altogether from the clamor of worldly affairs, he especially loved holy repose, in which he could more diligently engage with the matter of his soul. With the world dead to himself, as far as he was concerned, and showing himself crucified* to the blandishments of the world and to worldly enticements, with the success of his virtues advancing he continually raised himself up to the summit of divine contemplation, and he was wont to direct the high point of his mind there incessantly, where he wished with fervent sighs of longing to reach.

*Gal 6:14

43. The text has *sub medio* here, but the Vulgate has *modio*, "a measure."

44. A literal translation here would be "panting to contemplate his Maker's face."

Therefore, to say it truly, he was a victim pleasing to God,* an acceptable temple of the Holy Spirit,† and in fact a certain general workshop of blessed virtues: firm in faith, patient in hope, fervent in charity, grounded in humility, mild in modesty, moved by divine fear, cautious by the grace of discretion, shining forth in the splendor of chastity, preeminent in the understanding of spiritual knowledge, lamenting and groaning over the failings and perils of others' errors and especially the downfalls and dangers of the transgressions of brothers, as if over his own sins. By maintaining always the same countenance amid the countless vicissitudes of this world, he could not be corrupted by prosperous allurements[45] or altered by adversity. Continually pressing on with prayers and psalms, with frequent genuflections added, he did not cease from divine conversation and prayer night or day, and so he used to force the weary limbs of his body to serve the spirit with untiring obedience of devotion. Moreover, in his words he had such consolation and grace that whoever, situated in some difficulty and distress*[46] or, what is more serious, living in doubt about the sacraments of the Christian faith, approached him, that person went away fully comforted by the words of grace that used to proceed from his mouth.*

Finally, to add something as an example, a certain monk arriving from lands across the sea was dangerously shipwrecked[47] with respect to his faith in the Lord's body, which is consecrated on the altar by the grace of the Holy Spirit working through the utterance of words. As that man used to confess about himself, the speech of no just and religious man could

*Phil 4:18
†1 Cor 6:19

*see Ps 118:143, etc.

*Luke 4:22

45. We accept the editor's conjecture of *blandimentis* over the manuscript reading of *blandientis*, "of a flatterer."

46. Literally, "difficulty of distress."

47. Here the author retains the seafaring imagery from *transmarinus* above.

up to that time to any degree turn him aside from the aforementioned uneasiness of most pernicious hesitation. Immediately, at the very outset of a pleasing conversation, Hamo so completely delivered and released the man from every dark cloud of doubt that thereafter he kept the right faith about the truth of the Lord's body for the rest of his life, and he escaped the deserved destruction of everlasting death, which he was coming to without delay as a punishment for his faithlessness.

But truly, besides a common experience of human progress, a certain power of spiritual understanding so illuminated Hamo's spirit and perception as well that when, placed in any assembly, he saw anybody from a distance, although the person was utterly unknown to him before, through the Spirit he knew immediately at first sight from the person's appearance, with no one disclosing it, whether that person was involved in shameful acts of mortal sin. Indeed, I will prove this statement by a few examples.

Chapter 38

A certain bishop came to Savigny and stayed there as a guest; he was involved in certain shameful acts, horrible and intolerable beyond the custom of nature. He persisted in these for thirty years before his priest-

Dan 13:52   hood, and when he had grown old in evil days and ascended to the office of priesthood and afterward to no less than the summit of episcopal dignity,[48] he had never confessed them. And so, as Hamo looked upon this man but had not yet spoken with him, he told a certain elder, a man equally religious in every way, that although the bishop still remained in his body, yet in spirit he was already dead in the sight of God.

---

48. Literally, "the episcopal summit of dignity."

Therefore, having spoken to the bishop privately, with certain circumlocutions and figures of speech purposely drawn out indirectly, as it were, finally the two of them were able with difficulty to elicit from the bishop a confession of his own iniquity.

Thus by the prevenient grace of the Lord, with the foresight of his servant assisting and with the bishop himself at last firmly requesting that very thing, they received his confession, with the worst sins and those of his long-standing habit[49] that were weighing upon him disclosed on either side, and after the reparation of penance had been imposed, they sent him away to his own home. But afterward, this same bishop, departing from the present life around the middle of the very same year, showed clearly by the swift egress of death overtaking him that he had been invited to come to Savigny by the dispensation of divine grace so that he might be recalled to life by the admonitions and counsel of the blessed man rather than having been led there because of any other necessity, as was thought then.

Chapter 39

At another time, on a journey, when Hamo had come to a certain large crowd of people, with his eyes raised toward them he saw among the others a certain knight with venerable gray hair, but, contrary to the character of all goodness and contrary to the maturity of his age, he was involved beyond the custom of nature, as we said about the aforementioned bishop, in the heinous acts of Sodom and Gomorrah. And so when the man of the Lord spoke privately to this man who was in every way completely deprived of the life of God in his soul, after he had been pulled out of the

49. *Consuetudo* has the meaning "illicit intercourse" in certain classical writers.

throng, he urged him not to refrain from submitting to the remedy of penance by confessing his iniquities. Why say more?

At last, after the veil of useless shame had been with difficulty removed, the aforementioned knight decided to reveal his misdeeds to Hamo. He said, however, that he could by no means come to confession of these before death, because he could not restrain himself from them. But when he came to death, he would send word for the man of God to be summoned and would disclose to him in confession all the kinds of his shameful deeds, since he could confess these sins to no other than himself alone on account of the great shame of these acts. Indeed Hamo had this grace from heaven bestowed on him by the Lord, that sinners would not hesitate to reveal to him countless shameful acts and horrible misdeeds, among which, on account of an excess of shame, they would sooner resolve to die than to disclose them to another.

But to resume: through his great skill in spiritual doctrine, by indicating at one time the Redeemer's mercy, at another the Judge's severity, at another the uncertain and hazardous accidents of human mutability, Hamo prevailed upon the aforementioned knight, because without delay, after he had received permission from the bishop of Sées, in whose diocese he was living, the knight offered confession of his misdeeds to the good man with the highest devotion, likewise asking and strenuously imploring that he might deign to intercede with the almighty Lord for the remission of these same sins through his unceasing prayers.

Chapter 40

Likewise, at another time when Hamo was again sent on a journey and had stopped at the home of a certain powerful man, he saw there a certain woman as remarkable for the beauty of her body as for the nobility of her birth. She was living in such a great rage of hatred toward her husband that as soon as she sensed that she had conceived, more monstrously and more fiercely than all the wild beasts, she killed the very fetus in the womb, evidently so that offspring might not be born in her husband's name. And so when Hamo inquired closely about the state of her life in speaking to her privately, with a shameless countenance she declared that she would not be accused and condemned. Finally, after she had been sent away, the man of the Lord began to inquire very carefully about her life of those who were more intimately associated with her. From truthful assertions in their report he learned the things that we said above, just as he had perceived them beforehand in spirit. And indeed, we have directed our pen to relating these matters for this reason: so that from this the blessed man's holiness and the spiritual foresight in which he excelled might be made known more clearly, and if there are sinners who might be engaged in the aforementioned sins, or any other sins, they might quickly turn to the healing of confession and penance by trusting in the hope of forgiveness.

Chapter 41

Now, for the glory of Christ, who does not want the death of sinners but rather that they might be converted and live,* let us briefly report how the empress,[50] the mother of the king whom we mentioned above, was returned from the coils of the devil and the death of sin to life through the prayers and counsel of the blessed man, with the grace of Christ aiding him. For in fact, in a certain vision at night the blessed man saw

*Ezek 33:11

50. Empress Matilda, daughter of Henry I of England and wife of Geoffrey of Boulogne, was the mother of Henry II.

her coming toward him, standing before him in a blue gown and showing her hands as well as her feet completely bare; she was hideous and pale not only in her face but also in her whole body, and consumed by wasting, and in a certain way she seemed bloodless and already dead. And indeed this vision, in its ordered application of similitude, agreed in every way with the wretched life that the empress was leading at this time. For truly, she was so completely entangled and weighed down not only by the gloom of her immediate sins but also by the gloom of old sins and by inextricable chains of a long-standing habit[51] that as often as talk of divine matters took place to some degree when she was present, immediately, with her complexion changed, her lips trembling, and her heart pulsating, unable to bear the light of the Lord's preaching, as if the witness of conscience were reproving her, she shuddered at even a single sound of the divine word.

Therefore, after the aforementioned vision, at a time when an opportunity came to speak with her, the man of the Lord exposed to her and set before her eyes the foulness of her deeds, although she received this admonition of the blessed man with much annoyance and refused to listen. Yet afterward, sensing through the discernment of the man of the spirit that she had been foreseen in her iniquities and apprehended,[52] at last, with divine mercy illuminating her heart, in the pure, naked truth of confession she revealed all the misdeeds by which she was overwhelmed, insofar as she could remember.

In fact, rejoicing that the vision of her shown to him beforehand by the Lord had been fulfilled in the reception of her confession, at last, with the permission of

51. See note 49 on *consuetudo*.
52. *Deprehensam* echoes John 8:3-4, where a woman "caught in adultery" is brought before Jesus.

the archbishop, the servant of Christ imposed a wholly fitting remedy of penance on her. For indeed the nakedness of her hands and feet undoubtedly foretold the laying bare of her deeds and disposition and the nakedness to come in confession. And so, to speak briefly, after she had made the acquaintance and gained the friendship of the blessed man, and after she had received a penance from him, progressing from virtue to virtue and employing herself with the ardor of fervent faith in mighty works of justice and piety, at last, after a blessed end, as we believe, she found rest in the Lord.[53]

Chapter 42

At another time, relaxed in sleep on a certain night, Hamo saw a certain woman who was well known to him, one distinguished for her power in the world and her abundance of wealth, sitting on a very large horse. She was entirely covered by white garments so that no part of her body could be seen except her eyes alone. And so when the man of the Lord had addressed this woman in the customary way, wishing to lead her back to the way of rectitude through the reparation of penance, he set before her very many abominable and unspeakable signs[54] of her sins, which he in no way doubted that she had committed.

But in order that the truth of the aforementioned vision might be proved, while covering herself all around with a whitened garment of feigned justification and with the falsified coverings of excuses drawn over her on every side, by shamelessly denying what she had impurely and scandalously done, she made it

53. Empress Matilda retired to a priory of Bec; she died and was buried there in 1163.
54. The word *nota* was used by Roman censors to indicate acts of infamy or immorality.

worse. But though she covered her body so, yet her eye was visible, because although she might conceal the baseness of her past actions by careful speech to whatever extent she could, yet from his understanding of the spirit she could not hide her wicked purpose, because of which she was still languishing in sin.

Chapter 43

But since we have discussed the blessed man's way of life and his merits, while proceeding thus far with the grace of Christ granting, not so much with an embellished elegance of speech as in an unadorned and faithful narrative, we believe that it is not out of place if we bring forward from the side into our midst, as it were, for the advancement of our readers, some miracles brought about divinely through the relics of saints, which he used to bring together from every side with great care. And so once when the man of faith was dividing the relics of the most blessed apostles Peter and Andrew, whom not only their faith and suffering made brothers but also their relationship of flesh, it pleased him to join some of the blood of Saint Peter, which he had at hand, although a small amount, to the bones of Saint Andrew, clearly so that the simple and upright man might also preserve the brotherhood that they had entered into at birth by the uniting of their relics.

When he had done this, immediately, as a wondrous proof of divine power, the same blood united itself to the aforementioned bones and poured itself over them so much that in the twinkling of an eye* it made these same bones completely ruddy and blood red with a purple color of rosy beauty, so that in a divine and wondrous manner from the two substances directly joined together, rather a single species appeared. But without his knowing it, a small amount of this blood adhered to the nail of his thumb while he was han-

*1 Cor 15:52

dling it. Discovering it on the following day, when he wanted to cleanse this same nail of the stain of blood, now by rubbing, now by repeatedly washing it, and could not, finally, at the suggestion of a certain brother who used to help him in this task, he perceived that that little drop had been poured over his thumbnail from blessed Peter's blood, which he had been handling in the presence of the same brother. And so, as soon as he realized this, after the nail with the blood had been very carefully scraped evenly, he joined that which he scraped off to the aforementioned relics. But for what reason the providence of divine goodness, without whose command not even a leaf falls from a tree, willed these things to happen I have decided to entrust to the judgment of the reader rather than rashly to explain anything with respect to them.

Chapter 44

Also, when Hamo was engaged in similar employment at another time, he had decided to join certain others to relics of blessed Benedict and Scholastica, his sister, which were kept separately in a certain ivory pyx. As soon as he put them in it, the silver clasps of this pyx, with which it was not only fastened but also much adorned, were divinely broken, and both sprang apart from each other with wondrous speed. Moreover, when he had attempted a second time to do the same thing and he had closed the pyx after the relics had been put in, the bottom leapt far from it as if it had been struck by a forceful blow. Thus, since the man of the Lord had been absolutely astonished by the showing of this power, for a time he rested from the aforementioned task.

But returning to it after a few days had intervened, with a zeal for pious exploration as if he were another Gideon,* he strove to search for a sign in a third pyx. *Judg 6:36-40
When he had put in certain other relics, joining them

to the relics of the most holy Benedict and his sister Scholastica, as he had done before, no less did the lid of this pyx immediately, sooner than said, fly apart from it. But concerning the miracle repeated so often, although he did not attend to the cause of the same miracle enough for clarity, he strove to glorify greatly the grace of divine mercy and kindness with worthy commendations of praise.

Chapter 45

Once the same man of venerable life sent relics of blessed John the Baptist to a certain lay brother to be kept in a certain individual private house; no one stayed in it except a certain knight and the lay brother, who used to serve this knight diligently. Furthermore, the aforementioned knight was a man of very great age and a man of exceeding honesty and gentleness. And so when the feast of blessed John arrived, the same lay brother, roused in the customary way by the monks' signal, proceeded to church and left the aforementioned knight alone in the house. Thus while the honest man was keeping watch attentively, lying on his own bed in the peaceful silence of the night, all at once the whole house shone with a sudden brightness, when, behold, he saw a beardless youth with bare feet and shining with inestimable brightness enter the house. But when this young man, clothed in garments brighter than snow and bearing a wand of imperial authority in his hand, had drawn near to him, addressing him with a serene countenance, the young man said, "Lie still, lie still." And when for a while through the house, and especially around the chest in which were preserved his. . . .[55]

55. According to the editor, the life of Hamo breaks off here in the Cotton manuscript. The remaining chapters are found in three and sometimes four of the other manuscript witnesses to the *Vita*.

Chapter 46

The wondrous power of Christ and his wisdom should be wondrously proclaimed in his saints, through whom, while he brings to light the hidden guilt of wrongdoers, he often recalls these same wrongdoers from the abyss of sin to salvation. Therefore, since we reported the superabundant riches of God's grace that he deigned to confer on his servant for the manifold benefit of his followers, let us follow up about the rest as we have begun.

The servant of God was very friendly and well known to a certain community of nuns. To these he was kept bound by great affection on account of this above all: that in the judgment of religious as much as of laymen, they were believed to surpass all the nuns of this province in religion and holiness. Also, passing often among them and hearing their confessions, the servant of God used to applaud them very much for the position and the ardor to which they advanced with divine grace aiding them. But with the passage of time, now growing weak in his failing limbs and with time already hastening along to when he ought to go the way of all flesh, he heard what he did not want to hear, namely, that these women were cooling off from the ardor of their former way of life and had fallen into some idleness of negligence and lukewarmness. Thus, troubled at the unexpectedness of this news and grieving as well, he turns totally to God in prayer, begging and intently imploring that, if it were so, as was being said, he might deign to show him fully their way of life.

And so on a day when the man of the Lord was carefully pondering the things that were being said about them and he had not yet decided to give full credence to what was said, suddenly, as he was keeping watch, in ecstasy he sees himself sitting in the chapter of these women and them sitting all around in order in the chapter as well. And so he sees a thing unbelievable

to him before, that behind each one of them, radiant
and shining in their garments and countenance, there
came next four no less opposite, misshapen and black
in their whole body and habit, and thus he saw in all.
He recognized, however, none of these at all, except
one bright and shining in her garments and countenance whom he saw standing alone outside the chapter. Yet on each side she had one very severe welt. He
was much amazed and thinking to himself about the
vision; while he was still lingering in the same ecstasy,
a voice sent from heaven thunders forth to him, saying, "Do not doubt, servant of God, do not doubt,
servant of God, since as you see, so it is."

Again on another day, he observes himself sitting
within the circle of their chapter and sees one of them
whom he knew best coming directly opposite him;
she appeared horrible to see, with her garments and
her countenance very black. Made most certain by
revelations of this kind that they were in no way per-
severing in the service of Christ with the ardor with
which they had begun, but, as is the custom for very
many, they had in some measure fallen asleep through
negligence in their practices from the first way of religion they had undertaken, the servant of Christ, although enfeebled in body and already very near death,
yet drawn by bonds of that love that, as we read, is
Song 8:6   stronger than death, started on his journey to them.

Therefore, when he was situated in their chapter
and had clearly reported what had been shown to him,
for the future he admonished them to hasten soon to
the remedy of confession and penance, because very
many, and a large number of them, although still detained in the body, were already dead in the eyes of
God through the guilt of their negligence. Struck with
boundless terror after they heard these words, all accepted the admonition of the blessed man with rejoicing, just as if from an angel dispatched to them from
heaven, and immediately the individual nuns, fortified
with regard to the examination of their life and of

their own actions and not sparing themselves at all, through oral confession and good works threw out the earthiness of a harmful heap from the well of the heart.

And when he heard their confessions and gave boundless thanks to almighty God for their recovery, while that one who had appeared to him in the cloister was approaching among the rest, the man of God made known to her that he had seen her specifically so before the others, very black in her garments and her countenance, and bloodless. But heaving deep sighs from the depths of her heart, she confessed it to be truly so. Thus, openly revealing the private offenses of their hearts to Christ's servant through confession, this nun as well as the others received from him, as if from a faithful physician, with divine grace aiding him, a remedy of perfect health. Finally, inquiring diligently of the blessed man about the time of the aforementioned vision in which he had seen these things and learning from his report, instantly they perceived that at this time in which he had seen these things they had been living in an altogether more remiss and more dispirited state than they had been before.

Chapter 47

Likewise, when the man of the Lord had secured the acquaintance and friendship of a certain other community from passing their way often and from the ample generosity of his benefactions, spiritual as well as corporal, he began to be an altogether diligent and pious examiner of this community's accepted way of life and the way it continued in its manner of life in the sight of the Lord. And so after grace from heaven had been sought and gained in this matter through his pursuit of constant prayer and devotion, finally, transported into ecstasy, he observed himself situated in the cloister of the aforementioned community; at the same time he saw all the brothers of this monastery sitting together in the same place.

Of these, half were situated under the open sky, as it were, in a little grassy area of the cloister, and appearing dark with frightful countenances, they seemed wholly clothed in the blackest of garments. The remaining half were stationed in that part of the cloister that is near the chapter, appearing very agreeable, with pleasing countenances and shining faces and also with the brightest splendor in the garments that they were wearing; they presented in their appearance a certain solemnity of mind. Therefore, when he was seized with great astonishment over these whom he had seen to be black because, knowing the consciences of almost each one from their private conversations, he noticed that not one of them was persisting in deadly sin, at last he received this response from the prophetic utterance of a divine voice: "Do not doubt," it said, "Do not doubt, man of God, for those whom you observe to be stained by blackness have been made lax by negligence and lethargy. And although they outwardly simulate the habit of religious life, inwardly dead in the sight of God, they do not perform the works of religious life."

From this, therefore, let us acknowledge that we are wretched men, in fact more wretched than the rest of men, and let us not pay attention to the patches and aprons of divine justice, but by putting our hand to vigorous tasks, let us keep the law of the Lord in thought, word, and deed, and let us not take up the haughtiness of pride from this, from which we ought to acquire an increase of humility.

Chapter 48

When Hamo had understood the revelation mentioned above through the influence of the divine spirit, he began to think very carefully day and night and to turn over in the innermost part of his mind whether by chance the remaining countless multitude of the monastic order in a like condition, or certainly in a different one in the sight of the Lord, had received the grace of its way of life. And when an interval of time rolled along in its swift course and the man of the Lord was in no way turned aside from his purpose, at last he was not defrauded in his longing or confounded in his expectation. Finally, after many offerings[56] of prayers, Christ's servant saw himself being led by the hand of the Lord and raised, with the divine spirit guiding him, to a loftier part of the sky. When he had been led there, turning his eyes toward the depths, he observed almost countless assemblies of the monastic profession disposed separately below. When he was looking at them, he recognized them in the shape and form in which he had seen the forenamed community: namely, half of them, as it were, in every way appearing black in garments and in countenance, but the rest appearing in the whitest habits and with the greatest glory and very great beauty of countenance. One must not think, however, that in that blackness of the first half was foreshown to him their irreversible damnation, but, just as it was told to him about the brothers of the community recalled above, their immoderate negligence and slackness were made manifest. Unless they would repent of this, they would undoubtedly be heirs of everlasting death.

Chapter 49

With the Exaltation of the Holy Cross approaching, and then the solemn office of the dead following after the third day, as is the custom, the same servant of God was in the infirmary, surely gripped by a serious

---

56. *Holocaustomata*, literally "burnt offerings."

sickness. And when that night had arrived in which the solemn vigils of the dead follow after the regular vigils, near the end of the regular vigils there entered into his mind a question for careful thought about the status of those souls after death, how they might subsist or what aid the offices of human service might supply to them. And when, restless because of thoughts of this kind, he was diligently intent on celebrating the divine praises, suddenly, transported into ecstasy, he saw in the higher part of the sky a countless multitude of souls that he observed to be also naked and shining in great glory. Moreover, their faces were lifted up to heaven, as if in all their prayers they were begging for mercy from almighty God; he also saw that they were buffeted by fierce cold and winds.

Again on the third day he saw these same souls coming into view with a similar appearance, but now situated in much higher parts of the sky. And the higher they were ascending, so much the more were they avoiding the vexations of winds and cold. In any case, since they came into view with an appearance of brightness and yet were not completely free from torments and pain, what else must be supposed except that, departing from here, although they did not take with them the greater and often repeated offenses for which they would certainly be handed over to the most horrible punishments, yet they had dragged with them other negligence of slighter guilt that was cleansed even in their passage. But what he saw again after the third day, that having progressed to much more lofty heights they had now almost escaped the penalty of torment, what else does it signify other than the swift assistance of those who offer salutary hosts[57] to almighty God for their deliverance?

57. *Hostias* means "sacrificial offerings," here (as also in chap. 50) rendered as *hosts*.

Chapter 50

When a certain sister in the community of nuns about which I spoke above was nearing death, it happened that the man of God was present there. When she made her confession to him, straining out a gnat and swallowing a camel,* as the gospel parable says, she divulged the lesser and slighter sins but concealed the more serious ones by which she was greatly weighed down. Finally, after a little while, she was removed from human affairs. When the time of her burial had come and the man of the Lord was offering the salutary host for her while celebrating Mass, through the Spirit he immediately realized that this sacrifice for her was not accepted by the Lord. In fact, in the following year the man of God spiritually saw the soul of the aforementioned nun on high in the air being harassed by demons, and it was being cruelly tossed about by one or the other of them in turn.

*Matt 23:24

Chapter 51

Also, the servant of Christ entrusted money to a certain brother to be disbursed to the poor. And when it had been made known to him by a certain other one that the aforementioned brother had attempted to carry out fraud in the almsgiving, moved by a double pang of sorrow, namely, about the fraud carried out against the poor and the everlasting death incurred by that brother because of the guilt of his accursed theft, at last Hamo perceived for himself what he had heard through another. For he spiritually saw that brother, with his face in fact unchanged but inwardly, as if in his soul, drenched by the gloomy mist of a certain cloud and perplexed; indeed, in this vision, I believe, the brother's treachery was clearly condemned and his most wretched way of life indicated.

Chapter 52

Now indeed, who could worthily expound how great was the reverence and how frequent the care with which Hamo used to honor the memories of the saints? In short, with the utmost effort and utmost zeal he built very many basilicas; indeed, he dedicated these to certain saints whom he deeply loved in a special way. And in fact, no less did he build basilicas for the apostles and martyrs, confessors and virgins. Finally, when he had already harbored some hope concerning the future building of a new church in this place, though his confidence in this plan wavered somewhat in his soul on account of the magnitude of the task, at last, casting his thought before the Lord,* with diligent and constant prayers he begged from God, the very source of all good things, his counsel and help in starting and constructing this church.

*see Ps 54:23

In fact, he was not defrauded in his hope, but the Lord heard the longing of his heart. For one day, after his prayer of this kind was finished, while going from the church up to the dormitory, when he had arrived in front of his own little bed, unexpectedly he saw a silver penny lying in the middle of the way before the bed. When he had lifted it up from the floor, astounded and at the same time rejoicing, a voice, divinely flowing into his heart, spoke to him as follows: "Behold," it said, "your monastery, which you have asked for with such great longing." In truth, after a few days, what the Lord foretold to him in a figure[58] he wondrously fulfilled in the outcome of the subsequent work.

Chapter 53

Also, we should remember the fact that although Hamo by no means dreaded that common enemy of

---

58. *Figura* has the sense here of a diagram or architectural sketch.

human nature, death, at the time of his first profession of monastic vows on account of the great ardor of his longing, as he was wishing to be released and to be with Christ,* yet in his last years, with the weakness of that long illness weighing him down (from which he also died), he greatly feared death. But I also think that it is suitable to explain how divine grace, which nowhere abandons its saints, raised him up from anxious fear of this kind. On a certain day when he was praying at the tomb of a man[59] devoted to God named Peter, Hamo, suddenly transported outside himself into ecstasy, saw in the higher parts of the sky a countless multitude of saints shining brightly in conspicuous glory and great honor, and Peter rejoicing with mighty jubilation in their company. And when the man of God carefully directed the sharp point of his mind toward contemplation of them, that entire heavenly multitude turned their faces toward him most kindly and fully bowed to him respectfully. Now indeed, following this the man of God, made altogether more certain about attaining to their assembly, used to wish strongly for the hour of death, which before he used to fear.

*Phil 1:23

Chapter 54

Also, from some fellow members of the community about whose life and morals he was confident, he sometimes requested this: that they would appear to him after their death and inform him about how it was going with them. In fact, while not only in no way passing over the boundary prescribed by him they used to appear to him according to the agreed condition and make known what was going on with them, they even foretold to him what was going to be concerning his own salvation.

59. *Quoddam*. The man referred to is Peter of Avranches.

Chapter 55

Again, at some time, in spirit he saw the whole community of his monastery separated and divided in three ranks. The first group, which was lower, standing on the ground in a great crowd, appeared wholly black and misshapen not only in their garments but also in their entire body. But the second group, raised up in the sky a little from the ground, showed itself to the man of God in a different appearance, stained in its garments and no less in the diverse quality of countenances. Also, positioned above this one and standing in a higher part of the sky as if arranged by gradations, the third group was remaining fast, with the brightest and most pleasing splendor in its garments and with countenances directed toward heaven in great exuberance of glory. Moreover, there is no doubt that the triple difference of this vision was shown beforehand to the man of God according to the diverse quality of their manner of life and the merit of their way of life.

Chapter 56

Likewise, in the same way Hamo saw a certain rich man who was well known to him, but entangled in worldly vices, surrounded by eight demons. Before his sight a certain frightful fire, like a vast fountain boiling up, was extended upward into the sky; that rich man was believed to be destined to be cast into this fire after death, just as was seen in the spirit by the servant of Christ.

Chapter 57

As the time of his own death was drawing near, when he was reflecting on the status of souls, how they would ascend into heaven, that is, by themselves or with angels leading them, and how they would penetrate the firmament, while he was sitting, for pain prevented him from lying down, he saw four angels, and with them leading him he was raised up into the sky. Two of the angels were preceding him, but two were going on his right and left. Moreover, while ascending with them, he experienced no distress. And in that ascent, when he had arrived at that place where paradise was now near and, so to speak, was thought to be above his head, he sees a multitude of souls in a magnificent place, all covered by a very red and, as it were, fiery color. He saw that holy assembly of souls beseeching the Almighty with heads humbled and bowed, and giving thanks, as it seemed to Hamo, because with him calling and granting this favor, the servant of God was also about to come soon into the fellowship of that blessed multitude. Furthermore, returned to himself, he perceived that he was sitting as before, but he was undergoing less pain. Moreover, this vision brought him much hope and comfort.

Chapter 58

When Hamo was sensing beforehand that the time of his own death was imminent, it happened that places in which he had once lived came to his recollection, and in recalling them he was held fast by a certain sweet fondness for them. Moreover, when the inevitability of death was forcing him to depart from here, again the absence of those same places that he had pondered before brought to his spirit a slight taste of bitterness, which was washed away on the following night by a vision such as this: a very large palace was shown to him, within whose perimeter was observed a glorious multitude of souls; they were seen positioned next to the walls of the palace and clinging to the walls, so to speak. Furthermore, a radiance mixed with redness covered the palace as well as the individual souls. Moreover, in the middle of the palace was seen a tree adorned with branches but lacking leaves, extending into the sky so that his sight could not reach the top of that tree. For he was standing in a much lower place, but yet the souls standing in the palace were contemplating God, the sight of whom he could not attain, inasmuch as the site of his place was lower.

He seemed, however, to receive an answer, as if the Spirit of God were sharing words with the spirit of man: "Since you are about to inhabit after a short time, as an everlasting inhabitant and colleague, these places so pleasant, this blessed community of the just, to leave the dwelling of an earthly habitation ought to be an incentive for exultation in your heart, not an incitement[60] to sorrow. For if you should compare whatever is earthly to these places that you have seen, what glory or delight does it seem to have?"

Then moreover, after a few days had elapsed, on the feast of Saint Paul, when Hamo had implored the patronage of the same blessed Paul with the pious devotion of his heart and with sincere prayer, he was delighted once more by the appearance of the blessed showing, which divine largess enhanced with marvelous increase. Behold, he was again allowed to look upon the palace, the tree, and the souls, in their aforementioned state and site. In addition, he saw the Lord Jesus Christ with a very shining countenance, at a youthful age, so to speak, next to the tree that, as was said before, was placed in the middle of paradise. Moreover, when the Lord Jesus Christ had turned his eyes toward him, the rays of his eyes seemed to descend right into Hamo's heart with wondrous light and great power after penetrating his breast and vital parts.

---

60. I have retained the parallelism of *incentivum* and *incitamentum* here.

Moreover, though the individual aspects repeated in this mystery of the divine vision brought astonishment to him after he returned to himself, yet the recollection of divine regard was most pleasing and the cause of special exultation when Hamo remembered Jesus looking toward him and the rays of his eyes penetrating through his breast to his heart. For although he had been allowed to see the Lord Jesus in other revelations, yet up to this time the means of seeing his eyes had not been granted.

Furthermore, he used to say that he had obtained this vision through the merits of blessed Paul. But let no one think that this showing of a blessed vision was a mere dream, for in the hour in which these things were made known to him, he was free from the drowsiness of sleep, awake or almost awake, as he himself declared; he recalled, however, that he had been transported in spirit to look upon them. Hence the consolation granted for the present and the almost-certain expectation for the future produced in his heart certain firstfruits of the gladness that he is now believed to enjoy fully. Nevertheless, although so many venerable signs showed that this man was dear to God, although so many magnificent portents of his own salvation shone forth, he rose up against himself as a very harsh reprover, ardently accusing and rebuking himself for having ever dared to think, much less to say, that he, a sinner, earth, ash, a worm, had seen him upon whom angels long to look and that he had been seen by him so familiarly.

At last, after the course of the present life had been completed, in the year 1173 from the incarnation of the Lord, on the thirtieth of April, the same servant of Christ departed to the Lord, to whom belong honor and glory forever. Amen.